# Phenomena a book of wonders

The *Veilleux brothers (see p. 57) found this spontaneous image superimposed on a photograph of their kitchen in July 1968. It was later identified by Professor Charles Lyle as an Australian 'wondjina' rock painting featured in Erich von Däniken's* Return to the Stars, *and almost certainly unknown and unobtainable before this book was published in 1969. This precognition was not the only oddity noticed by Dr Jule Eisenbud in* Fate, *February 1976. Professor Lyle once described the rock painting as a 'pagan Last Supper'. 'He had no way of knowing,' wrote Eisenbud, 'that the picture on the kitchen wall, against which this picture was shot and which was totally obscured by it, was Leonardo's* Last Supper.'

# Phenomena
## a book of wonders

John Michell · Robert J.M. Rickard

with 119 illustrations

PANTHEON BOOKS

NEW YORK

First American Edition

Copyright © 1977 by Thames and Hudson
Ltd., London

All rights reserved under International and
Pan-American Copyright Conventions.
Published in the United States by Pantheon
Books, a division of Random House, Inc.,
New York. Originally published in England
by Thames and Hudson Ltd., London.

*Library of Congress Cataloging in
Publication Data*

Michell, John F., 1933–
  *Phenomena*
    Includes bibliographical references.
    1. Curiosities and wonders.  2. Occult
  sciences.
  I.  Rickard, Robert J. M., 1945–, joint
author.   II. Title.
AG243.M46  1977   001.9'4   77–2234
ISBN 0-394-41596-5
ISBN 0-394-73389-4 pbk.

Manufactured in the United Kingdom

Designed by Carl Willson

# Contents

# The phenomenal world

This is not just a book of wonders; it is a book of repeated wonders. It is about things which are experienced by people in every generation, themes in life which recur endlessly but contrive always to elude reasonable explanation. In terms of any rational system of belief they are impossible, yet they survive every attempt to exorcize or suppress them. They are repetitive and effective. They affect people mentally or physically, and for that reason we include them among the 'real' phenomena of this world. On their own level they correspond to the archetypal themes of mythology and the archetypal images in dreams. These also, because they pass the criteria of being repetitive and effective, we allow to be 'real', and we refer to them in drawing up the inclusive world-view which we call phenomenalism. This book is meant as an introduction to an expanded, phenomenal view of reality which, because it is based on life as experienced rather than as conceived, we offer as a more complete, practical and satisfactory way of seeing things than the physical world-view of modern science.

As phenomenalists, we accept everything; we believe nothing absolutely; we do not explain. Any theories we may offer are tentative and temporary. Our study is the content of human experience, things that happen, or are believed to happen, or are said to happen. Particularly we are interested in the enigmatic range of phenomena whose existence lies somewhere between the 'hard' reality of nuts and bolts, bricks and mortar and the 'psychological' reality of dreams.

The father of modern phenomenalism was Charles Fort (1874–1932), a world-changer, a cosmological revolutionary. From his lifetime's collection of anomalies and irregularities in the scientific world-image he identified many previously unrecognized types in phenomenal reality, such as the UFO, the fireball and the teleportation effect. More than that, he developed, subtly and humorously, a philosophical view of life capable of adapting itself to the widest possible range of experience. He delighted in all the products of nature and imagination. He accepted everything that happened in life and rejected all interpretive myths, even scientific ones. He valued first-hand witness above second-hand rationalization. Existence is one creature. Everything is related to and merges into everything else, with different levels of reality interpenetrating. There are no breaks in the spectrum of phenomena. All categories, all divisions, are man-made and arbitrary, for there is no such thing as an isolated event any more than there are isolated organs in the body. 'There's a shout of vengefulness in Hyde Park, London – far away in Gloucestershire an ancient mansion bursts into flames.'

In the continuous field of phenomena there are peaks, islands of a submerged mountain range. In the illustrated section of this book we have chosen phenomena which cluster round certain peaks, arranging them under different categories. These categories are artificial and for temporary convenience only, for each one can be infinitely subdivided or merged with others to produce different patterns of peaks or archipelagos in the geography of the phenomenal universe. One of our objects is to point out the rich variety of images that can be projected onto and drawn from experience of life. And we begin our justification of phenomenalism as the least inadequate of philosophies by suggesting that the best way for anyone to avoid turning into a mad bore, crank or obsessive is to recognize that nature is quite equal to the wildest flights of human imagination and quite capable of manifesting evidence to support the craziest theories that anyone can dream up. Only with this understanding, preferably confirmed by experiment in the style of Lewis Carroll's White Queen ('Sometimes I've believed as many as six impossible things before breakfast'), can one fully appreciate such scenes as the learned professor reproving the enthusiast for not viewing the world in the image of current pedantry and being screamed at in return for being blind to things that should be clear to any lunatic.

As phenomenalists we recognize no certainties. Yet all around us there are certainties variously contrived, the certainties of tyrants, psychiatrists, high priests of science and religion, cranks and fanatics, each one consisting of different selections from the common source material, the world of sensory perception, and each one a rival to the others. There are wars between world-views for the status of dominant reality. Mental imperialism. We think these certainties are best avoided. They are maintained by studied ignorance and selective blindness. Finally they have the same irritating effect as the wearing of blinkers. When the cherished beliefs of a lifetime are confronted with experience that contradicts them, the beliefs should know how to give way gracefully. Ourselves, we take pleasure in all beliefs and theories; we are benign to all interpretations and schools of thought, and we look kindly on stern orthodoxies and passionate heresies alike. Each one reflects an aspect of human nature and each one has a positive contribution to make to the stock of human understanding. Yet we would rather sample them all than swallow any one whole. Throughout this book we advance numerous theories to account for the odd events and apparitions assembled in it, but though all of them are useful in explaining some of the evidence, there is none which covers the full range of phenomena in any field. We appreciate theories as works of art, and we create our own in the same spirit, preferring always to study reality at its source, in the products of nature, rather than through the images people have made of it.

The advantages of a phenomenal world-view are demonstrated by the following event recorded in John Aubrey's *Miscellanies*.

In 1655 a man who should have been in Goa, the Portuguese colony in India, and who actually had been in Goa some moments previously, was suddenly found to be back in Portugal. He had been carried mysteriously through the air. He was given a fair trial, found guilty and burnt at the stake.

The ecclesiastical authorities in Portugal at the time, like all defenders of orthodoxies everywhere, were not phenomenalists. They wanted explanations, and they explained in terms of the dominant reality. That reality included magicians and witches, enemies of the faith yet part of it, a kind of official opposition. One of the characteristics of these enemies, by which they could be recognized, was their tendency to fly through the air. No one but a recognized saint or a magician did such things, and since the man from Goa was no saint he must be a magician. This logic was followed out to the point of burning him.

The tragedy was caused by the authorities' moralistic attitude towards phenomena. We can not now tell whether the man actually was transported through the air from Goa; there are no details, although the evidence at the time was strong enough to convict him. But we do not believe that he was necessarily a magician. In the seventeenth century there was sufficient proof, for anyone who cared to look for it, of LEVITATION AND SPONTANEOUS FLIGHT, and since that time many good cases have been recorded, from abductions of people attributed to fairies to modern UFO-linked teleportations. Examples are given in our sections STRANGE DISAPPEARANCES, TAKEN AWAY AND BROUGHT BACK and TELEPORTATION. Many of these appear to have occurred spontaneously rather than by magic and witchcraft; and we believe that the now fashionable UFO attribution is as arbitrary as the earlier explanations. Had the Portuguese authorities been able to review dispassionately the history of spontaneous levitation instead of merely accepting the current explanation of it, they could not have justified burning the man from Goa.

Many are the misunderstandings, injustices and miseries which could have been avoided at the time by a touch of phenomenalism: visionaries sent to madhouses, UFO contactees put out of work, scientists discredited for unorthodox findings, Joan of Arc and many others burnt for conversing with spirits. Fort recorded several instances where unaccountable disturbances of the 'poltergeist' variety were blamed unfairly on children in the household, often on some wretched servant girl who may have been the unconscious medium for such disturbances. Inevitably, with the modern confusion of all creeds and in reaction to the oppressive certainties of the great nineteenth-century theory-mongers, phenomenalism is becoming more generally appreciated for its inclusive approach to reality. With it comes a new and welcome tolerance. Policemen can spot pumas in Surrey or chase UFOs in Devon and still remain policemen. People mysteriously transported through the air are no longer burnt; sometimes they are even believed. Scientists view, and write papers on, such products of extra-scientific reality as fire-walking and spoon bending. Humanists, freed from such once obligatory concepts as spirits or the primacy of matter, study the divining rod and survival after death through the neutral evidence of their associated phenomena. There are even some psychiatrists who will listen uncensoriously to the impossible experiences of their patients. Meanwhile, exclusionism, as Charles Fort called it, the tendency to adopt a rationally coherent part of reality as a true substitute for the more than rational whole, still flourishes in the academic world which informs the political one. The only revolution we look forward to is that which will free the toiling masses of downtrodden phenomena, raise them from their condition of neglect, and allow them an equal say in governing our conception of reality.

**Phenomenal varieties and explanations**

We are concerned with symptoms rather than causes; with symptoms of existences that exist only in their symptoms; with objects falling from the sky, or disappearing into thin air, or being or not being where they should not or should be; with repeated occurrences of impossible creatures; with events and phenomena encountered on the physical plane yet obeying the laws of dreamland rather than those of physics. We conceive of three modes of reality, 'hard', 'psychological' and, between the two, 'phenomenal', all active and effective, all merging. Events on one level relate to those on the others, with causes and effects indeterminate. Does smoking cause cancer or cancer cause smoking or are they both of some other origin? Does the future air disaster cause the premonition or the premonition the air disaster or are they both provoked by something else? Throughout the different levels of reality there are correspondences. Strange objects in the sky, monsters by land and sea, humanoids and unearthly men. These are the archetypal stuff of dreams, creatures of universal myths and fairy stories, yet spilling over at times into phenomenal reality to shock or amaze human witnesses, and sometimes approaching though never quite achieving hard reality with such ambiguous credentials as strange footprints and blurred photographs. And among all the mass of evidence, the hints and apparitions, scarcely an item of 'solid' proof, scarcely a nut or bolt to convince those whose notion of reality is limited to such things. This aversion to giving hard evidence of their existence is a striking feature of our phenomena. It may be the best clue we have to their nature. Perhaps it is deliberate. We are led on only to be cut off. John Keel the UFO writer has some interesting things to say about the delusions visited – from somewhere – on the UFO prophets after an initial period of inspiration. Unidentified flying hoaxes in a cosmic send-up; a universal treasure hunt with clues in a dead language and the course booby-trapped. We will write again when we know.

Suppressions are another thing. Museum curators are rarely phenomenalists. They label in terms of other labels, or they reject. No one wants the odd piece that belongs to another jigsaw puzzle. When the religious people ran the museums, exhibiting sacred relics and objects of miraculous origin, the evidences of our phenomena were more prominently displayed. But they were explained, religiously. The explanation supported the myth behind the religion, and when the religion changed the explanation changed with it. And the process continues. Here is an illustration. Many of our phenomena are connected with certain spots, the sites of old churches and places traditionally sacred. As phenomenalists, we think that the sanctity of these spots arose in the first place from something that happened there, something that may happen there still. Mysterious lights, miraculous cures, visions and spectres: these are most commonly associated with ancient sacred places, and the association is a very old one. The various qualities of the spots later to be called sacred were recognized in very early times. Later they were explained. The cures or visions were attributed to local gods, then to other gods of other religions, then to saints or legendary holy men or Buddha or the Virgin Mary. A modern development of the tendency to explain in terms of current myth is the theory, born of the space age UFO cult, that identifies the great sanctuaries of prehistoric civilizations as the work of extra-terrestrial spacemen.

The two enemies of phenomenalism: suppressions and explanations.

Charles Fort, the connoisseur of phenomena, was a connoisseur also of explanations. In 1881 there was a storm over the English city of Worcester (see FALLS OF CREATURES AND ORGANIC MATTER). Tons of winkles and mussels, with a few crabs thrown in, fell from the sky, littering streets, back yards and gardens. Of course they did not really fall from the sky because there are no winkles, etc., up there in the first place. So a local explanation arose. A fishmonger with unsaleable stock had dumped them. The Worcester fishmonger became Fort's favourite character. He stood for all the inadequate, hopelessly overstretched explanations that rationalism, for want of anything better, must sometimes make do with. Fort painted a lively picture of the Worcester fishmonger, processing quite unnoticed through the city streets with his many carts loaded with superfluous shellfish. His assistants are busy shovelling them into the road. They climb walls and shovel them into back yards and onto roofs. This done, they vanish without trace. Enquiries showed that no winkles or other shellfish had been on offer that day in Worcester market.

As well as the Worcester fishmonger, Fort identified another common type of explanation, the partial masquerading as the total. A house is attacked by mysterious forces; a 'poltergeist' classic. Stones fly, objects float, fires break out, blows are felt – and then a boy is caught throwing stones. The phenomena cease, and obviously the boy was responsible for the entire episode.

A subtle principle in nature which Fort was the first, at least since the days of the old alchemists, to remark, is the tendency of scientific experiments to yield results gratifying to the experimenter. There was the trivial case of the obliging snails. In August 1886 snails fell out of the sky near Redruth, Cornwall. One correspondent to the *Redruth Independent* thought they were sea snails. He put some in sea water and they thrived. Another thought they were fresh-water snails. The ones he put in sea water died. We suspect no one of dishonesty, remembering the new doctrine of the sub-atomic physicists that the act of observation affects the thing observed. We know what they mean. Professor Paul Kämmerer for example. He had a theory, an heretical one, to do with the inheritance of acquired characteristics. To prove it, the toads in his laboratory should develop rough black feet. They did so. A specimen was sent to England for inspection, was inspected and found to be as stated. Other scientists disliked the heresy. They also inspected the toad, hoping to discredit it, and found the black feet doctored with Indian ink. The matter was explained by all parties, variously, but nothing in the explanations was more interesting than the phenomenon itself. Kämmerer desired black-footed toads and was answered. His opponents desired no such thing and they too were obliged. The Piltdown hoax: a similar sort of case. Darwin claimed it was only the imperfection of the fossil record that prevented the discovery of missing links between species. A generation of scientists strove to find the most important of the hypothetical missing links, the one between men and ape stock. Evolutionism and a world-view depended on it. There was intense desire for it. It was duly found, and in England too, matrix of empire and orthodoxy. For forty years the

Piltdown skull, half man half ape, only too literally so, stood as hard evidence of the truths of evolutionism. It converted the last waverers. Old Boyd Dawkins, an original opponent of Darwin, confessed his errors on the strength of it. In 1953 it was exposed as a clumsy fabrication, but who did it? The detectives say that more than one person must have been involved, all the suspects leading evolutionists and one, Teilhard de Chardin, promoter of an evolutionary religion. Perhaps they were all in it. The evidence points that way, but we find it hard to credit such mass, fanatical dishonesty so long maintained. We are left with the simple phenomenon: an ape-man skull was desired, and the desire was answered.

Many of our phenomena are like the Piltdown skull, wish-fulfillers, need-satisfiers, related to the thought-forms of eastern magi as creatures of the imagination made manifest. The sensitive folk of the Rocky Mountains dream of hairy giants living up on the high peaks. Not only do they dream of them, they actually see them. They even see them sober, and so the Himalayan yeti has an American cousin, 'Bigfoot', THE GREAT AMERICAN MONSTER, with his phenomenal credentials of footprints, strands of hair and inconclusive snapshot photographs. Psychologists have much to say on this sort of thing, all of it relevant, but when they descend to explanations they tend to allow the partial to masquerade as the total. Phenomena can not be explained away by describing them or their witnesses in clinical terms. Yet many of our phenomena are definitely related to the state of mind of the people to whom they occur. Fire-walking for example, or levitation; these are certainly physical feats but they can also be called imaginary ones since they are performed in states of trance or ecstasy. It is the same with apparitions – monsters, werewolves and so on – which relate to unconscious desires, to atavistic images and yearnings. But we do not follow the psychologists in locating the source of our phenomena in the unconscious mind. There is no certainty. It is no less likely that the images in the unconscious mind were imprinted there by phenomena in the first place rather than vice versa: that the thing preceded its reflection. True, philosophers give primacy to the mental world over the physical, but when it comes to such questions as whether perception preceded the perceived, futility overwhelms and we return to our present and sufficient source of madness, the study of phenomenal reality.

## A window on the phenomenal world

The trouble with rationalistic cosmologies is that they can never entirely accord with experience. The discrepancy sets up irritations and the innocent suffer. Normal people are declared or declare themselves mad; talents and genius are suppressed or distorted; the world appears duller than its natural hue; low-mindedness is institutionalized. No rational system can amalgamate and reconcile all our phenomena. So we must be rational ourselves and follow this conclusion by looking for an irrational cosmology. A religion seems the first obvious answer. Religious systems make room for the irrational,

are founded on it. But closer inspection shows that these irrationalities appear as such only from outside the system. Within all is sweet reason, because all is explained, relatively. The children at Fátima saw and spoke to a radiant lady. It was explained to them that they had been granted a shared vision of the Blessed Virgin Mary – in the jargon of phenomenalism a BVM sighting. There are many such records both within and outside religious contexts. Howard Menger in America during the early 1950s claimed contact and conversations with another (or the same) radiant lady. He wrote a book about her, *From Outer Space to You*, explaining her in the context of the UFO cult as a wish-fulfilling space missionary. The idea of the time conventionalizes her identity. She has been variously described as the Queen of the Fairies, as Isis or/as the White Goddess. Her names are legion but behind them all is the same experience – an encounter with a sympathetic lady, glowing.

There is something to be said for all conventionalizations that allow the phenomenon its due reality. People who see the radiant lady, whatever she is called at the time, are at least permitted to believe they have seen something. In many ways the modern psychological explanation is the least satisfactory of all, since by locating the source of the vision exclusively in the seer it reduces its content to the chance projection of a disturbed mentality. The experience becomes illegitimate, no longer a source of wonder but of shame, a symptom of sickness, a portent of evil, a suitable case for treatment. This way of seeing things is excessively low-minded. Psychology has made a useful contribution to the study of our phenomena by drawing attention to the relationship many of them have with unusual mental states; yet the phenomena themselves, fire-walking, stigmata, radiant bodies, land and water monsters, aerial battles and all, remain as they always have been, unexplained. Their one constant feature is the reality-status they all share – less than 'hard', more than 'psychological'.

An inclusive cosmology, that is what we have in mind: a total world-view which accepts, without moral judgments and without rationalistic censorship, the entire range of repeated human experience. Obviously there can be no such thing within the canon of science or organized religion. Both pretend to offer a total world-view but can maintain it only by suppressing experience or by explaining it in terms of their own basic assumptions. To find precedents for the sort of thing we are looking for, we must recede into the distant past, before the rise of dogmatic science and religion.

Charles Fort was very much a man of his time. He mistrusted the past. All his data were of contemporary or quite recent incidents. And from the data alone he developed a view of reality which seemed in his generation to be one of unprecedented craziness. Yet it was not unprecedented. There were Forts in antiquity; there have always been Forts; but in modern times they have been classed as heretics and suppressed by the religious or scientific orthodoxy. For respected, unsuppressed Forts we must look to the ancient philosophers, the humorous sages of Taoist China or the pre-

Socratic westerners. Socrates himself had the Fortean view that he was the most informed of men because he alone realized that he knew nothing, but by his time the high priests and defenders of orthodoxy were in control, and he was put to death for opposing relativism to the official certainties of state religion. He pointed out that there were other gods besides the state ones, as Fort pointed out other phenomena besides the scientific ones.

Showers of creatures and objects from the sky, for example. By all good accounts this is by no means a rare occurrence. Yet the modern treatment of this fairly harmless – and sometimes beneficial – phenomenon has been disgraceful. For all its impressive documentation it has been victimized by scientific certainty, excluded, suppressed or explained – partially. The same with many other types of repetitive events, such as those illustrated in our sections. We look for a cosmology which includes them all, not only to prevent the injustices which arise through ignorance of them but also because the science which is not informed on them lacks the complete data for its investigations. From the evidence gathered in this book we suggest there may be principles or active forces in nature which science has so far ignored because they are not strictly within the realm of physical law with which it deals. Curiously enough, science has begun to recognize the most insubstantial level of reality, the world of psychological types, before acknowledging the intermediate level of phenomenal reality, which has roots in the objective and subjective worlds alike. In the universe, which combines and harmonizes all levels of reality, we detect the characteristics of a living organism. Self-regulation is a feature of all living creatures. A wound activates the process of healing; needs cry out and are satisfied; deficiencies attract compensations, sometimes excessively. Cravings for water have led to people blowing up at oases. So it is universally. One year there is a shortage of toads, not that anyone cares very much; but there is compensation and next year a glut. Toads swarm out of the water, rain down from the skies; people shovel them out of their houses. We note with Fort this hermaphroditic tendency in nature to satisfy its own desires, a tendency which provides the mechanism of magic. Fort's worldview was a spontaneous revival of that which informed the writings of the old mystical philosophers. If one desires to attract anything in nature, wrote Plotinus in the third century AD, referring to the shrines and invocation centres of the ancients, one should construct a receptacle designed to receive it. For virtually the entire course of history this view of things has prevailed. Behind every magical act, ritual and prayer meeting is the idea that desires can be artificially implanted in nature to produce their fulfilment. Thus tribesmen dance to attract rain and bird-lovers hang up nesting boxes in their orchards. Many of our phenomena can be related to this self compensating, reflexive tendency of the universe to respond both to the needs which arise naturally within its parts and to those injected into it by concentrated human will. Some mixed examples: the newly dug pond, suddenly and unaccountably teeming with fish; the wedding ring stigmata appearing on the finger of a dedicated and virginal bride of Christ; manna from heaven to the faithful in the wilderness; a friend intensely thought about and soon afterwards heard of, or from, or encountered; all miracles, coincidences, inspired puns and poetic justices; the levitating force by which the ecstatic soars aloft after his thoughts; monsters in children's imaginations and in Loch Ness or the Himalayas; ape-men in the imaginations of Darwinians and in the Piltdown gravel beds.

An inclusive cosmology is the prerequisite for an inclusive science, one which is based on total observation. Such a science would deal in probabilities rather than pretend to certainties. It would detect rhythms, patterns in occurrences, correspondences between events unapparently linked. In ages past our phenomena were highly regarded, officially. Provincial governors in China and ancient Babylon were expected to include in their annual reports to the central government everything strange which had taken place that year, peculiar objects in the sky, apparitions, monstrous births, irregularities in nature, popular delusions or unrest, every subtle symptom of psychological and thus of social disturbance. The Chinese, and no doubt other administrations, had fixed tables giving the correspondences between the various symptoms and specified inadequacies in government and court ritual, and the symptoms were treated or accommodated by the appropriate changes in central orthodoxy. The advantages of this phenomenal approach to science are recognized by the present regime in China. Their system of predicting earthquakes, the only one in the world which actually works, depends on the ancient practice of observing omens. The giant pandas at Peking zoo are consulted, unusual developments are noted in the course of nature and, as we have just read in the newspapers, 3 June 1976, the Chinese claim that their success in predicting recent earthquakes is due to the peasants being encouraged to report strange behaviour in animals and changes in the levels of local watercourses.

One feature of a phenomenalist system of government which disturbs Fortean purists is its tendency to invent myths. A myth is a sort of explanation – a suspect word in phenomenalist circles. Yet we have already confessed our partiality to explanations and theories of all sorts, though on one condition, that they really do serve to explain, that they cover the phenomenon wholly, not partially. If they do this it does not matter how absurd and fantastic they are. If they make people laugh, so much the better. Children will like them the more, so will the old people, and everyone else can believe them or not as he or she pleases. If myths are necessary, as we suspect they are, they should be enjoyable and harmless, not taken too seriously by responsible people nor insisted upon as compulsory beliefs. An example of an explanatory myth which covers the phenomenon as experienced, does no harm and gives people pleasure is the old Japanese solution to the mystery of things dropping down from the sky. The reason given is that there is a hole in the sky and sometimes things just fall through it. Objects which have appeared in this way are preserved as sacred curiosities in Shinto temples. Different, equally bland reasons for the same pheno-

*The sea-serpent (see pp 118–19) conceived as a long-necked plesiosaur by P. H. Gosse in* The Romance of Natural History, *1860.*

menon are given by the official explainers of other societies, and they all do well enough. Fort's humorous but logically irrefutable myth of an atmospheric Super-Sargasso Sea as a receiver and occasional dispenser of terrestrial bric-à-brac is of the same traditional order. The least adequate approach to any aspect of experienced reality is to deny it, not even to explain it but to explain it away. The nineteenth-century treatment – which continues into the present – of the 'falls' phenomenon was to dismiss every incident as a hoax, delusion or error. Even at the start of this century there were authorities who denied the reality of meteorites on the scientific grounds that stones could not fall from a stoneless sky, and falls of other matter as described in our sections are still widely disbelieved from the same logic. Neglect of what actually happens in favour of what someone's theory says should happen has the effect of dividing people and authority in a way which benefits neither.

Neo-phenomenalism, the science of the future. With nothing to prove, no faiths, theories or taboos to inhibit, we shall look at the universe directly by considering all the evidence of itself it chooses to offer. There will be discoveries of other phenomenal archetypes, many more than we have illustrated in this book, of their periodicities and geographical associations and of the types of people and states of mind most commonly affected by them. A Bureau of Signs, Omens and Recurrent Freaks will collect and process our data and detect links. And behind the links we will find causes in the form of universal characteristics unapparent to the eye of reason. Perhaps, if it seems worth the effort, we will go on to become magicians, masters of levitation for personal and commercial transport, werewolves at will, invokers of lightning to kindle our fires, of fish showers to stock our ponds, of manna in the desert or ladybird swarms when the greenfly infest our roses. In any event we will make the world a richer place by extending recognition to every one of its picturesque realities, by widening the field of phenomenal experience which a sane person can admit to enjoying, and by finding significance in happenings which the officially encouraged, unnecessarily low state of mind of the present is conditioned to ignore or devalue.

# Showers of frogs and fishes

To frogs and fishes we add toads. On 23 September 1973, according to *The Times* next day, tens of thousands of small toads fell from the sky in a 'freak storm' onto the southern French village of Brignoles. *The Times* blamed it on recent tornadoes. At Châlon-sur-Saône, reported the *Daily News* of 5 September 1922, little toads fell for two days. A similar discharge was observed near Toulouse in August 1804: in the news item quoted by Charles Fort from *Comptes rendus* the toads are described as juveniles and tremendously numerous. It had been a bright, clear day, and then suddenly a great cloud appeared. Out of it, as people watched, fell the numerous little toads. Another such shower is recorded in a letter dated 24 October 1683 preserved in the Blickling Hall, Norfolk, manuscript collection. According to the writer, John Collinges, toads poured down on the Norfolk village of Acle. So he had heard. They had made a nuisance of themselves invading people's houses, and the Acle publican, unable to endure the smell of them, had thrown them by the shovelful into the fire or out into the yard. Next day they were all gone.

We have so many records of frog and fish falls that, if we let them, they would fill up a fat book. For a suitable advance payment we will prove it. We would start classically with Pliny, quote from the Annamese historical almanacks and proceed into the fourth century AD with Athenaeus who, in *The Deipnosophists*, chronicles such things as the continuous three-day shower of fish which inconvenienced the Chersonesus district of Greece and the fall of frogs so serious that the roads were blocked, people were unable to open their front doors and the town stank for weeks. The long chapter on reports from the Middle Ages would examine the theory, orthodox at the time, that frogs and toads exist spermatically in the soil and spring up with a shower of rain. The modern period

would begin with Jerome Cardan and his new explanation that frog falls are the work of water-spouts which pick the creatures off the mountains and rain them onto the plains. The nineteenth century would contribute hundreds of cases, many of them collected in the books of Charles Fort and the articles of the distinguished modern authority on falling frogs and fish, Dr E. W. Gudger. Nor would the present century disappoint us, with its potential for interviews with such people as the lady of Sutton Park, Birmingham, sheltering from the rain on 12 June 1954, who witnessed hundreds of little frogs bouncing off people's umbrellas and scaring everyone with their leaping and their proliferation. As an appendix to the book we would reproduce the article in *INFO Journal*, no. 10, which lists the fifty-three cases of modern fish-falls in Australia.

These living-rain cases are beloved by all connoisseurs of odd phenomena, not only for themselves but particularly on account of the fine crop of diverse explanations they engender. The theory inherited from Pliny and dominant until

after the Renaissance, that of frog seed in the soil and the refreshing shower of rain, fits in with one feature of the data, first noticed by Fort, that the frogs and toads are always small and young, never (though 'never' always allows for exceptions) full-grown frogs or tadpoles. It is of course inadequate for cases such as the one given by a golf caddy in a letter to the *Camden News* of Arkansas, published on 2 January 1973, of 'a shower of tiny frogs about the size of nickels' during a thunderstorm: 'The golfers and I could not believe our eyes as we watched thousands of frogs come right down with the rain from the sky.' The explanation currently popular is in terms of whirlwinds, but selective whirlwinds, which scoop up, transport and rain down frogs or fishes alone, rejecting such associated items of their environment as water, mud, slime, rocks, weeds and other animal species. Whirlwinds are not generally so choosy, nor do they answer for the many cases of falls from clear skies, on still days, on to very limited areas of ground, and continuing for a long time or repeatedly at one particular spot.

An explanation which often appears in cases of falling fish is that they were disgorged by high-flying birds. Another one is the earthquake. The famous naturalist, Count de Castelnau, described an intense rainstorm lasting several days in February, 1861, after which fifty acres of land at Singapore were found covered with a local species of catfish. The natives, gathering them by the basketful, said they had dropped from the sky, but the Count, with the advantages of education and of not having seen the thing himself, blamed it on an earthquake. He did not explain further, and in any case the earthquake had happened five days earlier. Another famous scientist of the time, Humboldt, denounced as medieval superstition the idea of living rains. (In his day, of course, even meteorites were frowned on.) In South America he came across 'boiled fish' strewn all over the

## A TUBFUL OF TOADS

### Part of Thousands That Fell in a Thunderstorm.

NORTH CHELMSFORD, Mass., July 21 (A. P.).—If you doubt it, Mrs. Lillian Farnham issued a public invitation to visit her home and see a tubful of the little ones.

Mrs. Farnham says that at the height of a thunderstorm last night toads by the thousands fell around her home. Each was about three-quarters of an inch long, she said.

---

### A Shower of Sand-eels.

ABOUT 3 o'clock on the afternoon of Saturday, August 24 last, the allotment-holders of a small area in Hendon, a southern suburb of Sunderland, were sheltering in their sheds during a heavy thunder-shower, when they observed that small fish were being rained to the ground. The fish were precipitated on three adjoining roads and on the allotment-gardens enclosed by the roads; the rain swept them from the roads into the gutters and from the roofs of the sheds into the spouts.

The phenomenon was recorded in the local news-papers, the fish being described as " sile." I was away at the time, but, seeing the account, I wrote to Dr. Harrison, and thanks to him, and especially to Mr. H. S. Wallace, I obtained a sample of the fish, and I was able yesterday (September 5) to visit the place in the company of the latter gentleman.    . . .

There can be no question, therefore, that at the time stated a large number of small fish were showered over about one-third of an acre during a heavy rain accompanied by thunder; we were informed that no lightning was observed, and that the wind was variable.

---

(*Left*) A chapter-heading from Olaus Magnus' Historia de gentibus, *1555, in which he discusses many falls of fishes, frogs and animals, events which have repeated in every age up to the present.* (*Left bottom*) An account from the Philosophical Transactions *1698.* (*Above left*) An American *toad-fall.* (*Above right*) An English eel-shower, *1918.* (*Below*) A woodcut of an *18th-century incident in Transylvania.*

ground. There was a volcano nearby on which Humboldt blamed both the fish and the boiling. In a much debated case near Aberdare, South Wales, on 11 February 1859, a dense shower of fish, the largest five inches long, covered yards and the roofs of houses. Specimens were sent to Dr Gray of the British Museum in London. He identified them as young minnows and explained the belief that they had fallen from the sky as most probably arising from a practical joke in which somebody had drenched somebody else with a bucket of water from a stream.

Charles Fort, of whom falls of little frogs were particular favourites, conceived from them the notion of the 'Super-Sargasso Sea' lurking in the upper atmosphere, which receives objects from earth and occasionally scatters them down. In *Lo !* he expressed an even more mystical idea which we find among the most fascinating of his conjectures. In 1921 there was a report from Sussex of a pond, newly filled with water in November, found to be swarming with tench the following May. In another case, from Maryland, a farmer dug a ditch which filled up with water during a week of rain. In the rain water were found perch of two different species from four to seven inches long. It seems, wrote Fort, as if the new pond, vibrating with the need for fish according to its nature, attracted fish in from somewhere. The fish that fall on land are perhaps near misses, intended for somewhere else. In mitigation of nature's errors in this respect there follows a Fortean classic: 'The sending of fresh water fishes to a salt water lake is no more out of place than, for instance, is the sending of chaplains to battleships.'

One of us remembers as a child hearing of dew ponds, freshly dug in the chalk of the Wessex downs and far from any other body of water, soon discovered to be full of fish; and we note other such mysteries as eels suddenly populating mountain lakes. Fort's suggestion was that TELEPORTATION – the phenomenon of things disappearing from one place and appearing at another – might be an active agent in the distribution of species. All new varieties of living creatures might originate from the Super-Sargasso Sea. There was, for instance, a fall of little frogs near Birmingham on 30 June 1892. They were not like the local ones but described as almost white.

In the letter to *Nature*, reproduced on this page, the correspondent argues that because the fish that fell in the incident described were dead, such happenings were unlikely to have any effect on distribution. True, there are many falls of dead fish, sometimes so long dead that they have taken the form of slime, indicating a lengthy sojourn in the Super-Sargasso Sea. See RAINS OF CREATURES AND ORGANIC MATTER. On the other hand, many falls or teleportations are of living creatures which continue to live in their new environment. The interesting thing about Fort's observation on the new pond which attracted fish is that it is in exact accordance with the ancient magical doctrine that a vacuity will naturally draw to itself that which is made to fill it. The mystical Neoplatonist, Plotinus, revealed that the way to attract whatever you require to attract is to fashion a vessel specially designed to receive it. Hang a nesting-box in the orchard and a wild bird will come and nest in it. Make a pond delightful to fish and they will inhabit it.

In case anyone should take him seriously, dig a fishpond and wait in vain for fish, Fort had his excuse ready. Suppose the development of life here to have been a process of population by bombardment; now that every corner of the earth is inhabited by the appropriate creatures, the force of teleportation has no further function. It survives as an atavism, weakly. Instead of elephants some occasional little frogs.

*Charles Tomlinson's* Raincloud and Snowstorm, *1864, gave the case of John Lewis of Aberdare, Glamorgan, caught in a fish-fall on 9 February 1839. Ten minutes later a second shower hit the same spot, a strip 80 yards by 12 yards.*

# Falls of creatures and organic matter

In 1930 five men fell out of a thunder-cloud on to the Rhön Mountains, Germany, frozen in layers of ice. In *Strange Stories: Amazing Facts*, 1975, it was explained: five glider pilots had been carried into the cloud by strong air currents, and had bailed out – becoming the nuclei of super-hailstones. But how to explain the six- by eight-inch gopher turtle that came down with a hailstorm, entirely encased in ice, at Bovington, Mississippi, an event respectably recorded in *Monthly Weather Review*, May 1894?

Most people know of the periodic suicides of Norway's lemmings, but we wonder how it is, if this death-urge is genetic, that some remain behind to renew the breed. After reading this and our other falls sections, readers may be less outraged by the notion of replacements raining from the sky, particularly in the light of other records of animal falls in lemming country, such as C. Tomlinson's reference in *The Raincloud and the Snowstorm* to a shower of rats 'transported by the wind' into a Norwegian valley. More specific was an article on the lemming cycle in the *Journal of Cycle Research*, January 1957, quoting historical sources. Thus, in 1578, 'in the entire surroundings of Bergen, there rained big yellow mice which swam ashore when they fell into the water'. Another mouse-shower occurred in the autumn of the following year. Popular beliefs in similar phenomena were based firmly on observation, though usually dismissed as 'folk tales'.

Thousands of snakes, 1 to $1\frac{1}{2}$ feet long, arrived during torrential rain in a fairly localized area (two blocks) of Memphis, Tennessee, on 15 January 1877, according to *Scientific American*, 36–86. None was seen to fall, but it was so improbable that so many snakes could be hiding in that small urban area to be brought out by the rain (it had never happened before), that people preferred to believe they fell from the sky. But none was found on roofs. That need not deter us – we know of far too many stories of things falling from appearing-points in mid-air to discount this one (see FALLS OF ARTIFACTS).

In 1896 the *Philadelphia Times* reported that many hundreds of birds fell into the streets of Baton Rouge, Louisiana, from a clear sky. There were wild ducks, cat-birds, woodpeckers, and many birds of strange plumage, some of them resembling canaries, but all dead. On one street alone, children collected two hundred birds. There was no doubting the reality of the thing; the town was cluttered with dead birds. W.L. McAtee, writing in the *Monthly Weather Review*, May 1917, theorizes in terms of migrating birds thrown off course by a storm somewhere – but, of course, this simply does not account for the fact that hundreds of birds of different species died and fell at the same time in the same place. This leads on to another mystery. In January 1969 something smashed hundreds of duck in flight over St Mary's City, Maryland. It was as though the ducks (canvasbacks, redheads and scaups) had flown into a silent, invisible explosion, though no one below heard or saw a thing except falling ducks. According to the *Washington Post*, 26 January 1969, they fell with multiple rib fractures and severe haemorrhages, acquired *before* they hit the ground.

Rains of blood are among the oldest prodigies known to man, yet despite many modern recurrences and ancient allusions (e.g. Homer and Plutarch) the phenomenon is still regarded as 'myth'. On 15 May 1890 a blood-like substance fell at Messignadi, Calabria. *Popular Science News* 35–104, reported that the Italian Meteorological Bureau identified it as bird's blood. They suggested that a flock of birds had been torn apart by a violent wind – but their own records contained no mention of such a wind, nor could they explain how there were no carcases of the supposedly mangled birds. On 17 August 1841 workers in a

(*Left*) *Flammarion saw all insect rains in terms of locust plagues (as here in Algeria), but remained puzzled by the huge numbers of moth eggs, spiders and caterpillars dumped on the snows of Savoy in January 1869. (Below) The Biblical rains of manna and quail may indeed have been based on fact. M. J. Teesdale, in* Science Gossip, *3–229, cites Turkish manna-falls including one of several days during a famine in 1846;* Nature, *January 1891, mentions another, of lichen which was made into bread.*

tobacco field in Tennessee were startled by the rattle of large drops on the leaves. Looking closer they saw that the drops were like blood, and that they fell perpendicularly from a peculiar red cloud overhead. They fetched the owner and a Professor Troost, and when they returned with these worthies they saw the field strewn with foul-smelling bits of matter. The *American Journal of Science*, October 1841, carried a report from Professor Troost in which he declared that the stuff was animal fat and muscle-tissue, though he would venture no opinion on the 'blood'. Later this learned journal said that it believed the event to be a hoax by the Negro workers who for unknown reasons had scattered a decayed hog over the field.

We read in *Scientific American*, March 1876, that on 8 March many witnesses in Kentucky saw flakes of meat drifting down from a clear sky. As in many of our accounts, including the Tennessee meat fall above, these flakes fell only in a confined area (an oblong field). An investigator found that the meat-flakes (one was 3–4 inches square) were 'perfectly fresh'. Bravely he ate some and found they tasted like 'mutton or venison'. Once more the public was treated to the spectacle of squabbling scientists, ignoring eye-witness testimony in favour of their own favourite theories, the winner being that the stuff was disgorged by a flock of buzzards. The most recent account in our files comes from the *Flying Saucer Review*, November 1968, quoting from Brazilian papers. For 5 to 7 minutes on 27 August in that year, meat and blood fell on an area of one kilometre square between Cocpava and São José dos Campos.

But just as we are sure there have been rains of blood and flesh, so we are sure that there have been coloured rains. *La Nature*, 28 September 1880, relates that Professor Brun of Geneva investigated reports of a blood-rain near Djebel-Sekra, Morocco, and found rocks and vegetation covered in dried red scales, which he identified as the remains of colonies of the minute organism *Protococcus fluvialis*. He explained that they had been deposited there by a whirlwind, but confessed he was puzzled by the extraordinary selection involved. They were all *young* organisms.

We do not doubt there have been falls of colonies of nostoc (blue-green algae) or infusoria, or the exudations and eggs of insects. Most instances of 'jelly falls' are in association with unexplained aerial lights. Chladni tells of a viscous mass that fell with a 'luminous meteorite' in Italy in 1652 – *Annals of Philosophy*, 12–94 – and of a 'gelatinous matter' that fell with a globe of fire on Lethy Island, India in 1718 – *American Journal of Science*, 26–133. *Scientific American*, 2–79, says that on 11 November 1846 a bright object, four feet in

(Above) A rain of blood at Lisbon in 1551, pictured by Lycosthenes in Prodigiorum ac ostentorum . . ., 1557. In 1869, blood, hairs and strips of flesh up to 6 inches long fell on a town in California (Los Angeles News, 3 August 1869). (Below) The account in the Worcester Daily Times, 30 May 1881, of the great fall of winkles two days earlier.

diameter, became or left behind a mass of 'foetid jelly' at Loweville, New York. And so on. The continuity of the phenomenon is well documented. For example, the Dublin *Evening Herald*, 7 February 1958, reported a strange light passing over West Meath and landing in a field. It was thought to be a UFO, but investigators rushing to the spot found only a mass of 'bog butter'. The Bishop of Cloyne writing in 1696 (quoted in *Philosophical Transactions*, 19–224) spoke of many such falls in his lifetime in Ireland, and said that this bog butter, whatever it is, was highly prized by the local people as a treatment for scalds. Professor McKenny Hughes wrote in *Nature*, 23 June 1910, that the notion that falling stars turn into jelly was very common; he claimed he had seen 'the rot of the stars' for himself, and that the Welsh called it *pwdre Ser*. Attempts to explain it as the gelatinous fungus *Tremella mesenterica* are inconclusive.

Fort advanced the idea that, just as nourishment is supplied to the developing parts of an egg, perhaps these falls are attempts to nourish our planet as an embryonic system, using teleportative processes, and that our environment was originally prepared for us by air lifts of material, food and life from somewhere else – a process that still continues intermittently as a survival of more active times. Eccentric though this notion may sound, it is quite in accordance with the evidence: for, as we hope we have shown, things do fall from the heavens, and many of them are alive and edible. There was, after all, a positive response to the Israelites' prayers for quails and manna, and, as far as we know, showers of edible lichen still occur in Asia Minor to this day.

The seeds that rained into the streets of Kirkmanshaws, Persia, were thought to be manna, but said by the London *Daily Mail*, 13 August 1913, to be like Indian corn. *INFO Journal* 8, 1972, tells of a rain of West African beans on a farm in north-west Brazil in the summer of 1971. In these cases and others, we remain astonished at the way the whirlwind theory is automatically brought out as an explanation even though it is consistently discredited on examination. Sometime in 1897 an incalculable number of seeds fell around several towns in the Italian province of Macerata. In *Notes and Queries*, 18 September 1897, they are identified as seeds of the Judas tree, a native of Central Africa, and most were in the first stage of germination. We boggle at the idea of any whirlwind that can pick up *only* these seeds in such a great quantity (no twigs, leaves, etc.), transporting them to Italy, keeping them together in the air and not dropping any on places in between! The *Philosophical Transactions*, 16–281, says grains of wheat fell in Wiltshire in 1686: the damned things were in hailstones.

# Missiles from the upper regions

Lavoisier, Gassendi and other great seventeenth- and eighteenth-century scientists investigated reports of stones dropping out of the sky. They touched them, probed them and examined witnesses to their fall, but could not face the implications of the evidence. 'There are no stones in the sky,' Lavoisier told the Academy of Sciences, 'therefore stones can not fall from the sky.' On 13 September 1768 a stone weighing 7½ pounds dropped with a loud explosion on to Luce in Maine, France. Lavoisier examined witnesses and then the stone itself, and decided it must be of terrestrial origin, probably unearthed by lightning. 'In spite of the belief of the ancients,' he wrote, 'true physicists have always been doubtful about the existence of these stones.' It is a good thing there were no true physicists around on 7 December 1491 when an enormous stone fell at Eisisheim before the entire army of Maximilian I.

It was only at the beginning of this century that the meteorite theory became totally accepted, but the stone falls that particularly interest us now are those of non-meteoric character and those which occur in odd circumstances or in connection with other phenomena. The Dhurmsalla Meteorite, a mass of stone covered with ice, fell on 28 July 1860. The Deputy Commissioner of Dhurmsalla, India, reported in the *Canadian Institute Proceedings*, 2–7–198, that within a few months of its arrival there was a fall of fishes at Benares, a fall of red stuff at Furruckabad, an earthquake, a dark spot on the sun's disc, an 'unnatural darkness of some duration' and peculiar auroral displays. The evening after the event he himself saw many lights in the sky that today would be called UFOs. Greg's catalogue of meteorites describes the Dhurmsalla fall as 'so intensely cold as to benumb the fingers and hands' (*Report of the British Association*, 1860).

Slow, personalized or portentous stone falls are so often recorded that we pick a few stories at random. *The Times*, 1 May 1821: showers of stones continue upon a house in Truro, Cornwall, despite many days of guarding and investigation by the mayor, soldiers and others. Records go back to the time when the Lord 'cast down great stones from heaven' on the Amorites (Joshua 10:11). Livy (I,3) tells us that when Tullus conquered the Sabines, rocks began to rain into a sacred grove atop Mount Albanus. The Romans sent observers, and the rocks fell in their sight. Greg's list contains about 2,000 entries back to AD 2, and many of these are clearly not 'true' meteorites. Fort chronicles hundreds more 'non-meteoric' falls and says that

he has many more but frequency will not make the truth any truer, and withholds them. Miriam Allen deFord, the American writer and one of Fort's longest-lasting correspondents, wrote in a biographical essay on Fort, published in *Fantasy and Science Fiction*, January 1954: 'In 1922 there was a celebrated series of stone falls at Chico, California. I went there and investigated for Fort, and myself saw a stone fall from some invisible point in the sky and land gently at my feet.'

In Charleston, South Carolina, stones bounced off the pavement outside the offices of the *Charleston News and Courier* on 4 September 1886. It was 2.30 a.m., and no one could see any likely miscreant, but the stones were found to be warm. The 6 September edition of the paper carried the testimony of the editor, who had himself witnessed two further showers of warm stones at 7.30 a.m. and 1.30 p.m. on the same day. He noticed that they seemed to come from a point overhead and were strangely confined to an area of about 75 square feet.

The *Rand Daily Mail*, 29 May 1922, carries an even stranger story. For several months a chemist's shop in Johannesburg, South Africa, was bombarded with stones, and the phenomenon was thought to centre on a Hottentot girl employed there. The police staked out the garden and the girl was sent into the shop. Stones fell in quantities vertically all around her. The police noted this verticality because they were hoping to trace an accomplice by the trajectory. They searched the locality nevertheless, and stones continued to fall in the girl's vicinity. Weeks of fruitless investigation followed, while large stones continued to fall around the girl as the police watched.

A disturbing case of a personalized stone fall was reported in *INFO*, 14. Two men fishing in a lake at Skaneatles, New York, on the evening of 27 October 1973 were disturbed by a large stone splashing into the water near them, followed by a second and third stone, each progressively larger. They searched the locality with their torches and

(Left) A Turkish painting of the famous incident in which a rain of stones, dropped by birds, saved Mecca from the attacking Yemenite army. Today's equivalent of this naturalistic explanation is the attribution of falls of blocks of ice to aeroplanes. (Above) This is a fragment of a massive ice-block that smashed a car at Pinner, Middlesex, on 25 March 1974 (below). In Weatherwise, June 1960, an atmospheric physicist, James McDonald, found that only two out of thirty ice-falls in the 1950s could be blamed on planes.

found nothing. Then a rain of small pebbles forced them to pack up, and followed them as they ran to their car. They drove off in a hurry. Later, when they stopped to change their clothes, stones fell on them again. They stopped for a drink and were again bombarded as they emerged from the bar. As they parted company outside one of their homes, stones fell in torrents. Analysis by the Geology Department of Syracuse University identified the falls as belonging to local rock-types.

Another type of stone fall is that which occurs within rooms and enclosed spaces. We mention similar effects in MATERIALIZATION AND FLIGHT OF OBJECTS, but here is a recent classic. For five days stones rained round a young Aborigine farmworker at Pumphrey, Western Australia. Pathetically, scientists were quoted, explaining away by means of 'freak winds'. The clincher came when two witnesses swore that while they were in a closed tent with the young man, stones fell at their feet. There was no trickery involved, and certainly no holes for stones or freak winds in the tent material. They were said to be 'just ordinary stones' (Daily Express, 22 March 1957).

A major 'falls' category features jagged chunks of ice. We warn against excessive reliance on the apparently rational explanation that they drop off aircraft. Flammarion refers to a mass of ice, 15 feet long, 6 feet wide and 11 feet thick, falling in the time of Charlemagne (L'Atmosphère, 1888), and even if there had been modern planes in the first half of the nineteenth century they could not have carried the weight of some recorded falls without themselves dropping out of the air. In 1802, 18 cubic feet of ice thudded into Hungary; in 1828 a block a yard wide fell at Candeish, India. The Times, 14 August 1849, reported that the previous evening an irregular-shaped mass of ice had fallen at Ord, Ross-shire, after an extraordinary peal of thunder. It was about 20 feet around and must have weighed nearly half a ton. Ron Willis compiled forty-six such cases, from Fort and more modern sources, for INFO, 3, and readers are referred to his tabulation and discussion of the aircraft theory, the ice-meteorite theory, and the theory that winds, if strong enough, can support these masses while they form.

There have been some spectacular cases. In November 1950, a farm on Exmoor, near North Molton in Devon, was found littered with lumps of ice the 'size of dinner-plates'. Among them was a dead sheep, its neck cleanly slashed by the 14-pound chunk embedded in the ground by its shoulder: London Evening News, 9 November 1950. But this does not compare with the thousands of sheep killed by ice bombardment in Texas, reported in Monthly Weather Review, May 1877; nor with the bizarre death of a carpenter on the roof of his house near Düsseldorf on 10 January 1951, skewered by a spear of ice 6 inches in diameter and 6 feet long, reported in Frank Edwards's Strangest of All, 1956.

The 'falls' record teems with singularities. We could mention blocks of foul-smelling ice; falls of coloured ice; falls of salt crystals, copper alloy, clinkers, and alabaster; hailstones of carbonate of soda and a rain of nitric acid, most of which date from before this sort of thing became commonplace with industrial pollution. There have been falls of metallic fragments that cannot be accounted for by meteorological theory: for example, a soft lump of what turned out to be fragments of glass and almost pure zinc fell at Cannifton, Ontario (Belleville Intelligencer, 11 November 1968). A puzzling ball of limestone landed near Bleckenstad, Sweden, on 11 April 1925, and burst, leaving fragments which, according to Professor Hadding of Lund University, contained marine shells, and even traces of an animal resembling a trilobite (The Exploration of Space, by P. G. Gittens). See TOAD IN THE HOLE for other accounts of animals in the hearts of rocks.

# Falls of artifacts

One of the strangest Christian traditions holds that the Pillar of Saragossa was carried to that place by angels in the company of the Virgin Mary (during her lifetime), and that from the top of it she gave instruction to the Apostle St James. The traditions of most cultures all over the world include artifacts, like the Pillar, that are alleged to have fallen from the sky. They used to be held sacred, preserved in temples or put to magical use. Nowadays they languish in museum basements, or in some forgotten display, labelled 'Stone Age ritual object'. We note with interest that Greg's meteorite catalogue in the *Report of the British Association*, 1860, lists a pillar-like worked stone that fell from the sky in Constantinople in about AD 416.

Pyramidal stones, called variously thunder-stones, thunderbolts, sky-axes and lightning arrows, are universally prized as talismans against lightning. We read in C. Blinkenberg's *Thunder Weapons*, 1911, that the natives of Burma, China and Japan believed these objects to be manufactured in the sky. Tallius, writing in 1649, alluded to the belief of some naturalists that thunder-stones 'are generated in the sky by fulgurous exhalation conglobed in a cloud by the circumfused humour'. Like many an explanation of strange phenomena today, this has the appearance of saying something. It would be some centuries before scientific orthodoxy was to accept that stones could fall from the sky.

Fort was particularly interested in the number of accounts in which 'axe-shaped' stones were found near lightning strikes or embedded in trees struck by lightning. Blinkenberg mentions that it was the native belief as far and wide as Jamaica, Norway, Malaya and the British Isles that these 'axes' came down with the lightning. Fort adds the similar beliefs of the North American Indians (*Primitive Culture*, 2–237) and those of South America (*Journal of American Folklore*, 17–203).

The Anglo-Saxons were in particular terror of 'elf-shot', or 'fairy arrows', tiny missiles manufactured and thrown by the fairies. We have looked for continuities in our data and seen them repeat in different countries and times. What is folk-memory now may once have been founded on real incidents, and, vice versa, what was once a fiction has a way of becoming fact (see COINCIDENCES). A fine modern account of 'elf-shot' is related in A. A. MacGregor's *The Haunted Isles*: 'A specimen of these fairy arrows was

picked up at Loch Maddy some years ago by a young girl, who on going out into the darkness for an armfull of peats, heard something whizz through the air and drop at her feet.' (For other stories of flying stones linked to the fairies, see THE LITTLE PEOPLE and PHENOMENAL HIGHWAYS.)

A disc of worked stone, *très régulier*, fell at Tarbes, France, in June 1887. The *Comptes rendus* (1887–182) attempted to explain it by a whirlwind, but it came down without attendant debris, and was covered in ice. In 1910 a controversy raged in the pages of *Scientific American* when Charles F. Holder announced that he had deciphered a deeply incised inscription on 'a strange stone resembling a meteorite' which had fallen into the Yaqui Valley, Mexico. Holder's assertion that the signs were Mayan was fairly easy to discredit, so the matter was conveniently dropped, leaving uninvestigated the original claim that a stone bearing inscriptions had descended to the earth.

Today, the phenomenon seems to have changed its form, and in keeping with this godless age the divine origin has been devalued to accommodate the most trivial products of modern technology. From our records we could relate tales of rains of foil and tinsel since 1911; of manufactured chemicals since 1842; nuts and bolts since 1936; plastic materials since 1955; a brass cube in 1961; and all kinds of balls, big and small, metal and plastic, since the early nineteenth century. At Bijori, India, beads of many colours and holed ready to string have fallen regularly, it is said, for nearly a hundred years. At times they are so plentiful that you can scoop them up by the handful. All efforts to trace the source (assuming transport by 'whirlwind' and that some factory or warehouse somewhere must have a regularly diminishing stock) have failed, according to *Fate*, January 1955. Similarly, a police investigation failed to account for the rain of golf balls during a storm at Punta Gorda, Florida, 3 September 1969 (*INFO Journal*, 7, 1970).

E. T. C. Werner's *Myths and Legends of China*, 1922, mentions an ancient story about Lei Kung, the Duke of

Thunder, in which he drops a bottle of healing lotion down from heaven to a woman who has been struck by lightning. The modern equivalent, though warped in spirit and form, can be seen in the deluge of mud, wood-chunks, stones, broken glass and pottery that added insult to the injury of the people Piñar del Río, Cuba, four times in 1968 (*Beyond* magazine, October 1969). Similarly, great quantities of nails dropped out of the night sky onto the wife of the lighthouse keeper at Point Isabel, Texas, on 12 October 1888. The *St Louis Globe-Democrat* of 16 October said the nail-shower was repeated the next night, but accompanied this time by clods of earth and oyster shells. The report attracted crowds of sightseers, and many people testified to seeing nails plummeting down near the lighthouse.

We have data on events which *seem* to be falls, although no one has seen any falling. According to the *St Louis Post-Dispatch*, 10 November 1965, a man in Louisville, Kentucky, heard an explosion outside his back door, and rushed out to find his yard covered in bags of cookies. Interestingly they were also found on his garage roof, which suggested to the neighbours that the things came from above, probably cargo spilled from a plane. However there was no means of identifying the manufacturers or the hypothetical plane; nor did any plane report a loss of cargo.

There was no doubt, however, in the mind of a woman driving along a road in Palm Springs, California, that a wheel dropped out of the sky, badly damaging her car roof. According to the *New York Times*, 17 April 1969, the authorities could find no report of any plane with a missing wheel.

Such falls are inexplicable enough, but when they repeat with the same material on the same spot, the problem is doubly damned. According to the *Philosophical Magazine*, 4–8–463, fragments of rusty iron fell at Orenburg, Russia, on 25 January 1824 – and four months later, they fell again, as recorded in the *Journal of the Royal Institute*, 1828. We jump from metal fragments falling in the open air to a rain of buckshot that fell at intervals over several days in an office at Newton, New Jersey. The *San Francisco Chronicle*, 3 March 1929, called it the greatest mystery in the history of the town; and there was no apparent means by which the shot could have entered. After a similar case was reported in the *Religio-Philosophical Journal*, its issue for 24 April 1880 carried a correspondent's description of bullets that fell at intervals in broad daylight in every room of his house in 1867. The falls of 'large birdshot' increased and began to last an hour or more. Whenever he went to gather them up he could never find more than half a dozen – the rest mysteriously vanishing.

Among our records of falls of pieces of furnace-made brick, we can match the buckshot rains quite easily. The *Bulletin of the Sri Aurobindo International Centre of Education* for February 1974 has a lengthy recollection by an eye-witness of falls of pieces of brick inside various rooms of the Sri Aurobindo Ashram at Pondicherry, India, in December 1921. Searches could reveal no culprit or cause, but bricks continued to rain down in the courtyard, kitchen and stairwell. The residents soon noticed that the bricks were visible only below the level of the roof, as though they simply came into being at that height, falling as soon as they materialized. Some of the residents noticed that the phenomenon seemed associated with a young boy, assistant to the cook. They locked him in a room with no apertures, and bricks fell around him, wounding him. Forty-one years earlier, in a schoolroom near Government House in Madras, bricks had also fallen, and had continued to fall in the presence of thirty investigators for at least five days. The *Madras Mail*, 5 March 1888, says that the clergy advised marking one brick with a white cross and placing it in the centre of the room. To their utter astonishment 'a brick of a corresponding size, but bearing a *black* cross, dropped out of the air onto the top of the first brick', so precisely that it stayed balanced there.

We must mention one other trick in this strange repertoire. Long ago, we are told, an ancient people prayed for 'manna' and got it (see FALLS OF ORGANIC MATTER), and as evidence of continuity we offer the modern equivalent: rains of money in the concrete wilderness. Some of our cases occur during 'poltergeist' hauntings: e.g., pennies fell in the company of pieces of soda and lumps of coal during the famous 1927–28 disturbance at Battersea, London, investigated and recorded by Harry Price in his *Poltergeist Over England*, 1945.

One of the most devastating poltergeists of all time must be that which completely demolished a house near the Sorbonne, Paris, with a continuous bombardment of building materials. The commotion continued every night for three weeks and is recorded in the official French police magazine, the *Gazette des tribunaux*, 2 February 1849, which contains an undated allusion to similar excitement in Paris, when 'a rain of pieces of small money drew together the loungers of Paris every evening in the Rue de Montesquieu'. Note that the phenomenon was repeated on several occasions.

Fort mentioned a fall of coins in Trafalgar Square, London, but did not give details; however, we can report that pennies and halfpennies dropped around children going home from school in Hanham, Bristol, according to the London *People*, 30 September 1956. At Meshehera, Russia, silver coins fell 'all over the district' during a storm – *Daily Express*, London, 5 August 1940. The *People*, 17 February 1957, reported that a Gateshead, County Durham, woman was in her yard when 'two objects whizzed past her head' – they were halfpennies; and about forty to fifty pennies came down in short bursts over fifteen minutes at Ramsgate, Kent. According to the *Daily Mirror*, 10 December 1968, 'You could not see them falling – all you heard was the sound of them bouncing off the pavement.' Curiously they were all bent – shades of Uri Geller. The *Bath Chronicle*, 6 January 1976, records that two clergymen at Limburg, West Germany, picked up 2000 marks in banknotes which they said fluttered down from a clear sky. But even that cannot match for grandeur the 'thousands' of 1000-franc notes that rained on Bourges, France. Despite investigation, said the *Sunday Express*, 15 April 1957, no one reported or claimed the loss.

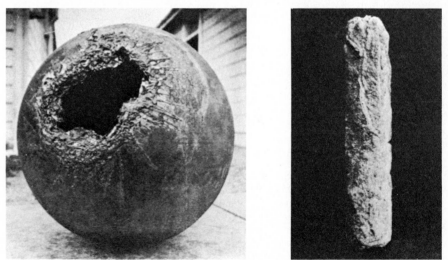

*(Left) A rain of crosses in 1503 reported by Lycosthenes, 1557. (Above left) A 16-inch metal sphere, thought to have fallen from space, found in New Zealand in 1972. (Right) An unusual 'meteorite', thought to be a 12-inch cylinder of marble that fell in Ohio in August 1910.*

# Images that weep and bleed

The old histories abound in references to idols and images that weep, sweat and bleed, events that were taken as powerful portents. It is recorded, for example, that on the eve of Alexander the Great's expedition of conquest, a cypress-wood statue of Orpheus, in Libethra, sweated profusely for several days. The sooth-sayer, Aristander, was not disconcerted; he delivered a favourable interpretation saying it was emblematic of the labour that future historians and poets would be put to in celebrating the monarch's exploits. Similarly, before the Sack of Rome in 1527, a statue of Christ was said to have wept so copiously that the fathers in the monastery where it was kept were continually employed in wiping its face. The same lachrymose tendency was attributed to a marble statue of St Lucy which wept during the siege of Syracuse in Sicily in 1719. Livy records that a statue of Apollo once wept for three days and nights; and Ovid tells of the dryad's oak at Eresicthon which gushed crimson blood-like liquid when it was sacri-legiously cut down.

All these old stories of bleedings and weepings by various sacred objects may sound too fantastic to be taken seriously, and yet the same phenomenon continues to be reported up to the present day. Even as we began to write this section, we received news of the bleeding statue of Christ at Eddystone, Pennsylvania (see illustration); and a few weeks before that the London *Sunday People*, 11 January 1976, contained an article on a 300-year-old wooden image of Christ, in the Brazilian village of Porto das Caixas, and the miraculous healings attributed to the blood which periodically streams from its painted wounds. Authoritative tests are stated to have established that the blood was real, though of an inde-terminate species. More interesting to us is the fact that, despite careful watches and examinations since the first ap-pearance of bleeding in 1968, the source of the flows has remained undetected. In 1972, a bleeding limestone crucifix attracted so many pilgrims that the Church had to warn the public that this was not a recognized miracle – yet! The

small crucifix belonged to the Pizzi family of Syracuse, Sicily, and the drops of blood formed on the statuette's breast, on the traditional site of Christ's lance-wound. According to Dr S. Rodante, president of the island's Catholic Doc-tors' Association, quoted in *Fate*, De-cember 1972, the blood coagulated instantly, whereas samples taken from the Pizzi family (presumably on the assumption that they might be per-petuating a hoax with their own blood) reacted in the normal manner.

Besides being a phenomenon in its own right, bleeding and weeping of images has occurred in association with other strange happenings. For example, on 21 August 1920, all the religious statues and pictures belonging to James Walsh, devout sixteen-year-old, began to bleed. He was lodging in the house of Thomas Dwan, in Templemore, County Tipperary, Ireland, and the statues in the house of Dwan's sister, Mrs Maher, were also found oozing blood after a visit by the boy. During the periods of bleeding, the furniture and other objects in Dwan's house moved on their own, in the best poltergeist tradition. In the months that followed many thousands of people saw these wonders. At first Dwan and Maher let small parties into their houses, but soon the great numbers became prohibitive, and they took to placing the statues in their windows as the columns of pilgrims trooped by, day and night. It was a strange scene amid the violent troubles in Ireland at the time. Many depositions were drawn up testifying to the miracle; and the *Tip-perary Star* rarely appeared without some new account of the wonder of Templemore. There was another man-ifestation here of interest too. In the earthen floor of the boy's room, there was a cup-shaped hollow which filled up with water. Thousands of pilgrims took away quantities, but no matter how often it was drained, the hollow was always full. There were no signs of any hidden spring (the water never overflowed), but just enough water to replenish the hollow was appearing as mysteriously as the blood on the statues. This turns our thoughts to the matter of 'holy wells' and the revered stoup-stones, the hollows in which always filled with fresh water said to have medicinal properties (see FALLS OF LIQUIDS).

Sometimes these mysterious ap-pearances of liquids take a bizarre form. The *Worcester Telegram*, of Illinois, 10 May 1970, reported that a 'watery blood' was oozing from the neck, hands and feet of the body of St Maximina, in St Adrian's Church, Chicago. St Maximina's 1,700-year-old bones are encased in a wax body portraying a beautiful lady, but the bones of the hands and feet are exposed to view; the whole in a glass coffin. This seems analogous to the so-called 'blood miracles' associated with many saints, whose blood was found long after their deaths to be fresh and still capable of flowing, and whose bodies remained uncorrupted. Father Herbert Thurston devotes several chapters to these aspects of hagiography in his *Physical Phenomena of Mysticism*, typical of which is the blood prodigy associated with St Nicholas of Tolentino. In 1345, forty years after the saint's death, a lay brother cut the arms off the saint's still incorrupt body, intending to carry them to Germany. Like the axing of Ovid's oak (ACCIDENTS TO ICONOCLASTS), this sacrilegious act was betrayed by a torrent of blood. The arms were recovered and enshrined at Tolentino in reliquaries, and are said to repeat their bleeding whenever some disaster threatens. Thurston had some doubts about the

tale of the severing, but added that 'there can be no reasonable doubt that from the two arms a curious exudation of a red fluid, described as "blood", did take place from time to time in the sixteenth and seventeenth centuries. In 1699 this discharge seems to have continued pretty constantly for four months'. That stringent critic and authority on miracles, Pope Benedict XIV, accepted the authenticity of this miracle.

In contrast, the Church has frowned on the way in which the miracle of the liquefaction of the blood of St Januarius has been popularly taken as a sign of luck for the city of Naples. Each year, phials holding dried particles of the saint's blood, kept in the Santa Chiara basilica, are supposed to turn liquid and froth for a while during services on the first Saturday in May, and on 19 September.

The miracle has sometimes been known to fail, and the Neapolitans fatalistically await a calamity on these occasions. In 1976, the two most violent earthquakes on record to have shaken northern Italy were both within days of the St Januarius festival. One happened in May on the sixth day of the failure of the miracle; the other happened in September during the week before a successful liquefaction, so take your pick. The earliest recorded liquefaction was in 1329, since when there have been many attempts to explain the event away. Sir David Brewster, in *Natural Magic*, speculates about compounds that would melt at low temperatures, so the 'blood' would froth from the heat of the hand holding its phial. Other investigators claim the phenomenon to be genuine.

Most apologists and critics of miracles tend to argue specific events in isolation; Fort and Thurston, on the other hand, suggested that the enigma may only be understood when the grand view of repeated and related events is taken. Fort was, of course, alluding to the TELEPORTATION of liquids, and we could extend this to include the well-documented perpetually damp 'bloodstains' that occur in 'haunted' houses (see MYSTERIOUS FLOWS AND OOZINGS).

Another manifestation is the weeping picture or statue. There is the recent example of a plaster cast Madonna owned by Mrs Theresa Taylor of Walker, Newcastle-upon-Tyne. According to contemporary newspapers, Mrs Taylor was praying before it on 10 October 1955 when she saw the Madonna's left eye open and a bead of moisture form there. Later neighbours were said to have seen a stream of tears. The last English case on our files involved a 16-inch crucifix, owned by Alfred Bolton of Walthamstow, London, which was observed to shed tears on at least thirty occasions between May and July 1966. A forensic scientist quoted in the *News of the World*, 24 July 1966, said he was quite baffled after a thorough examination of the statuette.

In March 1960, Mrs Pagora Catsounis was praying before a portrait of the Virgin in her Island Park, New York, home. She too thought she saw Mary's eyes open and tears flow. Her husband saw them too, and called the priest of St Paul's Greek Orthodox church in nearby Hempstead. When he arrived, he saw for himself tears forming under the glass and running to the bottom of the frame *where they vanished*. In relating this story, the writer in *Grit*, 26 July 1970, refers to other instances of weeping pictures. In 1953 several ikons of the Madonna wept blood in Italy: in Syracuse the flow lasted eight days, and in Mezzolombardo the blood had appeared on a newspaper photograph of a popular image.

*(Left) In 1911, this picture of Christ in a church at Mirebeau, France, began bleeding from the traditional sites of the stigmata. Tests at London's Lister Institute showed the blood to be a rare human type. (Below) The 'Weeping Madonna' of Syracuse, Sicily, 1953, whose flowing tears were found to be similar to human tears. (Below) A 28-inch plaster statue of Christ, now in St Luke's Episcopalian Church, Eddystone, Pennsylvania, started to bleed in November 1975. According to the* National Enquirer, *20 January 1976, the blood is human, though of great age. One investigator removed the solid chalk hands and found them continuing to bleed copiously.*

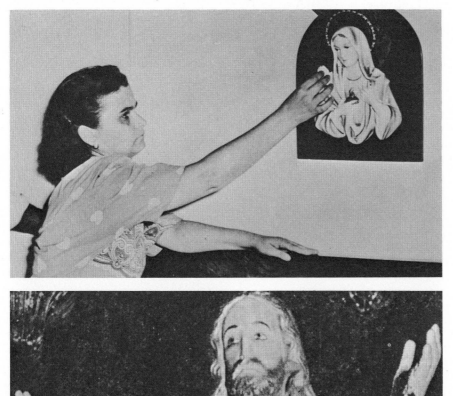

# Mysterious flows and oozings

Here we examine some symptoms of a mysterious, distributive force in relation to liquids – liquids which appear from 'nowhere' and ooze or flow from objects or drop down from mid-air. We note odd rains and localized repetitions, like the remarkable series at Geneva. The *Comptes rendus*, 5–549, carried a report that large, well-separated drops of *warm* water fell on Geneva from a clear zenith at 9 a.m. on 9 August 1837. This was repeated on 31 May the following year (*Yearbook of Facts*, 1839–262), and at 10 a.m. on 11 May 1842 (*Comptes rendus*, 15–290) and again that same day. During a series of quakes at Inverness in June 1817, *hot* water fell on the 30th of that month (*Report of the British Association*, 1854–112).

The mysterious phenomenon of intense, localized rain is called by meteorologists 'point rainfall'. As an example, *Symons' Meteorological Magazine*, 47–140, records a 'cascade' of water and hail upon an area of London of no more than 200 acres on 9 June 1809. The *Toronto Globe*, 3 June 1889, described the townsfolk of Coburg, Ontario, looking up to see a vast bag-like body of water crossing the town and flopping down two miles away. It was explained away as a 'waterspout'. Fort was fascinated with the idea of the TELEPORTATION of large volumes of water. For a torrent of accounts collected by him see Chapter 3 of *Lo!*

As alternatives to 'cloudbursts' there are steady flows. According to the *Comptes rendus*, 14–664, a stream of water fell from a stationary point in the sky over Noirfontaine, France, for at least two days in April 1842. The *New York Sun*, 24 October 1886, reported that water had been falling steadily for fourteen days out of a cloudless sky onto the same piece of ground in Chesterfield County, South Carolina. About the same time other papers were reporting similar falls at Cheraw and at Aitken, where the shower was confined to an area of ten square feet. The following month there was a fall at Dawson, Georgia, concentrated on a spot 25 feet wide. It was as if there were invisible, stationary taps left running in the sky.

Thirsty trees cry out for water, and the response, if response it is, is often erratic or absent-mindedly prolonged. The *Charlotte Chronicle*, of North Carolina, 21 October 1886, reported: 'Citizens in the southeastern portion of the city have witnessed for three weeks or more a very strange phenomenon. Every afternoon at 3 o'clock there is a rainfall in one particular spot, which lasts for half an hour. Between two trees at the hour named there falls a gentle rain while the sun is shining, and this has been witnessed every day during the past three weeks.' A Signal Service observer later sent a report on this to the *Monthly Weather Review*, October 1887, saying he had seen it himself over several days. The trees were red oaks, and 'sometimes the precipitation falls over an area of half an acre, but always appears to centre at these two trees, and when lightest, there only'. At Brownsville, Pennsylvania, it was a peach tree that received this watery manna. According to the *St Louis Globe-Democrat*, 19 November 1892, witnesses saw the water falling from a little way above the tree and covering an area round it of about 14 feet square. In July 1966, an acacia tree in the yard of a house in La Feria, Texas, had water, not falling upon it, but flowing out of it. The owner, Sam Morse, saw the stream coming from a knot-hole 20 feet above the ground, and collected 6 gallons in 12 hours. Other reports say the tree once pumped out 40 gallons over a 47-day period. *Fate*, February 1967, wryly recorded that the tree soon became an object of pilgrimage, and miraculous healings were attributed to its murky waters. Claims for the curative powers of mysterious sweats, tears and other exudations from unlikely objects, especially trees and images, extend far back into antiquity. The subject is pursued in our section IMAGES THAT WEEP AND BLEED.

Other, totally mysterious manifestations of liquids are called conventionally 'poltergeist flows'. In early February 1873, the Bank House at Eccleston, Lancashire, was the scene of an extraordinary series of events. Torrents of water rained down in the rooms, soaking the elderly inhabitants and ruining their furniture. Everyone who investigated the case was impressed by the genuine misery the phenomenon caused; there was no question of imposture. The report in the *Chorley Standard*, 15 February, noted that 'the most singular feature of the affair is that the ceilings themselves were quite dry'. On 9 September 1880, a reporter from the *Toronto Globe* described his investigations of improbable occurrences at a farm near Wellesley, Ontario, where windows were broken by unfindable missiles and furniture moved about on its own initiative. He later told of such volumes of water falling in the house, often when the rooms were full of sightseers, that the family's effects were ruined. Yet neither walls nor ceilings bore any trace of the water's passage. Frank Edwards in *Strange World*, 1964, describes the liquid plagues of the Waterman family (appropriately named), which only developed nine years after they moved into their house near Windsor, Vermont. One morning in September 1955 they found beads of moisture on their furniture as though a heavy mist had settled on it. According to Edwards they sponged the strange dew off, but it repeatedly returned, sometimes copiously. Checks made by service engineers found all the pipes tight and dry; but still water collected hour after hour. One day, says Edwards, as Dr Waterman 'transferred a shallow dish of grapes from one room to another, it filled with water during the transit'.

An article on mysterious flows of all kinds in *Grit* (USA), 26 July 1970, mentioned a watery persecution that drove the Martin family from their house in Methuen, Massachusetts, in 1963, and resumed its harassments in their new home in another city. Water was described as 'spurting' from different points throughout the house, as well as weeping from the walls and ceilings. We know from many studies of 'poltergeist' cases that the activity can transfer to the new home, but we also know of cases where the disturbances have remained with the house to plague the next family. The following case of Eugenio Rossi is reminiscent of other 'persecution' cases, such as where people have been the centre of attention for fires (FIERY PERSECUTIONS), stones (MISSILES FROM THE UPPER REGIONS) and other sinister hazards (INVISIBLE ASSAILANTS and STIGMATA). Nine-year-old Eugenio was in hospital in Nuoro, Sardinia, for a liver complaint, when, according to *The Sun*, 30 November 1972, large quantities of water began to seep through the floorboards around his bed. He was moved five times, each time for the same reason: water came through, or appeared on, the floor around his bed. Again we read of baffled officials and service engineers failing, despite a thorough search, to find any acceptable cause. Those people who, even though unwillingly, possess this natural affinity with water must surely have been the water-finders and rain-makers of ancient societies.

The classic case of a 'liquid poltergeist' occured at the Rectory at Swanton Novers, Norfolk, and was chronicled in most of the leading English papers and journals of the day. On 30 August 1919, it was noticed that oil was seeping through the ceilings of some rooms, or rather collecting in patches on the ceilings. In the next few days these seepings became constant flows and even, as some witnesses described, spurtings from the walls. It was suggested the house was built over an oil well, but it was not crude oil that was falling, but paraffin (kerosene) and petrol (gasoline). It arrived at the rate of a quart every ten minutes, and one report dated 2 September said that about 50 gallons had been caught in receptacles. Of the thirteen showers on 1 September, two were of water; others consisted of methylated spirits (alcohol) and sandal-wood oil. Not only was everything in the house ruined, but the vapours became so dangerous that evacuation became necessary. Walls were torn open and the ceilings probed and exposed, but no clue was ever found. The Rector, the Rev. Hugh Guy, employed a young house-maid, and attempts were made to implicate her. *The Times*, 9 September, declared that Oswald Williams, an 'illusionist', had gone to investigate, and that he had solved the mystery: he saw the girl throw water on the ceiling. In 12 September *The Times* printed an interview with the girl. She had gone into the house with Williams, and when water appeared on the ceiling Williams accused her. He gave her one minute to admit it, or he would see her in prison. Later she brought a charge against Williams and his wife that they had beaten her. The case was dismissed. It was never explained how the girl could transport 50 gallons of oils onto a ceiling in the midst of investigators without being detected, or where and how she could have obtained them.

*(Left) Point rainfall as an allegory in a 17th-century alchemical tract. (Below) Witches provoking a hailstorm in a 15th-century woodcut.*

*The ceilings at Swanton Novers Rectory, from the* Daily Mail, *3 September 1919 (see text). The rector, Rev. Hugh Guy, said to a reporter who noticed drops of paraffin, 'Next time it will be methylated spirit, or just water. I'm sorry you can't see it gushing . . . gallons of water came from that ceiling . . . the queer part is that the ceiling, the paper, and the laths are quite dry.'*

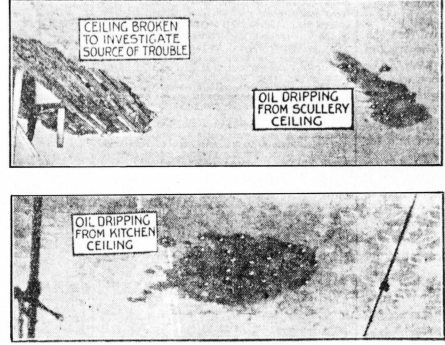

# Human glow-worms

Our subject here is light emanating from sources from which one would not expect it to emanate – human bodies, for example. As with many of our phenomena, incidents can be given from antiquity to the present day. The data comes from three directions, from medicine, religion and folklore, but the effect is the same throughout – people are lit up.

In May 1934, the 'Luminous Woman of Pirano' was a sensation that spilled out from the squabbles of the Italian medical press into the newspapers of all nations. Signora Anna Monaro was an asthma patient, and over a period of several weeks she would emit a blue glow from her breasts as she slept. Many doctors came to witness the phenomenon, which was visible for several seconds at a time. One psychiatrist said it was caused by 'electrical and magnetic organisms in the woman's body developed in eminent degree', which is one way of saying you don't know. Another doctor ventured 'electromagnetic radiation from certain compounds in her skin'. This was a reference to then-current theories of bioluminescence (see for example E. N. Harvey, *The Nature of Animal Light*, 1920.) Dr Protti who

made a long statement on his observations of Signora Monaro, postulated that her weak condition, together with her fasting and religious zeal, increased the amount of sulphides in her blood, and that since the normal radiant power of human blood is in the ultraviolet range, and that sulphides can be stimulated into luminescence by ultraviolet radiation, here was a reasonable explanation. (See *The Times*, 5 May 1934.)

Clearly this did not explain the strange periodicity or localization of the blue flashes, and the embarrassed investigators fell silent. Harvey himself talks of luminous bacteria that feed on nutrients in sweat, but by Protti's own testimony Anna Monaro would break into a heavy sweat only *after* the light emissions, during which her heart rate doubled. Numerous toxicology textbooks discuss 'luminous wounds', some in terms of bacteria, and others in terms of the modern view that the secretions contain the biochemicals luciferin and luciferase and a substance called ATP (adenosine triphosphate), which are normally kept apart, but when brought together give off a faint luminescence. The identical process lights up the glow-worm and firefly. Yet, if this theory were

applicable the Signora would have glowed all over.

In *Death : its Causes and Phenomena*, Hereward Carrington tells of a child who died of acute indigestion. As neighbours prepared the shroud they noticed the body surrounded by a blue glow and radiating heat. The body appeared to be on fire; efforts to extinguish the luminescence failed, but eventually it faded away. On their moving the body, the sheet below it was found to be scorched. Were it not for the numerous cases in our SPONTANEOUS HUMAN COMBUSTION section, one would find this incredible, and even among these records such conflagrations in a dead body are rare. Medical records of the human glow-worm effect are almost always in reference to pathological cases. For instance, Gould and Pyle in their monumental *Anomalies and Curiosities of Medicine*, 1937, tell of a woman with cancer of the breast : the light from the sore could illuminate the hands of a watch several feet away. The only occurrence of light emission from an otherwise healthy person that we have on file (apart from saints) is in a letter to the *English Mechanic*, 24 September 1869 :

'An American lady, on going to bed, found that a light was issuing from the upper side of the fourth toe on her right foot. Rubbing increased the phosphorescent glow and it spread up her foot. Fumes were also given off, making the room disagreeable ; and both light and fumes continued when the foot was held in a basin of water. Even washing with soap could not dim the toe. It lasted for three quarters of an hour before fading away, and was witnessed by her husband.'

Sometimes human radiance seems to be connected with inexplicable electromagnetic phenomena, and in ELECTRIC PEOPLE we give several accounts of luminous infants. But no amount of disease-based cases can match the show of luminosity put on by the mystics. The halo or shining aura is everywhere the attribute of the spiritual man ; and we can only suppose that this universal symbol is derived from a universal phenomenon of common experience. Holy men glow, sometimes blazingly. Even in everyday speech we refer to faces 'shining' with happiness. That this is not always simply a figure of speech is very warily accepted by the Church. Pope Benedict XIV wrote : 'It seems to be a fact that there are natural flames which at times visibly encircle the human head, and that also from a man's whole person fire may on occasion radiate naturally, not however like a flame which streams upwards, but rather in the form of sparks which are given off all around.' (*De . . . beatificatione*).

As one of many examples we can quote Thomas à Kempis's biography of St

Lidwina: 'And although she always lay in darkness, and material light was unbearable to her eyes, nevertheless the divine light was very agreeable to her, whereby her cell was often so wondrously flooded by night that to the beholders the cell itself appeared full of material lamps or fires. Nor is it strange if she overflowed even in the body with divine brightness.' (*St Lydwine of Schiedam, Virgin*, 1912.)

Father Herbert Thurston admitted: 'There are so many stories of holy priests who lit up a dark cell or whole chapel by the light which streamed from them or upon them, that I am strongly inclined to adhere to the more literal interpretation. . . . It is unquestionably true that there are hundreds of such examples to be found in our hagiographical records, and although a great number of these rest upon quite insufficient testimony, there are others which cannot lightly be set aside. . . . There can, therefore, be no adequate reason for refusing credence to the report of similar phenomena when they are recorded of those whose eminent holiness and marvellous gifts of grace are universally recognized.' (*Physical Phenomena of Mysticism*, 1952.)

Perhaps the most interesting thing in Father Thurston's statement is the reference to light streaming 'from them or upon them'. Both kinds of light are clearly implied in the passage about St Lidwina. Thurston goes on to relate the following story which is worth some detail, about the Spanish theologian Father Francis Suárez at the Jesuit College at Coimbra in Portugal. An elderly lay-brother, Jerome da Silva, came to tell the Father of the arrival of a distinguished visitor. The outer room of his quarters was in darkness, shuttered against the afternoon heat. Suárez's biographer Father R. de Scorraille (1911) records da Silva's account of the incident:

'I called the Father but he made no answer. As the curtain which shut off his working room was drawn, I saw, through the space between the jambs of the door and the curtain, a very great brightness. I pushed aside the curtain and entered the inner apartment. Then I noticed that the blinding light was coming from the crucifix, so intense that it was like the reflexion of the sun from glass windows, and I felt that I could not have remained looking at it without being completely dazzled. This light streamed from the crucifix upon the face and breast of Father Suárez, and in this brightness I saw him in a kneeling position in front of the crucifix, his head uncovered, his hands joined, and his body in the air five palms [about 3 feet] above the floor on a level with the table on which the crucifix stood. On seeing this I withdrew . . . as it were beside myself . . . my hair standing on end like the bristles on a brush, and I waited, hardly knowing what I did.'

About a quarter of an hour later, the Father came out, surprised to see the Brother waiting: 'When the Father heared that I had entered the inner room, he seized me by the arm . . . then, clasping his hands and with eyes full of tears, he implored me to say nothing of what I had seen, at any rate, as long as he lived.'

They shared the same confessor, who suggested da Silva write his account and seal it with the endorsement that it should not be opened and read until after the death of Father Suárez. All three parties were well-known for their piety – they had nothing to gain by deception – and the account has a ring of honesty.

In the same manner St Francis of Assisi was lifted and lighted, and the radiance of Saints Philip Neri, Catherine de Ricci, Francis of Paula, Alphonsus Liguori, and many others who were holy but never beatified, shines out of their biographies. Some legends might not, then, be as mythical as it is comfortable to suppose. When Moses came down from Sinai (Exodus 34:29–35) it is said that 'the skin of his face shone' so brightly that all who beheld it were afraid to go near him. For some time after, in the presence of others, he had to wear a veil.

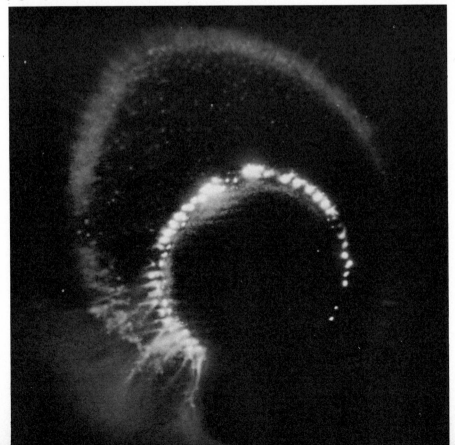

*(Left) Every religion has seen the power of its holy persons expressed in a bodily light. Mohammed is seen in a golden flame. (Above) St Francis of Paola (d. 1507) is one of many saints whose haloes are well documented. (Below) Modern photographic techniques have revived interest in the aura: a finger-tip seen with the Kirlian high-voltage method.*

# Mysterious lights

Lights in the sky, under the sea and in caverns deep beneath the earth. Mysterious lights that flit across marshes, hover over graves or haunt the paths to the graveyard. Lights that enter houses by way of the chimney, bright lights that swoop and hover, lights menacing or innocuous, gaseous or animate, casual or purposeful.

There are many names for the phenomenon – UFOs, fireballs, spirits of the dead, fairies, wills-o'-the-wisp, corpse candles, luminous serpents – but we suspect most of them as implying explanations for the unexplained. Ball lightning is a comfortable name for floating balls of light, but there is no agreement as to the nature of the phenomenon it is supposed to explain, nor on the characteristics to be expected in it. As recently as 1943 W. J. Humphries in *Ways of the Weather* was still of the traditional opinion that light balls were 'a humbug' or optical illusions. Here are the views of two other authorities:

'Floating ball lightning is not dangerous to human beings, even when it appears in the middle of a group of persons; it appears to avoid them [as] it avoids good conductors.' (Professor B. L. Goodlet, *Journal of the Institute of Electrical Engineers*, July 1937.)

'It is very dangerous to touch a fireball. An inquisitive child once kicked one and thereby caused an explosion which killed eleven cattle and threw the child and a companion to the ground.' (Frank Lane, *The Elements Rage*, 1945.)

Mr Lane illustrates the 'ball lightning' phenomenon with the following recorded incident:

'A young girl was seated at a table when she noticed a large ball of fire moving slowly across the floor of the room in her direction. As the fireball neared her it rose and commenced to spiral round her. It then darted towards a hole in the chimney and climbed up it. On reaching the open air it exploded just above the roof with a crash that shook the entire house.'

Tradition associates the appearance of floating lights with death, and many instances are recorded in support of this belief. Several of these were collected from witnesses by the former US Consul in Wales, Mr Wirt Sikes, author of *British Goblins*. On one occasion three of the pale lights the Welsh call 'corpse candles' were seen by all the passengers

*(Above) A fireball seen during a storm in Salagnac, France, in September 1845.*
*(Below) A 'ghost light' photographed in Basle Zoological Gardens in 1907.*

on the coach from Llandilo to Carmarthen as they crossed the river bridge by Golden Grove. A few days later three men were drowned at the spot when their coracle capsized. It is said that the number of the lights foretells the number of deaths to be expected. In John Aubrey's *Miscellanies* is the story of a woman who saw five lights in a room occupied by five maids in the house where she worked. The room had been newly plastered, a fire was lit to dry it, and the fumes stifled the girls in their beds. The appearance of corpse candles on the path leading to a burial ground is supposed, on the strength of numerous anecdotes, to signify that a funeral will shortly pass that way.

Baron von Reichenbach, famous for his earnest inquiries into the nature of the 'magnetic' light which some people see as auras or energy fields, was curious about the lights, wraiths, spectres or whatever, commonly apparent in graveyards. One of his lady colleagues, Miss Leopoldina Reichel, was gifted with the sight of such things. They appeared to her as dancing lights, some as big as men, others small, 'like dwarfish kobolds'. She was able to move among them and whisk them about with her skirt. Reichenbach, who believed himself to be the discoverer of an essence he called odic energy, brought his theory to bear on the evidence and came up with this resounding explanation of graveyard luminescence:

'It is a carbonate of ammonium, phosphuretted hydrogen and other products of putrefaction, known and unknown, which liberate odic light in the course of evaporation. When the putrefaction comes to an end, the lights are

quenched – the dead have atoned.'
(*Letters on Od and Magnetism*, 1926.)

Baring-Gould in *A Book of Folklore* also invoked 'phosphuretted hydrogen' as the explanation of graveyard lights. On one occasion his brother's overcoat, thrown over a grave, became impregnated with the stuff, causing him to faint. Baring-Gould quotes several instances of lights which have appeared to give warning of death by travelling along the coffin route or entering the house of the doomed person; but though he is prepared to accept the reality of stationary lights above graves, he rejects the moving variety: 'That these flames should travel down roads and seek houses where there is one dying is, of course, an exaggeration and untenable.'

The moving lights which are called ball lightning when they occur indoors become wildfire or wills-o'-the-wisp in the open air. They are variously explained as combusted methane (marsh gas), fairies or spirits, but there is no proof for any theory, or disproof, and according to the 1970 *Encyclopaedia Britannica* 'no entirely satisfactory explanation has been put forward' for the phenomenon. It may be significant that as the fairies disappeared from their once familiar haunts, so did the will-o'-the-wisp. In 1855 a correspondent in *Notes and Queries* asked whether in fact such a thing existed outside poetic tradition and was answered by several people claiming direct experience and providing descriptions. Dermot MacManus in *The Middle Kingdom* tells of personal encounters with 'fairy lights', which he says are different from the will-o'-the-wisp because they are of many colours and 'as bright and stable as electric lights'. One procession of such lights was seen to fly in formation from their usual haunt on a 'fairy fort' named Crillaun near Castlebar in the west of Ireland to another such earthwork on the opposite side of a lake. About the nature of the will-o'-the-wisp MacManus is undecided. Sometimes it seems to be inanimate and may be kicked or whisked about like von Reichenbach's kobolds; yet there was a girl he knew, 'very intelligent and well balanced', who was followed by a moving light, coming for her at running speed and changing direction to pursue her home. 'To this day she is convinced that it was directed by real intelligence.'

A most terrifying moving light chased and caught Mr Terry Pell of Spalding, Lincolnshire, as he drove his vegetable lorry towards Warminster in Wiltshire in the early morning of 10 August 1965. Warminster at the time was undergoing one of its periodic plagues of weird aerial visitations, details of which are faithfully chronicled by local journalist and author, Arthur Shuttlewood, in his book *The Warminster Mystery*. Forty five minutes before Mr Pell had his adven-

ture, at 3.45 a.m., Mrs Rachel Atwill a few miles away, saw what many others in the district have reported seeing, a bright staring light in the sky. She was awakened by a loud droning noise, looked through the window of her bungalow and saw the light, dome-shaped on top, hovering over the range of hills opposite. It stayed there for twenty-five minutes, humming and flickering, then vanished. Mrs Atwill suffered a headache and had to drink brandy. She recognized the shape in a photograph taken nineteen days later by Gordon Faulkner of Warminster and published in the *Warminster Journal* and the London *Daily Mirror*. When Mr Pell saw the light it was floating fifty yards in front of his lorry, having flashed into view from over the hills to his left. It was red and looked like a giant headlight or a human eye. It advanced on Mr Pell's lorry and fastened itself to the windscreen, vibrating. The lorry stopped. Its sleeping passengers, Mrs Pell and daughter Wendy, woke up to see the

light ball soar aloft and away. They were frightened but unhurt.

This incident is far from unique; for the UFO literature abounds in modern events of the sort which, when they have happened in the past, feature in collections of folk- and fairy-lore. Here is a report from Brad Steiger's *Flying Saucers are Hostile*, 1967, where it is given, as is customary in the folklore books, without reference to its original source. Mr William Howell of Texas was driving home at 11.15 one evening in the summer of 1965. Like Mr Pell he had two sleeping passengers, his brother's children, and he was also near a prominent local landmark, Foggy Hill. A light appeared overhead:

'It seemed to head directly for my car. It gave off a bluish light that became so bright the entire car seemed bathed in a blue haze. If that thing would have been a meteor, it would have landed with a big crash. It didn't. It made a sharp turn to the southwest and shot off in a burst of speed.'

*Explanations for the will-o'-the-wisp vary from ignited marsh gas to spirits of the dead. Often it is said to display intelligence or purpose, sometimes malevolent but sometimes revealing treasure. Its two followers, below, are about to learn how it stands in their case.*

# Asbestos people and fire-genii

*Time* magazine, 7 April 1947, included this brief story: 'In Woodstock, Vermont, a fire broke out in the basement of the Walker home on Sunday; the staircase caught fire on Monday; an upstairs partition blazed on Tuesday; the jittery Walkers moved out on Wednesday; the house burned down on Thursday.' We know a few briefer ones. Twenty-eight fires of unknown origin in one day forced the Hackler family to flee their Odon, Indiana, farm (*Collier*'s, 19 April 1941); and about forty fires in *a few hours* drove the Hoyt family from their home in Woodstock (another Woodstock), New Brunswick (see FIERY PERSECUTIONS). What interests us here is the notion that some people are fire-prone, or somehow catalysts for a process that manifests outbreaks of fires in their vicinity. Charles Fort called any such person a fire genius: 'By genius I mean one who can't avoid knowledge of fire, because he can't avoid setting things afire.' These genii, he thought, might have been very useful in the days before men knew how to make fire artificially. In this section we examine some of the evidence which suggests that human beings can both generate and project fiery heat and also something called (for lack of any better description) FIRE IMMUNITY, one aspect of which we illustrate in connection with the fire-walk.

As an example of fire immunity the case of Nathan Coker, a blacksmith of Easton, Maryland, is of great interest because, unlike some other famous fire-handlers, he needed no trance or preparation to demonstrate his powers. Three authorities, Gaddis, Fodor and Father Thurston, accepted the validity of the account, in the *New York Herald*, 7 September 1871, of Coker's testing before many prominent local officials. A shovel was heated to a white glow, and when all was ready, Coker 'pulled off his boots and placed the hot shovel on the soles of his feet, and kept it there until the shovel became black'. Coker also swilled molten lead-shot around in his mouth until it solidified; held glowing coals in his hands; and took a red-hot iron out of the fire with his hands. He told them: 'It don't burn. Since I was a little boy, I've never been afraid to handle fire.' This talent may be more common than we think. In *Mysterious Fires and Lights*, 1967, Gaddis mentions the report of a New York physician, Dr K. R. Wissen, who met a shy backwoods boy while on a hunting trip in the Tennessee mountains in 1927, and found that the boy could pick up and hold firebrands without injury. He said he had discovered the ability by accidentally picking up a red-hot horseshoe in his uncle's smithy. We are reminded of a story quoted by Thurston in *The Physical Phenomena of Mysticism* about a Canon charged to investigate reports of the immunity to fire of St Francis of Paola, who died in 1507. The Canon witnessed St Francis's performance but made light of it, saying that it was easy for him to bear the heat because he was not of 'gentle blood' but a peasant 'used to hardship'. St Francis replied that that was quite true. 'He bent down to the fire, which was a big one and burning fiercely. Filling his hands with the brands and live coals, he held them there while he turned to the Canon and remarked: "You see, I could not do this if I were not a peasant."'

Whatever the explanation may be, the phenomenon of fire immunity is ancient and universal. Mircea Eliade in *Shamanism*, 1972, says that it is a common practice for the smiths of the Dogon tribe to handle red-hot metal 'to re-enact the practices of the first smiths'. Nor do we doubt that there are some genuine performances among professional entertainers, such as that recorded by Max Freedom Long in *The Secret Science Behind Miracles*, 1948. Long was so astonished by the fiery conjurings of a magician that he obtained a private performance and brought along with him a dentist to examine the man's mouth, for as part of his fire-handling repertoire, the magician would play the hottest flame of a welding torch over the inside of his mouth, keeping his jaws wide open to allow close inspection. He also heated an iron bar to red heat and, gripping the glowing part with his hands

*Anne of Jesus, a companion of St Teresa of Avila, seen here holding a burning brand during an ecstasy, was known for her abnormally high body heat.*

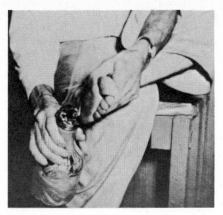

*(Above) Bradley Shell, one of the 'Saints' of the Pentecostal Holiness Church, of Kentucky, who demonstrate their faith by drinking strychnine, handling snakes and placing their limbs in fire, holds a flaming torch to his foot. (Below) Josephine Giraldelli, billed around 1800 as 'The Original Salamander', handling red-hot iron shovels.*

*In* Man, Myth and Magic, *1970–72, Kenneth Grant tells that a disciple of Anandamayi Ma (below) asked her to show her power and burn him to ashes. As she joined him under a sunshade he felt a fierce heat beat down upon his head. It grew so intense he begged her to stop. Grant says the man's umbrella was quite burnt in parts.*

and teeth, bent the bar up and down. Long and his expert were convinced the feat was genuine.

We think this demands the reconsideration of some historical evidence, not just the many tales of the fire exploits of holy men, but also, for example, the sort of incident recorded by John Evelyn in his *Diary* under the date 8 October 1672. Evelyn, who had a scholarly interest in the curious, had been invited to dine with Lady Sunderland, who afterwards sent for the entertainer Richardson, then well known in Europe.

'He devoured brimstone on glowing coales before us, chewing and swallowing them, he melted a beare-glasse and eate it quite up; then taking a live coale on his tongue, he put upon it a raw oyster, the coale was blown on with bellows till it flamed and sparkled in his mouth, and so remained until the oyster gaped and was quite boiled; then he melted pitch and wax with sulphur, which he drank down as it flamed; I saw it flaming in his mouth a good while; he also took up a thick piece of yron, such as laundresses use in their smoothing-boxes, when it was fiery hot, held it between his teeth, then in his hand . . . with divers other prodigious feates.'

A confirmation of Richardson's abilities is quoted in Olivier Leroy's *Les Hommes salamandres*, 1931, from the *Journal des savants* of 1677. During a test he held 'a red-hot iron in his hands for a long time without any mark being left upon it afterwards'.

Daniel Dunglas Home performed similar feats on demand and in clear light under scientific scrutiny (see Jean Burton's biography *Heyday of a Wizard*, 1948). Sir William Crookes wrote in the *Quarterly Journal of Science*, 1 July 1871, of seeing about thirteen different types of phenomena, including some astonishing displays of fire-handling, which proved to him the existence of an unknown 'Psychic Force'. When his full 'Notes on Seances with D.D. Home' finally appeared in the *Proceedings* of the Society for Psychical Research in 1889, he had 'nothing to retract or alter', despite eighteen years of merciless ridicule from his colleagues. Lord Adare in his *Experiences with D.D. Home*, 1924, bears witness to many of these events and says that Home would allow other people to hold coals without injury, after making 'passes' over their hands.

At the opposite pole to people who are immune to fire are those who, willingly or not, attract it or project it. In reviewing some of these cases we are reminded of the old belief that combustion depends on the presence of latent 'seeds of fire', and that there is a magic by which they can be made to blossom. There is the celebrated case of A.W. Underwood, of Paw Paw, Michigan, about whom Dr L.C. Woodman wrote in the *New York Sun*, 1 December

1882: 'He will take anybody's handkerchief, hold it to his mouth, rub it vigorously, while breathing on it, and immediately it bursts into flames and burns until consumed.' Underwood would strip, rinse his mouth out and set any cloth or paper alight by his breath. It was most useful, he said, when he was out hunting; he could have his camp fire going in seconds.

If that sounds far-fetched, consider the fate of a young Negress, Lily White, of Liberta, Antigua, whose clothes would suddenly burst into flames. Fires attacked her garments when she was at home and also in the streets, leaving her naked. The *New York Times*, 25 August 1929, reported that she had become dependent on neighbours for things to wear, and that even as she slept her sheets burnt up; yet she herself was never harmed by the fires that consumed all around her. Consider also the strange story in the *Daily Mail*, 13 December 1921, of the boy who, with his mother, was driven from their home in Budapest by 'alarmed' neighbours who claimed that some of them had seen flames flicker over him as he slept, singeing his pillow. It was said that since the boy's thirteenth birthday furniture had moved and fires had repeatedly broken out in his presence (see FIERY PERSECUTIONS for other cases of poltergeist incendiaries).

The Soviet parapsychologist Dr Genady Sergeyev referred in an interview in the *Sunday People*, 14 March 1976, to the powerful telekinetic medium Nina Kulagina: 'She can draw energy somehow from all around her – electrical instruments can prove it. On several occasions, the force rushing into her body left four-inch long burn-marks on her arms and hands. . . . I was with her once when her clothing caught fire from this energy flow – it literally flamed up. I helped put out the flames and saved some of the burned clothing as an exhibit.' For more on Mrs Kulagina and others manifesting strange para-electrical forces, see ELECTRIC PEOPLE.

There is also evidence to suggest that the tendency to attract or be immune to fire can be brought under human control. Max Freedom Long's exotic magician (see above) said that, although he was of white parentage, he was orphaned in India and adopted by local fire-walkers, who trained him from an early age.

He was taught to meditate on a burning lamp, to 'sense the God behind the flame' and thus enjoy his protection. To many gods is attributed the power to confer fire immunity. The Hindu invokes the protection of Agni, the Kahuna calls on Pele, and the Greek villagers dance on fires clutching icons of St Constantine and St Helen. All their different invocations are effective, but so also were those of Home and Richardson, who asked no favours of any god.

# Fire-immunity and the fire-walk

No one in his senses would attempt to walk barefoot across a pit of fiery coals or hot stones, so we can only suppose that the people who do so are not in their normal senses but in some other state. We have no idea how people can so delude themselves as to the nature of physical reality that they voluntarily undertake this impossible feat, yet the fact is that they do so, universally and with impunity. Fire-walking is one of the last remaining tokens of the power over nature attributed to the ancient magicians; and modern shamans, says Professor Eliade, especially value it for that reason.

In *The Miracle Hunters* (1959), George Sandwith gives several detailed accounts of the Hindu fire-walks that he witnessed while a government surveyor on the island of Suva, Fiji. After one dramatic ceremony he returned to his hotel with another spectator, a banker, who was obviously deeply disturbed by the experience. 'Very grudgingly he admitted the fire-walking was genuine, for he had thrown something on the pit and it caught fire at once, but he was strongly of the opinion that the Government ought to stop it! When asked why he became very annoyed replying that it does not conform with modern scientific discoveries. When I suggested that something of value might be learned from the fire-walkers, he was so furious he turned on his heel and left me.'

This turning on the heel and leaving is a reaction commonly found among people confronted with the types of phenomena described in this book.

One of the first 'scientifically controlled' fire-walks was held at Carshalton, Surrey, in September 1935 under the auspices of the University of London (see *Fifty Years of Psychical Research*, 1939, by Harry Price, who rationalized that the secret lay in brief contact and the low thermal conductivity of the burning wood). The walker was a young Indian Moslem, Kuda Bux, who strode across the twenty-foot trench four times without signs of burning. We recently saw some unpublished notes on the incident, made at the time by Harold S. W. Chibbett, which include many of the bigoted rationalizations that he overheard that day. One doctor loudly pronounced that anyone could do it, as, despite appearances, the temperature was only that of a cup of tea (it was over 800° Fahrenheit). He was invited to try it if he was so sure of his theory, but declined, saying he was not suitably dressed for the occasion.

Andrew Lang, the great folklorist, was one of the first to point out the ubiquity of the fire-walking ritual. He collected many modern instances from

*The most difficult and impressive firewalk is, like this Polynesian ceremony, done over visibly radiant stones, not ashes or wood. By normal standards the walker should have been horribly crippled, even killed, after his first two steps.*

widely separated countries but the practice was already old when it was recorded by Plato, Virgil and Strabo. Eliade pushes its antiquity back to the very origins of shamanism, and in *The Forge and the Crucible* he has much to say on fire-immunity rituals. These are practised in different forms by many people, from the fire-dancing Navajo Indians of North America to the Hindus, and even occur within a nom-

inally Christian tradition in Europe. To this day, on the feasts of St Constantine and his mother St Helen, the villagers of Langadas in Greece dance on glowing coals, clutching icons of these saints.

Many earlier examples of fire-immunity among devout Christians are given in Thurston's *The Physical Phenomena of Mysticism* (1952); Olivier Leroy's key work on the subject, *Les Hommes salamandres* (1931), gives even more cases; for example it is reliably recorded that when St Polycarp of Smyrna was put to the stake in about AD 155, the flames formed an arch over him, and he was unscathed until a soldier thrust him with a spear. The Protestants are also reported to have had their fire heroes. Gaddis in *Mysterious Fires and Lights* says that during the Huguenot revolts in seventeenth-century France, Claris, a Camisard leader, was condemned to be burnt yet continued unsinged and still talking in the midst of the flames. When the fire died down, 'not only was he unhurt, but there was no mark of fire on his clothes'. The Camisard general, Jean Cavalier, and other witnesses confirmed the story when they were later exiled to England.

Behind the universal demonstrations of the fact of fire-immunity lies a bewildering variety of methods by which it is achieved. Trance and religious ecstasy seem to be a vital prerequisite in the Hindu rituals (whether in India, Ceylon or Fiji), yet Kuda Bux and many others have reproduced the effect without trance. Sometimes there are elaborate preliminaries involving chanting, dancing and sexual abstinence, yet there are many other cases in which the walking has been performed without preparation or after a merely perfunctory ritual. E. G. Stephenson, a professor of English Literature, attended a Shinto ceremony in Tokyo and was seized by the urge to cross the 90-foot charcoal trench himself. An officiating priest insisted that he must be 'prepared' and took him to the nearby temple where the priest sprinkled salt over his head. Professor Stephenson later described how he walked, in quite a leisurely way, over the fire, feeling only a tingling in his feet (*Journal of Borderland Research*, 2–8 and 5–4). He mentions one interesting detail, that during his crossing he felt a sharp pain in one foot and later found a small cut, evidently made by a sharp stone. Dr Harry B. Wright wrote in *True*, March 1950, of a firewalk he witnessed on Viti Levu, Fiji, over a 25-foot pit of heated stones. He imagined the walkers to be in a painsuppressing state of ecstasy, but when he examined their feet before and immediately afterwards, he found them ordinarily sensitive to prodding with a pin or his lighted cigarette.

The majority of fire-walks are over beds of coals – though Dr Brigham, whose adventuring in Hawaii is described later, walked on lava; and Mircea Eliade refers to the Lolo shamans of China whose speciality was a walk over glowing ploughshares, recalling the medieval Christian 'trial by ordeal'. Dr B. Glanvill Corney, chief medical officer of the Fiji Islands, wrote in *Notes and Queries*, 21 February 1914, that he had seen five mass walks over red hot stones and had found no burnt feet among the walkers.

Now we come to two of the central mysteries of fire-immunity: the apparent selectivity of the fire in the matter of what it will or will not burn; and the ability of certain people to bring this selectivity under their own control.

Leroy's 'Human Salamander' was the sobriquet of Marie Sonet, one of the *convulsionnaires de Saint-Médard* in Paris in the 1750s (of whom a good account is given by Dr E. J. Dingwall in *Some Human Oddities*, 1947). She would lie rigid over a roaring fire for long periods of time, supported at head and feet by stools and wrapped in a sheet. She would thrust her shod and stockinged feet into a brazier of coals and withdraw them only when the hosiery was completely burnt away. Just why the shoes and stockings should burn when the sheet did not remains a mystery, but we do know that something similar happens in a fire-walk. Max Freedom Long in *The Secret Science behind Miracles*, quotes the account by Dr John G. Hill of a walk over red-hot stones on a Tahitian island, in which a white man took part. The pit was so hot that his face peeled, yet the glowing rocks made no impression on his leather boots.

Leroy's *Les Hommes salamandres* is also the source for what is probably the classic fire-walk, which took place near Madras in 1921 in the presence of the Catholic Bishop of Mysore (who sent the account to Leroy) and the local Maharajah. The proceedings were conducted by a Moslem, who never went into the fire himself, but conferred immunity on those who did. Many went through voluntarily; others were literally pushed into the fire by the Moslem, and the bishop tells how their looks of terror gave way to astonished smiles as they completed the walk. The Maharajah's brass band (all Christians) were induced to march through the flames, and they were so thrilled at their success that they went through a second time, trumpets blowing, cymbals clashing, etc. – a performance we would have gone far to attend. According to the bishop, the flames rose up, licking their instruments and faces, yet their boots, uniforms and even sheet-music were all unscathed.

Max Freedom Long gives a detailed account of how his mentor, Dr W. T. Brigham of the British Museum, was taken onto fresh boiling lava near a volcano on Kona island by three Kahunas the local magicians. They instructed him to take his boots off as they would not be covered by the Kahuna protection, but he refused. As he watched one of the three walk calmly onto the lava flow, the other two suddenly pushed him and finding himself on the hot lava, he had no choice but to keep on running to the other side. In the course of the 150-foot dash, his boots and socks were burned off. The three Kahunas, still strolling barefoot on the lava, burst into laughter as they pointed out the trail of bits of burning leather.

What does go on in a fire-walk? Dr White expresses the widely held view that the walkers are in an exalted state of mind which suppresses pain, as achieved in experiments with hypnotism. Yet there are fire-walks without trance or ecstasy. Neither is there any evidence to suggest that damaged tissues heal up so rapidly that they are not noticed (a process sometimes observed among Dervish, Hindu, Balinese and other body-piercing devotees). The boldest clue we have found in the discussion is in *The Crack in the Cosmic Egg* by J. Pearce, on the perception of different orders of 'reality'. Pearce suggests that the fire-walk is a classic illustration of the creation of a new reality (albeit temporary and local) in which fire does not burn in the familiar way. As long as this reality is maintained all is well, but the history of the fire-walk contains many accounts of gruesome fatalities and shocking damage to those whose faith snapped so that they were plunged back into the world where fire burns. The magical state of affairs in which flesh, and sometimes other material, is immune to fire is created, it seems, by the person who officiates at fire-walking ceremonies. Leroy's Moslem writhed on the ground in agony as soon as the Maharajah announced the end of the proceedings. It was explained to the bishop that the man had taken the burning upon himself. In *Women Called Wild*, Mrs Rosita Forbes describes a fire-dance ceremony in Surinam, presided over by a virgin priestess, among descendants of African slaves who had intermarried with the local Indians. The priestess was in a trance for the duration of the fire-dance, and if she had emerged from it unexpectedly, the dancers would no longer have been immune from the flames. We have to agree with Dr Corney that psychical and psychological theories alone do not account for what happens, and that some physical phenomenon takes place which has not been understood or explained.

Pearce's theory of fire-immunity as a product of a state of temporary reality invoked by a magician explains why the fire-walk has so shocked and offended those who depend on using the reality they have grown accustomed to as a bulwark against the apparition which Freud called 'the black tide of occult mud'.

*Saints Cosmas and Damian, two early martyrs, were brother doctors whose ministrations to the poor were unpopular with the ruling elite. Legend says that they were unsuccessfully drowned, crucified, stoned and burnt (as in this painting by Fra Angelico) until they were finally beheaded.*

# Fiery persecutions

Spontaneous outbreaks of fire are a familiar feature of 'poltergeist' disturbances. In the dramatic case of the Dagg household in 1889 (see INVISIBLE ASSAILANTS and MATERIALIZATION AND FLIGHT OF OBJECTS), the investigator, Woodcock, made a public statement citing no less than seventeen witnesses, to the effect that 'fires have broken out spontaneously throughout the house, as many as eight occurring in one day, six being in the house and two outside; that the window curtains were burned whilst on the windows, this happening in broad daylight, whilst the family and neighbours were in the house'. The statement is quoted in full in Thurston's *Ghosts and Poltergeists*, 1953.

The *New York World*, 8 August 1887, says that as many as forty fires had been found in two hours in the Hoyt residence in Woodstock, New Brunswick, and that they had burnt themselves out or had been inexplicably confined to very small areas. They began on 6 August, and no origin could be found for them: 'Now a curtain, high up and out of reach, would burst into flames, then a bed quilt in another room: a basket of clothes on a shed, a child's dress hanging on a hook.' Fort mentions a case in which fires broke out in the presence of a girl adopted into the MacDonald household, of Antigonish, Nova Scotia, until in March 1922 their house finally burned to the ground.

This brings us to a significant aspect of many 'poltergeist' cases and outbreaks of inexplicable fires. They generally seem to involve the agency of young girls, often, as Fort observes, girls who had been adopted or working as maids in the afflicted households. In many cases, as we shall observe, these involuntary fire-agents are bullied by authorities into 'confessing' their responsibility for mysterious fires, because this suits the authorities' convenience. In April 1908, Margaret Dewar, a retired schoolteacher of Whitley, Northumberland, was bullied by the coroner, the police and the gossip of neighbours into changing her story that on 22 March she had found her sister burned to death in a bed untouched by signs of fire. Her terror was taken to be the incoherence of intoxication, and when she told the story again under oath in court, it was again suggested that she was drunk. She persisted and the coroner adjourned the inquest until she would come to her senses: see *Blyth News and Wansbeck Telegraph* for 23 and 24 March and 3 April, 1908. The *New York*

*Herald*, 6 January 1895, tells of twenty fires the previous day in the home of Adam Colwell in Brooklyn. Policemen investigated and saw furniture break into flames, and one even stated he had seen wallpaper near Colwell's son, Willy, suddenly begin to burn. It was thought that the family's adopted girl, Rhoda, was responsible, but there was simply no way in which she could have started so many fires in full view of the firemen. A man came forward the next day to say that during the period Rhoda had been employed in his house in Flushing, New York, as a maid there had been fires, which had ceased after he had expelled her. The same paper on the next day records how the girl 'sobbed' her 'confession' when faced with the 'facts' during a long interrogation. We wonder how many other confessions have been imposed on bewildered children by authorities in need of a tidy solution to an untidy mystery.

What confuses the issue is that this agency is sometimes so blatantly indicated, though not in a form comfortable to consider. Fourteen-year-old Jennie Bramwell was an English girl adopted by Robert Dawson of Thorah, Canada. According to the *St Louis Globe-Democrat*, 19 December 1891, the

St Martin of Tours (d. AD 400), celebrating Mass in Tours Cathedral, once saw a 'globe of fire' hover over his head. Despite the full house, only five others saw it. His successor, St Gregory, recorded other encounters, including one at St Martin's death and one during a parade of his relics.

*(Left) In 1713 the Abbé Girolamo Leoni de Ceneda was terrified by a flame which suddenly burst with a roar from the ground in a village near Venice. It hovered over the spot for a while and then vanished. There are several records of the same phenomenon elsewhere.*
*(Above) In Chinese and Japanese traditions persecutions by ghosts and fox-spirits often took the form of balls of light or flames. In this painting by Kunichika of a scene from a Noh play, the poltergeist-like fox-fires, Kitsune-bi, attack a character called Yayegaki Hime.*

girl went into a trance after an illness. 'Look at that!' she would exclaim, and the place on the ceiling at which she pointed would start to flame. As Mrs Dawson and the girl sat facing a wall, the wallpaper began to blaze. In the week that followed there were many fires in the girl's vicinity; her dress, the furniture, and even once a kitten's fur. In 1932 there were many fires of undetectable origin in the house of C.H. Williamson, of Bladenboro, North Carolina. His daughter seemed to be the centre of the disturbance, and once, standing in the middle of a room, with no fire near her, her dress suddenly ignited – *New York Sun*, 2 February 1932. And again, it was told of twelve-year-old Willie Brough in the *San Francisco Bulletin*, October 1886, that he set things on fire 'by his glance'. His parents thought he was afflicted by the devil and threw him out. A local farmer took him in and sent him to school: 'On the first day, there were five fires in the school: one in the centre of the ceiling, one in the teacher's desk, one in her wardrobe, and two on the wall. The boy discovered them all, and cried from fright. The trustees met and expelled him that night.' We have on file corroborating stories of fire-prone people. Consider, for example, the case of Barbara Booley, who was involved in seven different fires in Devon, Gloucestershire and Somerset within four years: *News of the World*, 19 October 1975.

Let us now look at a few cases of a more sinister nature, in which the outbreaks of fire actually seem to be directed at some poor individual. In *Poltergeist over England*, Harry Price tells of a case that happened near his home. On the night of 18 November 1943, Mrs Madge Knight's screams awoke the other occupants of her house. They found her in bed, bare but covered by the bedclothes; the skin had peeled off her back, but otherwise there was no smell or evidence of burning. A doctor identified the injury as a severe burn and administered morphine. According to the *West Sussex Gazette*, 23 December 1943, Mrs Knight died from toxaemia on 2 December. At the inquest forensic experts testified that despite a thorough examination, no evidence of fire or corrosive compounds or liquids could be found on her clothes or the bed linen. The jury gave an open verdict.

This recalls a more horrifying incident in Marylebone, London, 123 years earlier. On 5 January 1820, and thereafter, fires broke out in the Wright household, where a ten-year-old girl, Elizabeth Barnes, was employed as a servant. Twice Mrs Wright found her clothes on fire while sitting in the kitchen with the girl. Once Mr Wright, hearing his wife's screams, found her in flames when the girl was not present. The Wrights' daughter moved in to 'guard' her mother, who still caught fire by 'some unknown means' and 'was so dreadfully burned she was put to bed'. Wright had accused Elizabeth of causing the fires, but Mrs Wright had defended the girl. They put Mrs Wright to bed, and upon leaving the room, Wright and his daughter were immediately brought back by her screams, and found her in bed surrounded by flames. The Wrights had Elizabeth arrested. The *Annual Register*, 1830–13, ends its account of this remarkable case with the magistrate saying that he had no doubt the ungrateful girl was responsible in some way, but would adjourn the matter until Mrs Wright, who had always believed the girl innocent, was well enough to testify.

At Binbrook Farm, near Market Rasen, Lincolnshire, for nearly two months objects had been thrown about rooms or moved on their own, and fires broke out in unexpected places, and this time the girl, whom the farmer 'had taken from the workhouse' to be a servant, was in no condition to be dragged to the police station. The farmer himself told the *Louth and North Lincs News*, 28 January 1905, that he saw the girl sweeping the kitchen, at the opposite end of which there was a well-guarded small fire. 'I suddenly came into the kitchen, and there she was, sweeping away, while the back of her dress was afire. She looked around as I shouted, and, seeing the flames, rushed through the door. She tripped, and I smothered the fire out with wet sacks. But she was terribly burned, and she is at the Louth Hospital, now, in terrible pain.' It was believed that the fire must have been burning her back for some time if the extent of the injury is to be accounted for; and the girl continued in her belief that she was nowhere near the fire when she ignited. During this case something was killing the farmer's chickens in a horrible way (see CATTLE RIPPERS, SHEEP SLASHERS AND MYSTERIOUS MUTILATORS). The girl's trance-like ignorance of the fire seems remarkably like the strange lulling in fatal cases of SPONTANEOUS HUMAN COMBUSTION. Curiously, earlier that same month, something burned a woman, Elizabeth Clark, in the Trinity Almshouse, Hull, not many miles from Market Rasen. The *Hull Daily Mail* for 6 January 1905, reported that on hearing groans from behind a partition in the dormitory at 6 a.m. the woman's fellow-inmates discovered her covered in burns; 'Not a shred of her nightdress remained.' The bed was untouched and during the actual burning she had uttered no cry. Elizabeth Clark could give 'no articulate account' of what happened and died shortly after.

# Spontaneous human combustion

The phenomenon of a living human body suddenly bursting into flames and rapidly becoming ashes has a long history; yet no one has discovered how and why it takes place and the reasons behind its selection of victims. For a body to take fire in this way from no apparent outside source is quite as miraculous as the opposite phenomena in our section on FIRE-IMMUNITY. A popular nineteenth-century theory was that people seized on by spontaneous combustion were drunkards who had somehow saturated their bodies with inflammable spirits. The ancient belief characterized both fire and lightning victims as sinners in receipt of divine retribution, and this view is still held by the Chinese and other traditionalists. There was however at least one dissenting voice in antiquity, that of Lucretius. 'Why,' he asked, if the gods are responsible, 'do they not ensure that those who have perpetrated some abominable outrage are struck by lightning and exhale its flames from a breast transfixed, for a dire warning to humanity? Why, instead, is some man with a conscience free of sin shrouded undeservedly in a sheet of fire, trapped and entangled without warning in the flame from heaven?'

A strange feature in cases of people killed by lightning is the rapid decomposition of the corpse. With spontaneous combustion the process is even more immediate. It is a strange fire that consumes only living flesh, normally the most incombustible of materials, leaving almost untouched the victim's clothes and other surroundings. Since the work of Davy and Lavoisier on the theory of combustion the notion of such a fire has been scientifically regarded as preposterous. However, in defiance of the scientific view, cases still occur where people are suddenly attacked by fire from 'nowhere'.

The best documented case is that of Mrs Mary Reeser who departed this life on a pillar of fire on the night of 1 July 1951. The next morning, her landlady took her a telegram, but found the doorknob to Mrs Reeser's apartment in St Petersburg, Florida, too hot to touch, so went for help. Two painters working nearby managed to open the door and were met by a blast of hot air. They could see no sign of the plump, sixty-seven-year-old lady. Her bed was empty, and though the room bore signs of a fire, there was only a little smoke and a feeble flame on the beam of a partition that divided the single room from a kitchenette. Firemen easily put out the flame and tore away the burnt partition. Behind it, instead of Mrs Reeser and her armchair, they found a blackened circle on the floor, a few coiled springs, a charred liver, a fragment of backbone, a skull shrunk to the size of a fist, and just on the edge of the scorched patch, a

black satin slipper enclosing a left foot burnt off at the ankle.

The case was investigated in detail by firemen, arson experts, pathologists and insurance men. Appliances and wiring were checked but no cause for the fire could be found. Strangely, there was no sign of fire except in the vicinity of the chair, but there it had been unnaturally intense. A mirror on a wall had cracked with the heat, plastic switch-plates had melted, and in the bathroom more plastic items were damaged. At the inquest it was said that crematoria normally use a temperature of $2,500°F$, sustained for up to four hours, to incinerate a body, and even then they have to resort to grinders to disintegrate the remains to the state in which Mrs Reeser's body was found. Assuming that a heat of this intensity was somehow generated, why, it was asked, was the wall not scorched behind the chair, and why was a pile of newspapers less than a foot away not burnt? The FBI released a statement on 8 August, suggesting that Mrs Reeser had taken her usual sleeping pills and fallen asleep in the chair while smoking (this report is quoted in full in Vincent Gaddis's *Mysterious Fires and Lights*, 1967), but experts testified that even if her clothes had caught alight they could only have burnt her superficially, and that neither they nor the smouldering armchair stuffing could have generated and sustained anything like enough heat to ignite a human body.

By coincidence, one of America's foremost pathologists specializing in deaths by fire, Dr Wilton Krogman, was on holiday nearby and joined the investigations. He remained completely baffled by the event, regarding it as the most amazing thing he had ever seen, for never in his great experience had he seen a human skull shrunk by intense heat, which normally has the opposite effect.

There are many references to spontaneous combustion in the work of eighteenth- and nineteenth-century writers, including de Quincey, Dickens, Marryat, Melville and Zola. These were often based on famous cases like that of Countess Bandi of Casena, of whom only a head, three fingers and both legs were found in a heap of ashes, four feet from her bed, sometime before June 1731 (the earliest account being in the *Gentleman's Magazine* of that date). Many similar accounts can be found in the early textbooks on medical jurisprudence, as such fires have often given rise to suspicions of criminality. For example, the *Enzyklopädisches Wörterbuch* (Berlin, 1843) mentions the reduction to the scant remains in a pile of ashes of the wife of a Frenchman called Millet, of Rheims, in 1725. Millet had a very pretty servant girl, so he was charged with murdering his wife and using fire to conceal the evidence. At the inquiry, however, it was acknowledged as a genuine case of spontaneous combustion and Millet was vindicated.

What sort of fire can it be that consumes a body unnaturally, yet leaves clothing and surroundings unnaturally intact? Cade and Davis in their *Taming of the Thunderbolts* suspect that an *atomic* fire, similar to those of plasma physics, may be involved. But there is no accounting for the strange selection involved in many cases. For example, the *Madras Mail*, 13 May 1907, tells of two constables carrying a woman's body, still smoking, to the District Magistrate near Dinapore, India, after she had been consumed by flames. Her room was untouched by fire, and the clothes she was wearing were unscorched on her burnt body. This astonishing detail is met with time after time. The *New York Sun*, 24 January 1930, reported an inquest on Mrs Stanley Lake, at Kingston, New York, at which the coroner said: 'Although her body was severely burned, her clothing was not even scorched.' In our other sections on strange fires we notice this same selectivity at work.

There is another constantly recurring aspect of this phenomenon, that the victims seem to be in a kind of trance. In *Cosmos* 3–6–242 is an account by a Dr Bertholle to the Société Médico-Chirurgicale of his investigation of the case of a woman found burned to death in an almost unscorched room in Paris on 1 August 1869. He said that it was as if the body had been in an intense furnace, yet only the floor under the body had been scorched. He could not understand why the woman had made no outcry to be heard by the other occupants of the house. Another case: the charred bodies of five men were found sitting in casual positions in a car in a backroad near Pikeville, Kentucky. The account in the *Syracuse Herald-Journal*, 21 November 1960, does not describe the condition of the car, but quotes the coroner as being baffled at the absence of any sign of a struggle to escape.

The strangest case of this kind was summarized by Fort from an English paper, the *Dartford Chronicle*, 7 April 1919. At 2.30 that morning the well-known author, J. Temple Thurston, was found dead, scorched from the waist down. There was no trace of fire on his clothes nor in his room; but outside the door of that room, firemen found a blaze and could not understand how it started or why it should be confined to that spot. Thurston was fully clothed and alone in the house. He still had money in his pockets, and there was no sign of the fire being used to mask a robbery. The inquest produced a verdict of death by heart failure brought on by inhaling smoke, and once again surprise was expressed that, if Thurston had been up and about when he discovered the fire, he had not escaped or called for help from his neighbours.

Eric Frank Russell used the phrase 'ultra-rapid holocaust' to describe this phenomenon; indeed much of the circumstantial evidence points to a quick and intense combustion. Dr B.H. Hartwell told the Massachusetts Medico-Legal Society that on 12 May 1890 he was driving through Ayer, Massachusetts, when he was flagged down and called into a wood. In a clearing he saw the crouched form of a woman with flames blazing from her shoulders, abdomen and legs. There was no evidence that she had set herself alight, and neither Hartwell nor the other witnesses were able to say anything other than that she had just burst into flames. A report was later published in *Science*, 10–100, 1890.

Dr E.S. Reynolds, addressing the Manchester Pathological Society on the topic of spontaneous combustion in 1891, resorted to the current theory that most victims are inebriates. Today it is said they fall asleep while smoking, ignoring the cases where the victim neither smoked nor drank. Reynolds tells of one case where a woman's legs were carbonized *inside* her unscathed stockings (see *British Medical Journal*, 21 March 1891, p. 645). In the London *Daily News*, 17 December 1904, is an item on the case of Mrs Thomas Cochrane of Rosehall, Falkirk, who burned to death in her chair, surrounded by unconsumed pillows and cushions and without uttering a cry. Clearly there is a mystery about such cases, with hints of occultism, that inhibits serious investigation by doctors and scientists.

*(Left, top) In 1888 Dr J. Mackenzie of Aberdeen attended this case of an old soldier in a hayloft burnt to a crisp, resting on a beam (the floor had burnt away), and surrounded by unscathed bales of hay. No fire had been seen, no cries heard, and, from the preserved features of the face, no pain felt. (Left bottom) Illustration, by 'Phiz', of the famous SHC scene in Dickens's* Bleak House. *(Below) A photograph showing the localized burning typical of SHC.*

# Electric people

One of the earliest scientifically investigated cases of an 'electric person' was that of Angélique Cottin of La Perrière, France, whose strange condition began when she was fourteen, on 15 January 1846, and lasted ten weeks. When she went near objects they retreated from her. The slightest touch of her hand or dress was enough to send heavy furniture spinning away or jumping up and down; and no one could hold an object she also was holding without its writhing from their grasp. A study group was appointed by the Academy of Sciences, and the famous physicist François Arago published a report in the *Journal des débats*, February 1846. He noted that her power seemed to be like electro-magnetism (compasses went wild in her proximity), was stronger in the evening and seemed to emanate from her left side, particularly her left wrist and elbow. Poor Angélique would often convulse while the phenomenon was active, her heartbeat rising to 120 a minute, and she was so frightened by it that she repeatedly fled from the scene.

We have no way of knowing just how many historical poltergeist cases were in fact instances of the high-voltage syndrome. Dr E.J. Dingwall presents a collection of accounts of compass-deflection and movements in furniture, etc., in his four-volume history of *Abnormal Hypnotic Phenomena*, 1967, the earliest case referred to being in 1786.

Cases continue to be reported in modern papers. In her teens, during the 1890s, Jennie Morgan, of Sedalia, Missouri, was highly charged; sparks would fly from her to nearby objects, animals would avoid her, and those people forgetful enough to shake her hand or touch her were often knocked unconscious. Caroline Clare, seventeen, of London, Ontario, became ill in 1877. Her weight dropped to ninety pounds and she would suffer dramatic fits, describing faraway places she had never seen. When she recovered about a year and a half later, her life, like Jennie's, was made a misery by strong discharges of electricity. Objects in contact with her (e.g. her corset stays) became magnetized. Cutlery would stick to her skin and had to be pulled off by another person. She was the subject of an investigation and report by the Ontario Medical Association in the summer of 1879.

Frank McKinstry of Joplin, Missouri, was also a subject of study in 1889. When he felt charged he had to keep moving, because if he stopped his feet became glued to the spot and he had to ask passers-by to lift his feet and release the charge. Similarly, sixteen-year-old Louis Hamburger was studied by the Maryland College of Pharmacy in 1890. He too was a 'human magnet' and could make metal objects dangle from his skin. With the tips of three fingers he could lift a glass jar full of iron-filings weighing about five pounds. These cases and those of a few other electric people have been briefly chronicled by Frank Edwards, Vincent Gaddis and others. Drs Gould and Pyle in their monumental *Anomalies and Curiosities of Medicine*, 1937, also deal with electric humans. For example, in 1938 the Universal Council for Psychic Research met in New York to offer a prize of $10,000 for demonstrations of psychic phenomena not reproducible by trickery. An elderly lady, Mrs Antoine Timmer, showed how cutlery stuck to her hands as if her skin were magnetized – but her case was dismissed because the chairman, the illusionist Joseph Dunninger, said he could do the same himself with a concealed thread. Thus another opportunity for research was lost for ever.

Perhaps the most famous case from that astonishing period in America in the late nineteenth century was that of Lulu Hurst, who actually made a stage act of her powers between 1883 and 1885 as 'The Georgia Wonder' before she quit to marry her manager. The phenomena began, as in a classical 'poltergeist' case, shortly after she was fourteen. China would smash in her presence, and at night there would be knocking sounds and frighteningly heavy thumps in the bedroom she shared with a younger sister. Soon it was discovered that questions spoken in the room were answered by raps for 'yes' and 'no'; the Fox sisters had founded modern spiritualism about forty years earlier in the same way. The day after the noises started, Lulu handed a relative a chair. As the chair twisted in Lulu's grasp four men tried to hold it, but the forces were too great and the chair broke into pieces, and they were flung violently backwards. Lulu, like Angélique, ran screaming from the house. Within two weeks her parents had persuaded her to turn her affliction into an act. In it she presented variations on the theme of a little girl thwarting several grown men. She would hold one end of a billiard cue while two men struggled and failed to

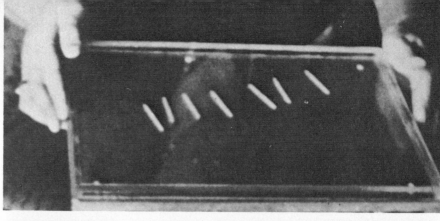

force the other end to the ground. She could also lift three men sitting on each other's laps on the same chair, merely resting her open palms on its back. She would then lightly touch the chair while five men tried in vain to budge it from the spot. Edwards in *Strange People*, 1961, quotes from many contemporary accounts. She would allow investigators as close as they wished, and they consistently found no evidence of strain or trickery in the girl. Fort mentions two other 'immovables' from that period: Mrs Annie Abbott who demonstrated her powers in London, November 1891, and Mrs Mary Richardson in Liverpool, September 1921. Holms investigated both cases for his *Facts of Psychic Science* and concluded that the ladies did not resist pressure, but that in some inexplicable way pressure against them did not reach or touch them. Forces without reaction seem to crop up in most 'poltergeist' cases (see MATERIALIZATION AND FLIGHT OF OBJECTS), yet we urge caution in explaining away these effects as products of unusual bio-electrical fields. We know of so many cases of poltergeist activity in which there is no known human agency; others occur in the absence of any pubescent youth; indeed every attempt to establish a constant factor in our phenomena can be countered by contrary cases, as though the phenomena delighted in teasing us. It is astonishing that little research, if any, has been done on the pathological causes of para-electrical effects, irrespective of their similarity to poltergeistery.

The only analogies for appearance and discharge of these high voltages are in the bio-electric processes of animals like eels. Each cell in our body can generate a small charge. Dr Mayne R. Coe (*Fate*, July 1959) believed that a cubic inch of human muscle cells could (in theory) generate 400,000 volts of very low amperage, but it would need a highish amperage to cause the effects that we have mentioned, and they are still unexplained. The pubescence

*(Far left) In 1908–09 a young Polish medium, Stanislawa Tomczyk, achieved fame by manipulating objects through 'invisible rays' from her fingers. (Above left) Angélique Cottin causing furniture to move (see text). Today Nina Kulagina, a Russian housewife, wears the telekinetic crown. Stills from a Soviet film (above) show tests in 1967 in which she moves a row of matchsticks without touching them. These ladies all demonstrate at will effects which, if spontaneously arising, would be attributed to a poltergeist.*

theory is scotched when we remember that Gould and Pyle mention a six-year-old Zulu boy who gave off intense shocks, exhibited in Edinburgh in 1882, and Fodor in his *Encyclopaedia of Psychic Science* tells of a baby born at Saint-Urbain, France, in 1869, who badly shocked all who touched him. Luminous rays would shoot from his fingers, and when he died, just nine months old, a radiance was observed around his body for several minutes. Douglas Hunt, writing in *Prediction*, January 1953, gives two other cases of high-voltage infants: one was able to charge up a Leyden jar, and the other caused 'vibrations' in objects held near him, and was also seen to be surrounded by a soft, white radiance. For other cases of luminosity in humans see HUMAN GLOW-WORMS and MYSTERIOUS LIGHTS.

Another curious piece of the jigsaw appeared in the *Electrical Experimenter*, June 1920, in which Dr J. B. Ransom, chief physician at Clinton Prison, New York, reported on thirty-four convicts suffering from botulinus poisoning. One had tried to throw away a piece of paper and found it stuck to his hand; soon all

the afflicted were in the same highly-charged condition, varying in intensity with the severity of the poisoning. Compasses went wild in their vicinity and metal objects were deflected from their grasp; but these effects faded as they recovered.

The history of the poltergeist shows many electro-magnetic interferences, from dimming lights to gadgets running without power, as seen in a famous case at Rosenheim, Bavaria, from November 1967. Translations of the investigation by Professor H. Bender, Dr Andreas Resch and others can be found in *The Journal of Paraphysics*, vols 3 and 4. Interferences with telephones, electric power and lights were centred on a girl, Annemarie Schneider, and the phenomena stimulated by her presence included many of the 'normal' mechanical tricks of the poltergeist repertoire, like bulbs unscrewing themselves from sockets, drawers opening, pictures rotating on the wall, etc. From this case alone, with its mass of documentary and even filmed evidence, it is clear that the 'electric people' phenomenon exists, whatever the explanation.

37

# Bodily elongation

We have records that under certain circumstances, usually in ecstasy, a body is seen to elongate, or change shape. For example, in the *Summarium* to the Congregation of Rites for the beatification of Sister Veronica Laparelli (d. 1620) are depositions taken during the lifetimes of witnesses to her phenomena. One states that while Sister Veronica was reciting her Office, apparently 'with some invisible being, she was observed gradually to stretch out until the length of her throat seemed out of all proportion, in such a way that she was taller than usual. . . . This we have seen with our own eyes, all of us nuns who were in the chapel.' The nuns looked carefully to see if she were levitated; she was not. To make sure, they measured her (the event happened many times during ecstasies lasting up to three days in which she also levitated), and measured her again later, to find that she was at least a 'span' (ten or more inches) shorter. The Devil's Advocate, in the same process, warns us to be careful in accepting this event since at times her levitations were at first mistaken for elongations. However, we note the observation by several pairs of eyes of the extension of the neck, and being free of the necessity of arguing for or against Divine Intervention, also see the case alongside several others, some of which happened outside any religious context.

Canon Buti's *Life* of Mother Maria Constante Castreca quotes from the copious notes of her confessor, that about the year 1700 she was praying before a statue of the Infant Jesus when she was seen to grow considerably taller, her body trembling all the while. The same was recorded many times of the Venerable Domenica del Paradiso, about two centuries earlier, by her biographer, Borghigiani.

Sometimes this elongation takes place in the limbs, a phenomenon which, according to his 'spirit-control', D. D. Home was to manifest at least thirty times in his lifetime, many of these being impeccably witnessed. The official *Life* of St Catherine of Genoa, who died in 1510, tells that during the torment prior to her death, in which she suffered sensations of an intense internal fire (see ASBESTOS PEOPLE AND FIRE GENII), she had a violent pain in one arm 'in such wise that the arm grew more than five inches longer than it was by nature'. This was evidence given under solemn oath, as are all depositions by the Religious to the Congregation of Rites in the canonization process. Her equally dramatic contemporary, Blessed Stefana Quinzani, was observed, in 1497, re-enacting the Passion of Christ, and her *Life* (1784) contains the depositions of twenty-one distinguished witnesses. After enduring the scourging at the pillar, she flung herself to the floor; there was no one near her throughout the drama. 'The right arm is extended as if the hand were being really and immovably nailed, and at once the muscles are seen stretched and tense, the veins swell and the hand grows black, just as if she were indeed being fastened with a nail. She utters a shriek followed by a piteous moaning. Then the left is extended . . . but stretched considerably beyond its natural length.' We are told that when her right hand was 'pierced', her whole frame seemed to contract in that direction, and when her left arm was violently jerked to the opposite side 'her bosom was clearly seen to open'. Father Thurston, in his *Physical Phenomena of Mysticism*, says that it is impossible to determine beyond argument whether this means simply that her habit was stretched and torn, 'or whether the writer wished to suggest that there was some sort of physical rupture in the sternum and the adjacent tissues'. In our opinion the latter is a distinct possibility. Hardly less astonishing is that Sister Stefana seems to have gone through this ordeal *every Friday*, during which she was abnormally emaciated. When it was over she was restored to her usual plump round-faced self once more. The evidence of some of our other sections seems to suggest that the normal causal processes of reality can in fact be re-arranged, or even bypassed; and, if this is possible, might we not also expect to see gross and fundamental disruptions of the metabolic and psycho-physical processes of the body?

Many stigmatics have displayed a notable sagging of a shoulder, as though they carried a Cross of great weight. In the case of St Veronica Giuliani (d. 1728), a post mortem revealed that her shoulder-blade was bent and depressed to an extraordinary degree, so much so that the two surgeons declared in their formal depositions that they found it inexplicable that in life she had had the full natural use of the arm, as at least one of the surgeons, who also attended her in life, could verify. During her fatal illness in 1510, St Catherine of Genoa was subject to frightening fits in which acute hypersensitivity accompanied distortions of her body. Her *Life* says of one

attack: 'This was so violent that her whole frame seemed to be in a tremble, especially her right shoulder which appeared as though severed from her body, and similarly one rib seemed to be forced out of place with so much pain, anguish and racking of muscles and bones, that it was a terrible thing to look upon, and it seemed impossible that a human body could endure it.'

Rib displacements were also recorded of St Paul of the Cross (d. 1775), Gemma Galgani (d. 1903), and St Philip Neri (d. 1595), whose *Life* says that in great fervour of love he would clasp his friends to his chest and they would feel a great throbbing there. There are many witnesses to the fist-sized swelling that would appear on his left breast at such moments, palpitating violently and accompanied by such a sensation of heat that he would swoon, or bare his breast to the ground in an attempt to cool it. In the post-mortem examination the surgeons found two ribs in this area broken and thrust outwards, an injury that was evidently of some age. We have notes of people who are wounded in mysterious ways; those cases that seem to refer to the Passion of Christ we have included in our STIGMATA section; and those which have no apparent religious context we have dealt with under INVISIBLE ASSAILANTS. Clearly all these manifestations are somehow related.

Dr Imbert-Gourbeyre witnessed a disturbing event on 27 September 1880, during his long study of the stigmatic, Marie-Julie Jahenny. He writes, in his *La Stigmatisation*, 1894, that with five other witnesses he saw a trance come on her, and her head appear to sink into her body, below the level of her shoulders which now stood out at right angles to the collarbone. Her tongue swelled to an incredible size, forcing itself out of her mouth. Her whole frame contracted into the thorax so that she seemed like a lumpy ball of flesh. Then her right side, from the arm-pit to the hip, expanded greatly, and at the same time her left side appeared to shrink to practically nothing. Dr Imbert confirmed the impression by feeling through her nightdress. It goes without saying that the doctor, a professor of pathology, was profoundly shaken. Even assuming various psychosomatic and metabolic processes in an extreme form, the series of events had followed one another in such a short space of time that there could be no explanation within the current terms of medical science.

Unusual this may seem, but it is not unique. The classic poltergeist case at Amherst, Nova Scotia, during the year following August 1878, centred on nineteen-year-old Esther Cox. Walter Hubbell's contemporary account, *The Great Amherst Mystery*, reports that one night, Esther, who slept with her younger sister, was flung into the centre of the

*(Left) Gemma Galgani (d. 1903) was one of many Christian victims of rib displacement. (Above) H. D. Jencken told the* Spiritualist Magazine, *January 1868, that in the company of Lord Adare and others he had seen and measured inexplicable lengthenings of the arms, legs and body of the medium D. D. Home.*

*(Above) An ability to control by will the body's size was something Alice lacked, but is claimed by the* Shiva Sanhita *to be one of the eight* siddhis *or powers gained by supreme yogic attainment. (Below) St Veronica Giuliani (d. 1728), a stigmatic, had one shoulder deformed as if by the weight of a cross.*

room, taking all the bedclothes with her. 'What's the matter with me?' she groaned. 'My God! I'm dying.' Her hair was standing on end, her face was blood-red, and her eyes were bulging out of their sockets. The sister screamed and other people arrived in time to see that Esther was swelling visibly. To their horror, arms, legs and trunk were all inflating before their eyes. There were four loud sounds, like claps of thunder in the room, and Esther was instantly back to normal, and 'sank into a calm state of repose'. This was repeated on several occasions, along with classic examples of other classes of 'poltergeist' phenomena.

The Neo-Platonist philosopher Iamblichus wrote, in the fourth century AD, of the trances of mystics, in which: 'the body also is seen lifted up, or increased in size, or borne along in mid air' (*De Mysteriis*, III–iv–111). Though some scholars interpret the Greek word used as meaning merely *appearing* distended, we are inclined, from evidence of the phenomena from other sources, to believe it is a direct reference to these baffling elongations and distortions. In the modern era D.D. Home and the revered mystic Anandamayi Ma of Dacca have provided well-witnessed examples. Of Anandamayi Ma, also known as Mother, Kenneth Grant writes in his biographical note in *Man, Myth and Magic*: 'In earlier years, during the celebration of kirtan (religious chanting and dancing) Mother would often go into a state of trance during which her body underwent the most amazing contortions. Her devotees claimed that her body, rolling on the ground, would appear to grow unusually large and then, as suddenly, contract to almost nothing. At other times her body behaved as if it were boneless, bouncing up and down like a rubber ball.'

This power of elongation at will is listed among the 'eight Siddhis' (magical powers aquired by yoga) in most of the classical treatises on yoga, but as Grant points out, Anandamayi Ma did not practise yoga. We have met this enigma before in other sections in this book; stigmata and levitations, like elongations, are widely held to arrive during trance or ecstasy, but a survey shows that, although the majority of cases do occur under these conditions, the phenomenon is not dependent on it, nor on holiness. This latter is the main reason why the Church refuses to beatify on the evidence of miracles alone.

We have no doubt that spontaneous cases of elongation or bodily distortion have, within the context of different mythologies, coincided, or given rise to, genuine beliefs in transmogrification and shape-shifting. Perhaps a more gentle form of this can be seen in the occasional alterations to voice, face and posture of mediums during seances and priests during exorcism.

# Invisible assailants

In May 1876 there was panic in the streets of Nanking, China. Invisible demons were on the loose, snipping off people's pigtails. The citizens took to walking about with their hair clutched in their hands for safety. The terror spread to Shanghai and then to other towns, and another panic developed, the 'crushing mania', fear of being crushed while sleeping. This particular rampage of the 'hair-cutting fairy' lasted for nearly three years. Others have occurred since, and the phenomenon has a long history. According to De Groot's *Religious Systems of China*, 1892, the first recorded outbreaks of the hair-snipping panic were under the Wei dynasty in AD 477 and 517.

Newspaper reports of these panics in China raised many a smile at English breakfast tables, but these were wiped away when in December 1922 a similar scare broke out in London. Young ladies were being seized by a man who hacked off their hair and then disappeared 'as if by magic', eluding the bands of would-be gallants who came rushing to the rescue. We have heard psychological explanations for this and respect them on their own terms, but they do not account for the physical fact that people have suddenly and mysteriously been deprived of their hair in the public street in broad daylight. Thefts of hair seem to feature in psychic attacks of all kinds from poltergeists to UFOs. Carlos Díaz (see STRANGE DISAPPEARANCES) had some of his hair removed during his UFO experience, though without damage to the roots; and at the haunting of the Dagg family (see MATERIALIZATION AND FLIGHT OF OBJECTS), the *Brockville Daily Times*, in Ontario, 13 November 1899, reported that one of the little girls 'felt her long braid suddenly pulled. She cried out, and the family found it almost cut off, simply hanging by a few hairs. The same day the little boy said that something pulled his hair all over. Immediately it was seen by his mother that chunks of his hair, also, had been cut off'.

In *The Other Side*, 1969, Bishop James Pike tells of the strange disturbances that followed his son's suicide. In one incident, a female assistant awoke one morning to find some of her hair singed off in a perfectly straight line. This was repeated again the next morning, and three weeks later one of the burned-off locks mysteriously appeared on a bedside table. An even stranger case can be found in the *Religio-Philosophical Journal*, 4 October 1873. During a succession of poltergeist-type happenings at Menomonie, Wisconsin, a young girl was standing by her mother with no one else present when her hair was sheared off in chunks close to her scalp, vanishing as it was cut.

We now turn to a more shocking sort of violation, the symptom of which is the appearance of wounds, as if the victims had been stabbed or shot with invisible weapons. The *New York Times*, 8 December 1931, printed a story by the captain of the German steamer *Brechsee*, which had put in at Horsens, Jutland, the day before. The captain had seen a man unaccountably wounded during a storm. Before his eyes a four-inch-long wound appeared on the man's head and he fell unconscious to the deck. On 16 April 1922, a man was brought to Charing Cross Hospital in London with a stab wound in his neck. All he would (or could) say was that he had strolled into a turning off Coventry Street, received a wound, and fallen to the ground. A few hours later another man was brought to the hospital – same wound, same story; and that same day a third man was unaccountably wounded in that same turning off Coventry Street. There was a report of all this in *The People*, 23 April 1922.

Charles Mackay, in *Extraordinary Popular Delusions and The Madness of Crowds*, relates in detail the alarm in Paris in March 1623 at the rumoured powers and antics of the newly arrived Rosicrucians. The Marais du Temple quarter soon aquired a bad name, for 'no man thought himself secure of his goods,

## BLOWS INVISIBLE.

MR. Brograve, of Hamel, near Puck-ridge in Hertfordshire, when he was a young man, riding in a lane in that county, had a blow given him on his cheek: (or head) he looked back and saw that no body was near behind him; anon he had such a-nother blow, I have forgot if a third. He turned back, and fell to the study of the law; and was afterwards a Judge. This account I had from Sir John Penruddocke of Compton-Chamberlain, (our neighbour) whose Lady was Judge Brograve's niece.

*(Left) Kaspar Hauser, after mysteriously appearing in Nuremberg in 1828, was fatally stabbed on 14 December 1833 by a 'black-cloaked man' of whom only the snowy footprints were found. Hauser's coat shows the traces. (Above) From Aubrey's* Miscellanies, *1784 edition. (Below) Invisibly inflicted wounds on 13-year-old Romanian Eleonore Zugun in 1926. (Right, above) Elf-shot (p. 18) from a medieval 'phantom sniper'.*

no maiden of her virginity, or wife of her chastity ... and people were afraid to take houses in it, lest they should be turned out by the six invisibles of the Rose-Cross'. Similarly, on 26 September 1923, the *Daily Mail* facetiously reported that Indian coolies in Lahore believed that a *mumiai* was abroad, an invisible thing that grabbed people in broad daylight. In 1890 the *Religio-Philosophical Journal* reported a scare from Japan, in which an 'invisible' was blamed for slashes about an inch long that appeared on people's necks. This reminds us of the tale told in the second branch of the Welsh *Mabinogion*, in which Caswallawn, son of Beli, donned the Veil of Illusion to slay some rival chieftains, who could see nothing of the assassin, only the sword as it materialized seconds before cutting them down.

Frank Edwards, in his *Strangest of All*, 1962, details the case of Jimmy de Bruin, who worked at Farm Datoen,

South Africa, and who seemed to be the centre of poltergeist disturbances in August 1960. During an investigation the Police Chief, John Wessels, and three constables heard twenty-year-old Jimmy scream with pain. He was wearing shorts and they could see cuts appearing on his legs even as they watched. The next day, in the presence of two officers, a deep gash appeared on his chest, although nothing had pene-trated his shirt. These cuts continued for several days. They were clean, as though made with a razor or scalpel – and all who saw them agreed that the young man could not have inflicted them on himself. Fort advanced the idea that if other things could be teleported, then perhaps wounds could be projected to appear on people. It is a common detail in cases of invisible assailants that the wounds appear on flesh beneath clothes which show no signs of penetration. The phenomenon seems to be a continuation of our STIGMATA section.

The poltergeist connexion was more clearly established in the celebrated Phelps case in Stratford, Connecticut, in 1850. The disturbances centred on Dr Phelps's twelve-year-old son Harry. In *Ghosts and Poltergeists*, Father Thurston's summaries of some events read like attacks on the boy – stones would be pitched at him, and a violent force would lift him off the ground to strike his head on the ceiling. Once he was thrown into a water-tank; and be-fore the eyes of shocked visitors he was caught up and suspended in the bran-ches of a tree while his clothes were methodically torn to ribbons by some-thing invisible. In a pamphlet published in 1800, *A Narrative of some Extra-ordinary Things that Happened to Mr Richard Giles's Children*, by a Mr Dur-bin, extensive attacks by invisibles on the children are detailed – only these left teethmarks in young flesh, like the case of Eleonore Zugun (see illustration). The witnesses describe the horrific sight of the little girl throttled by an invisible hand, seeing the sides of her throat pushed in, but without any obvious contraction of her neck muscles. Later the children were pushed and pulled, slapped and spat upon. On one occasion, five witnesses saw 'their arms bitten about twenty times that evening ... they

could not do it themselves as we were looking at them the whole time. We examined the bites and found on them the impression of eighteen or twenty teeth, with saliva or spittle all over them, in the shape of a mouth ... very wet [and] clammy like spittle, and it smelt rank'. Attacks by poltergeists, or what-ever they are, do happen, and more often than you might think.

We have many reports of 'phantom snipers' whose bullets, like phantom teeth, leave no other trace of themselves than a wound. In Chapter 12 of *Wild Talents*, Fort mentions three murders in which the police could only sus-pect that the murderers had changed the clothes of the victims, for they had bullet wounds with no penetration of their clothes. The oldest similar account we can find is of a man pushing a cart near Berigen, Germany, on 2 October 1875. According to *Popular Science*, 15–566, he heard a whirring sound, inaudible to his two companions, and found that his right arm had been shot through as if by a musket ball.

Here is the most gruesome account we know of assault by 'invisibles'. In 1761, five women were returning from collect-ing sticks near Ventimiglia, in northern Italy. Suddenly one of them cried out and dropped dead. Her companions were shocked by what they saw. Her clothes and shoes were torn into fine shreds and scattered up to six feet around her. There were wounds on her head that exposed the skull; the muscles on her right side had given way exposing her intestines; her sacrum was broken and most internal organs were ruptured or livid; her abdominal region bore many deep and parallel incisions, and the flesh of one hip and thigh was almost carried away, exposing the pubic bone and the broken head of the femur which had been forced from its socket. This horrific event was reported to the French Academy of Sciences by M. Morand, and the *Annual Register* for that year quotes him as noting that these grievous effects took place with no sign of penet-ration of the woman's clothes, nor was there any blood on the scene, nor any sign of her missing flesh. It was as though she had been the focal point for an instantaneous, silent and deadly explosion.

41

# Stigmata

In 1837 the *Annali universali di medicina*, vol. 84, of Milan published a study by Dr Dei Cloche on a girl he had examined three years earlier who had developed an astonishing degree of hyperaesthesia after a traumatic shock. All her senses were heightened so that she was in constant pain, dazzled by lights, and deafened by sound. For the rest of her life she took no nourishment at all, and she remained bedridden till her death in 1848. In the same year in which his paper appeared, Dei Cloche was called back to Capriana in the Italian Alps to see the girl, Domenica Lazzari. She had developed stigmata.

He saw wounds in her hands, feet and side, and a row of punctures across her forehead. Her hands were tightly clasped all the time, and on their backs he saw, between the middle and fourth fingers, a black, domed lump, perfectly circular, like a blackened nail about an inch across. The palms had deep incisions in the corresponding places, from which blood flowed copiously. Lord Shrewsbury stated in his *Letters*, 1842, that he had no doubt that the wounds perforated her hands. Overcoming Domenica's reluctance to reveal the sources of her constant pain, he 'distinctly saw the wounds and the blood and serum, quite fresh and flowing down over the wrist'. Looking at her feet he noticed that 'instead of taking its normal course, the blood flowed upwards over the toes, as it would do were she suspended on a cross'. This curious (anti-gravity?) effect was corroborated many times. T. W. Allies's *Journey into France and Italy*, 1849, records the author's visit to Domenica with two friends. One of them, J. H. Wynne, wrote: 'The Doctor has seen her feet a hundred times which are marked like the hands, but the blood runs up towards the toes, as it does up [to the tip of] the nose, as we saw.'

Like many other stigmatics, Domenica bled every Friday, and in the eleven years during which she bore her painful stigmata there was never any suggestion of trickery. On the contrary, all who visited her took away impressions of great suffering. Her hypersensitivity continued, and Lord Shrewsbury once saw her face covered in blood that flowed from the punctures in her forehead, as though from an invisible crown of thorns. He wrote that her face was never washed because she could not bear the sensations of water and wiping, and that the blood seemed to disappear 'of itself'.

The earliest recorded stigmatic was St Francis of Assisi, who received his marks in 1224, two years before his death. These were described in the *Tractatus de miraculis* (ascribed to Thomas de Celano, and written not later than four years after St Francis died) as having the appearance of black nails which protruded considerably, as though a real nail pierced the limb with its point and head projecting on either side. Celano says they were maintained long after death, and he gives a bizarre description of pilgrims filing past the radiant and still pliant body of the saint, seeing 'not the prints of the nails, but the nails themselves formed out of his flesh and retaining the blackness of iron . . . marvellously wrought by the power of God, indeed implanted in the flesh itself, in such wise that if they were pressed in on either side they straightway, as if they were one piece of sinew, projected on the other'. St Bonaventure's *Legenda minor* (pre 1274) goes into further detail on the projecting points, saying that they were clinched over, and projected so far that the soles of the feet could hardly be placed on the ground. We would be inclined to doubt this if we did not also know of Domenica Lazzari's hard, black, nail-like formations, though these did not project as far. Similarly, a wit-

ness for the beatification of Giovanna Bonomi (d. 1670) described how 'the flesh of her hands stood out like the head of a nail'. Though not in the usual category of stigmatization, the phenomenon of the 'Divine token of espousal' must involve the same psychogenic processes. The effect here is of a wedding ring around the appropriate finger, manifesting variously as a vivid red line, a thick ridge in the skin, or a depression, completely around the finger.

The arguments about stigmata are voluminous and complex, but there is no doubt that the phenomenon exists. A.R.G. Owen's summary article for *Man, Myth and Magic* suggests there have been at least three hundred cases. Father Herbert Thurston, the soundest authority, suggests there may be many more, because many genuine and devout recipients would conceal them, or pray that they might suffer the pain but show no outward sign of the wound to excite the curious. He chooses about fifty cases as having adequate documentation and presents them in his *Physical Phenomena of Mysticism*. Father Thurs-

(Left) The first major stigmatic was St Francis of Assisi, who received them in 1224 during a vision of a seraph (as in this woodcut by Dürer), although the notion of stigmata seems to have been known before this time (St Paul: 'I bear in my body the marks of the Lord Jesus', Galatians 6 : 17). (Above) A photograph of Teresa Neumann (d. 1962) 'weeping blood'. Her stigmatic phenomena were vigorously challenged throughout her life but imposture was never proved. She lost nearly a pint of blood from hands, feet, side and forehead, and 8 lb in weight, every Friday in an enactment of Christ's Passion, and fully recovered by Sunday. Her stigmata conformed to the description of St Francis's wounds. (Below) Nineteen days before Easter 1972, Cloretta Robertson, of Oakland, California, became the first black, and the first non-Catholic, stigmatic. Nor was she a brooding mystic; just a normal healthy 10-year-old girl. Drs L. Early and J. Lifschutz found that the blood appeared through her skin for a few minutes several times a day (General Psychiatry, May 1974). It ceased that Good Friday and never reappeared.

ton, more than any other, has urged us to be careful about using the word 'hysteria' in connection with stigmata. It is unfortunate that the word has many misleading connotations involving violent, extreme and uncontrolled emotional outbursts. In a clinical sense hysterical disorders are not confined to the overtly neurotic, the unbalanced, the weak-minded, or pathological liars. The records of many famous stigmatics disagree with the opinion of D.H. Rawcliffe (*Psychology of the Occult*, 1952) that the only 'true' stigmata are what he calls 'topoalgic hallucinations' (i.e. localized pain without visible injury), and that all else is a mixture of imposture, gullibility and delusion or 'purposive self-mutilation during hystero-epileptic attacks followed by amnesia'. The impeccable accounts of the sufferings of St Teresa of Avila, Padre Pio, and other stigmatics who have shown no obvious symptoms of hysteria, plainly show that suggestion-neuroses, so-called, are not incompatible with lives of the deepest sanctity. Furthermore, Father Thurston has shown that, as with Domenica and Palma Matarrelli (1825–88), stigmata are not always the product of excessive devotion or morbid brooding on the sufferings of Christ; we add the example of Cloretta Robertson.

Every theory of stigmatization that we know of breaks down when tested against the wide variety of the cases. It seems obvious that psychogenic processes are involved, and this has led to many experimental attempts to reproduce stigmata by hypnosis. In 1933 Dr Alfred Lechler published *Das Rätsel von Konnersreuth*, in which he ventured to explain the stigmata of Theresa Neumann with reference to his experiments on a young Austrian girl. Dr Lechler induced all the classic stigmata on her by suggestion during hyponosis, including sweating blood, tears of blood, the 'crown of thorns', and an inflamed shoulder caused by her imaginary carrying of the cross. But despite this result and numerous other less dramatic experiments, induced stigmata cannot compare in intensity, persistence and detail with the genuine spontaneous cases.

Stigmatization seems to involve a degree of selection in its imagery that suggests some subjective involvement in the process. The wounds themselves range from small red patches that never bleed to the deep and sometimes completely penetrating holes reported of Domenica or St Mary Francis of the Five Wounds (1715–91), of whom her confessor wrote: 'As the apostle St Thomas did, [I] have put in my finger into the wounds of her hands, and I have seen that the hole extended right through; for inserting my first finger . . . it met the thumb . . . underneath' (quoted by Thurston). Sometimes the wounds

are holes, sometimes straight cuts, and square, oval and oblong shapes have been recorded. In some cases the 'nailheads' are said to be in the palms; in others they appear on the back of the hand or on a foot. 'Lance-wounds' have been found on right sides and left, and also assume different shapes, from deep slashes and holes to the cross-shaped scar that bled at its edges on Padre Pio's left side. Catherine Emmerich (1744–1824) bore a unique Y-shaped cross on her breast resembling the equally unusual cross in the church at Coesfeld where she meditated as a child. Gemma Galgani (1878–1903) manifested bleeding 'scourge-marks' identical to those depicted on a large crucifix before which she often prayed.

We would suggest that this mysterious process is related to other phenomena in this book, which may simply be different aspects of the same forces. For example, we record the spontaneous appearance of images on bodies in MYSTERIOUS IMAGES and of mysterious woundings of people and animals in INVISIBLE ASSAILANTS and CATTLE-RIPPERS. Another correlation, noticed by Fort, is with records of liquids falling or oozing from invisible sources. He suggested that wounds could be teleported on to both bodies and statues (see FALLS OF LIQUIDS).

Whether or not these theories are acceptable, some process analogous to Fort's TELEPORTATION is demanded by the effects. Gemma's stigmata began as red marks. A fissure would open slowly, visible beneath the skin, until finally the skin tore, revealing the cavity filled with congealed and flowing blood. This happened every Friday, and the hole would be healed by the Sunday. The *Religio-Philosophical Journal*, 17 May 1890, reported a scare in Japan in which inchlong slashes appeared on people's necks in broad daylight. Another variation of the stigmata effect has wounds appearing *inside* the body. The heart of St Teresa, kept as a relic at Alba de Tormes, bears a wide horizontal fissure, conforming to her vision of being pierced by a 'fiery golden spear'. We could fairly disregard this but for the story of Caterina Savelli, stigmatized during communion in 1659 by five rays that shot from the host. After her death in 1691, two surgeons performed an autopsy before many clergy, and found a deep wound 'of old date' on her heart. Similarly, the heart of Blessed Charles of Sezze (d. 1671), examined by a postmortem under papal orders, was found to be completely pierced by a wound, and bore a facsimile of a crucifix on its surface, and of a nail, four or five inches long, buried within it. So we are informed in Imbert-Gourbeyre's *La Stigmatisation*, 1894, which quotes from affidavits signed by the doctors and surgeons involved.

# Cattle-rippers, sheep-slashers and mysterious mutilators

In 1973 panic and strange rumours spread across the American Mid-West. Rustlers were using unmarked, cargo-type helicopters to spot vulnerable herds of cattle from the air and radioing information to hidden ground crews. There were hundreds of reports that these machines had been seen hovering over herds and rising from cow-pastures. Farmers were warned to bring their livestock in at night and some even began taking potshots at anything that flew over their property.

Stories of these phantom rustlers lasted into 1974 when they were swamped by an even more thrilling development: UFOs were landing and mutilating cattle. One of the first accounts was in the *Miami Herald*, of Florida, 16 October 1973. Police at Dayton, Ohio had received about eighty reports of flashing UFOs in the area, one of them from a woman who claimed 'hysterically' that a UFO had landed, killing a couple of cows. By 1974, reports of strange lights and unidentifiable helicopters had become inextricably tied up with the ever-growing numbers of stories about mutilated cattle from North Dakota, Minnesota, Mississippi, Pennsylvania, Iowa, Missouri, Arkansas, Illinois and Nebraska.

Many of these cases are detailed in *INFO Journal*, 14, and by Ed Saunders in *Oui* magazine, August 1976. The most striking feature of the outbreak was the nature of the mutilations. Ears, eyes, lips, udders and tails would be removed and occasionally internal organs were surgically extracted in a purposeful, even ritualistic manner. Some carcases were found entirely drained of blood. In one case the intestines had been drawn out through a hole in the cow's side and piled neatly by its head (recalling a similar gesture by Jack the Ripper). A sinister aspect of these mutilations was the absence of footprints or bloody trails: an encouragement to the UFO theorists. Evidently gangs of mad, air-borne butchers or surgeons were abroad; many believed that a well organized and financed occult fraternity was responsible. The press had a field day, revelling in gory descriptions and stoking up the paranoia, even hinting at secret human sacrifices. Several investigators of the mystery claimed they were being threatened by 'satanists'.

Tom Davies, writing in the *Minneapolis Tribune* on 20 April 1975, attempted to scotch the occult and UFO theories. About 400 cases, he claimed, could be explained by a peculiar combination of blood disease (accounting supposedly for the complete absence of blood in most cases) and predators, which naturally go for the soft flesh first. But the data nag. Many authorities have confirmed the surgical precision of these mutilations. The draining of blood is a feature still unexplained, and so is the lack of tracks or footprints around the carcases, which were often found on snowy or muddy ground. Besides, the authorities could not explain why, if disease was a factor, it was not more widespread, and clearly predators could not account for many of the above bizarre details.

There are so few historical sources for this kind of thing that we offer no apologies for referring readers to chapters 13 and 14 of Charles Fort's *Lo!* Fort was fascinated by the winter of 1904–05, during which time, against a background of ghosts and poltergeists, outbreaks of religious revivalism in Wales, and swarms of strange aerial lights and airships, there occurred wave after wave of dreadful attacks on animals. At Hexham, Northumberland, something was killing sheep nearly every night, sometimes on *both sides* of the River Tyne on the same night. That winter there was more slaughter at Gravesend in Kent and Badminton in Gloucestershire, involving 'terrible losses for poor people'. Yet worse was to come.

In May 1910, something began killing six or seven sheep a night, biting into their necks and sucking their blood, but leaving the bodies untouched. In 1874, sheep were killed in a vampiric manner around Cavan, Ireland; as many as thirty a night had their throats 'cut and blood sucked, but no flesh eaten'. Wolves were blamed (the last wolf in Ireland was killed in 1712), and finally a dog was shot. This time the killings continued in the same region. Something killed over sixty sheep in two nights in 1906 at Guildford and Windsor in the SURREY PUMA country. At Llanelly in 1919 something entered hutches and broke the backs of rabbits. In 1925 a strange black animal 'of enormous size' tore sheep apart, terrifying the Edale region of Derbyshire into fears of WEREWOLVES. Cases occur to this day.

The UFO link to mutilated or kidnapped animals can be traced back to the rustlers from the land of Magonia in the clouds alluded to in the ninth century by Archbishop Agobard (see PHANTOM SHIPS). Other modern cases are mentioned by John Keel in chapter 13 of *Strange Creatures from Space and Time*, 1970. The heroes and gods of many cultures, too, were not above visiting this earth for a little rustling and mayhem – as were the fairies.

Sometimes there are features in these mutilations (e.g. back-breaking, blood-siphoning, removal of specific organs) that bring to mind elements of shamanistic or Mithraic sacrifice; but, as in the classic pattern of UFO paradox, the matter is devastatingly elusive. In their *Devil Worship in Britain*, 1964, Peter Haining and A. V. Sellwood confess they did not get far investigating the discovery of a pile of the heads of six cows and horses in a wood near Luton, Bedfordshire. The eyes had been extracted, the jaws wrenched open and two jawbones removed. Nearby were two rings of trampled grass round a gnarled tree. There were no other tracks, no blood and no sign of the bodies.

The heads were heavy enough to have needed two people to carry them down the two-mile bridle-path to the spot, suggesting to the police a conspiracy. No farmer for miles around admitted to losing any animals, and the case remains unsolved. The trampled rings recall similar patches reported from the sites of

*(Left) The mysterious death of a horse called Snippy during the 1966–67 UFO flap. No explanation was ever found for Snippy's bizarre wounds, the missing brain and vital organs, and the skin stripped cleanly from head and neck. (Above) At Quarouble, northern France, on 10 September 1974, a group of Oriental-looking aliens abducted some chickens.*

many of the Mid-West mutilations and also the ground markings associated with UFOs. The *Sunday Mirror*, 9 November 1975, tells of a black sheep, at Bray, Berkshire, found stripped of skin and meat from the neck down in a manner that suggested skill at flaying. This seems to be a reversal of the fate of Snippy (see illustration). There had been two other mutilations at Bray the weeks before. Phantom helicopters too are familiar objects in the UFO repertoire (see *The News*, 3 and 7, for notes on Canadian and British sightings); and indeed their *modus operandi*, with silent night manoeuvrings and powerful spotlights, is reminiscent of the great airship flaps of the late nineteenth century (see PHANTOM SHIPS).

Other cases link animal mutilation to another of our sections, THE GREAT AMERICAN MONSTER and its foul-smelling mystery anthropoids. In *The Unidentified*, 1975, Jerome Clark reports on his investigation into a series of bizarre animal killings around Rochdale, Indiana, during which about fifty people claimed to have seen a 'gorilla-like' thing in the area. On 22 August 1972 two members of the Burdine family returned to their farm to discover about sixty chickens ripped apart but not eaten. After a close encounter with the 'thing' they saw it again, by the lights of their car, framed in the door of the chicken coop. They shot at it as it lumbered off. Inside the coop all but thirty of two hundred chickens were 'ripped open and drained of blood'.

Now, as if to confound the UFO-link argument, we bring in the weirdest correlation of all. Fort had an inkling of what he called an 'occult criminology'; that all these attacks on animals were part of one mysterious phenomenon, including 'attacks some of them mischievous, some ordinarily deadly, and some of the Jack the Ripper kind, upon human beings'. Perhaps, like all great fictions, the terrifying destructive 'monster from the Id', in the film *Forbidden Planet*, is a mirroring of a repressed fact. In our INVISIBLE ASSAILANTS section we review some cases where wounds appear mysteriously on human bodies. Fodor, echoing Fort, suggested that childish passions of anger, hate, jealousy and frustration could be 'exteriorized' and vented on objects or people in the vicinity, causing the smashing, burning and spoiling pranks of poltergeists. In FIERY PERSECUTIONS, for example, we tell the story of the girl in the kitchen at Binbrook Farm, who was severely burned on her back although quite unaware of the fire consuming her. In reporting the incident, the *Louth and North Lincs. News*, 28 January 1905, mentioned incidentally the bizarre killing of 225 chickens on the property. Despite a constant watch on the hen-house, 'whenever examined, four or five birds would be found dead'. They were all killed in the same way: 'the skin around the neck, from the head to the breast, had been pulled off, and the windpipe drawn from its place and snapped.'

# Freak plagues and mass panics

In 1906, members of several families in New York were stricken with typhoid. A girl, Mary, was found to have worked in all these households as a cook, and the authorities branded her a carrier of typhoid germs, although, curiously enough, she herself was immune. They detained her for observation but released her after three years certified free of germs, though banned from food-handling jobs and required to report for regular check-ups. She absconded. About five years later, twenty-five cases of typhoid occurred at a New York maternity home. Once the health authorities learned that 'Typhoid Mary' was working in the kitchens they looked no further. The conclusion, they said, was obvious, and she was detained again. What is less obvious is where, if she was free of germs, did she get re-infected, if indeed she was ever infected at all? And why were no cases traceable to her during the five years she used aliases to get kitchen-work, and before 1906? Can a girl spontaneously attract or develop germs? If so, perhaps this explains other mystery infections.

We have an idea that this phenomenon of mysterious outbreaks of disease over-laps with some of our other sections. In STIGMATA and INVISIBLE ASSAILANTS we mention cases where marks and wounds have been inflicted on people's bodies by some non-physical agency, producing effects that are 'medically impossible'. If wounds can be teleported, why not germs? We suspect that 'Typhoid Mary' was one of those unfortunates, mentioned in some of our other sections, who are somehow the focus of unexplained fires, accidents, lightning strikes, bombardments of stones, etc. It may seem

that with this we abandon Occam's Razor – the rule that the simplest explanation should always be preferred – for unbridled chaos; but simplicity is relative and is often judged by partial and incomplete information. Any explanation is simple and obvious if one is conditioned to believe it in the first place.

The germ theory that damned 'Typhoid Mary' should have killed John Peck; but Dr Arthur Waite's attempts to kill Peck, his father-in-law, brought medical theory near to farce. In New York City in 1916 Waite fed the old man on diphtheria; then gave him a nasal spray doctored (had you ever wondered about that word?) with tuberculosis. Peck was still standing, so Waite weakened him with calomel and loosed typhoid on him, then influenza. In the end he gave up and poisoned him with arsenic. We can only speculate on what Waite, a professional bacteriologist, must have thought about germ theory. He had plenty of time to brood on it in prison. But even poison doesn't work invariably; Peck died, but Rasputin lived on after eating enough poisoned cakes to kill a regiment and had to be finished off by being shot twice, beaten with an iron bar and pushed through a hole in the ice into a freezing river. He was found to have drowned. Recently a woman spent a whole week-end trying to poison her husband. According to the London *Daily Mail*, 4 October 1975, Mrs Kathleen Kendall ground a whole box of tranquillizers into a bottle of Bacardi, dissolved a box of sleeping-tablets in a pot of tea, put packets of mouse-killer in his porridge, and weed-killer in his fairy-cakes, and gave him a Bacardi and Coke with fifty

aspirins added. He couldn't understand why he kept passing out, and went for a check-up. The hospital tests confirmed that he had digested most of what she had given him.

If some people don't die when they ought to, others have died when there seemed no reason why they should. Marjory Quick, daughter of the Bishop of Sheffield, drank what she believed to be medicinal paraffin, vomited and died immediately. The report in the *Daily Express*, 3 October 1911 says that no trace of paraffin could be found in the cup, her throat or mouth. It seemed 'obvious' to the authorities that she was in a suicidal state, whatever that may mean. An AP press report in most American papers, 18 January 1968, said that army Sergeant Robert Rush's wife woke him up at 6 a.m., screamed out and died immediately. The inquest disclosed that her sister had expired in the same mysterious fashion five years earlier. She had climbed out of a swimming-pool, looked around her wildly with a horrified expression, screamed and dropped dead. Autopsies on the sisters failed to find the cause of death. See *The News*, 5, for a collection of modern stories of sudden, double and triple deaths. Some of these stories develop a weirdness which 'rational' experts do their best to avoid. When Mrs Penelope Gallereault moved into a flat at Oakley Court, Bray, Berkshire, in 1972, friends warned her the place was 'spooky' – indeed, it had been used as a location for several horror films. Within three years her cat was killed in a strange manner; a neighbour was found dead, lying undetected for a week; one of her sons drowned in his bath and the other at a place on the Thames (which goes through the grounds) where a man had died a short time before. Police admitted that they were not satisfied with the results of their inquiries, and there were frequent allegations of witchcraft ceremonies in the locality. As the London *News of the World* went to press on this story, 30 September 1973, another man fell into the Thames and drowned at the same spot where the others had died.

When the Massachusetts State Commissioner of Health, Dr G. H. Bigelow, spoke after a supper at the Harvard

*(Left and below) Frenetic convulsive dancing has seized the minds and bodies of people in many ages and countries. In Apulia, Italy, there is a tradition that it was the cure for the bite of the tarantula. The dance was later formalized by Neapolitan composers into the Tarantella. (Bottom) One dancing epidemic began in the Netherlands in 1374 and spread to Central Europe, lingering until the 16th century. Some towns banished the colour red, or pointed shoes, on the grounds that these brought on the seizures. When the epidemic struck, there was nothing to be done but play music in the streets to accelerate its passing.*

Medical School, Boston, thirty students and doctors fell ill. Food poisoning was suspected but no cause could be discovered. The experts then declared it was paratyphoid, and lo! another twenty were struck down. The circumstances were strange, yet no evidence of any communication of the disease could be found. We note with some amusement that the subject of Dr Bigelow's speech was 'Food-poisoning', a fact which did not go unnoticed by the headline writers of the *New York Herald Tribune*, 30 January 1932. We have many similar reports: 15 girls at a school in Bournemouth, Hampshire, grow feverish (*Daily Express*, 3 October 1973); 150 children collapse at a carnival in Hazelrigg, Northumberland (*Daily Mirror*, 10 July 1972); 20 wedding guests vomit at the Drake's Drum, Kingstanding, Devon, site of a similar incident the year before (*Birmingham Evening Mail*, 18 July 1972); swimmers at Rickmansworth, Hertfordshire, break out in painful rashes (*Daily Mirror*, 10 July 1970); all thought to be caused by untraceable bugs or chemicals.

Sometimes people have collapsed complaining of strange fumes. The magazine *Human Behaviour*, January 1975, admits that 'accounts of victims gassed by undetectable vapours dot the annals of psychology', and details one case in March 1972 when 39 women at a data-processing centre in Kansas became dizzy, swooning and vomiting. Analyses of air, blood and urine failed to find any trace of the 'gas' they said made them 'feel hot', their eyes sting and heads reel. The next day they again dropped like flies. On the third day the management, under advice from psychologists, announced that the cause had been located; it was only 'atmospheric inversion'. The trick worked and the trouble ceased; or the trouble ceased despite the trick, for our records show that these attacks may repeat but rarely last more than a few days. The psychologists concluded that these cases 'are examples of mass hysteria – a sort of

psychic contagion'. See *The News*, 8, for a collection of phantom smell stories involving large numbers of people collapsing in nausea in factories, homes and cinemas.

Perhaps there is something to the notion of 'psychic contagion', not as those glib psychologists used it, but as applying to some human equivalent of, for example, the great sheep panic of 3 November 1888 near Reading, Berkshire. According to accounts in the papers shortly after the event, thousands of sheep throughout an area measuring 25 miles by 8 miles were found one morning scattered far and wide, panting with terror. Consider the great hunt in America in June 1899 for the 'kissing bug' that caused thousands to seek medical attention for their lips, swollen and with tiny punctures. Writing at the height of the flap in *Popular Science Monthly*, 56–31, Dr L. O. Howard noted that only six species of insect in the country could give such bites, and since this was the work of none of them, he dismissed the whole affair as 'a senseless scare', like the hysteria which occasionally sweeps southern Europe about imagined tarantula bites.

The panic phenomenon was certainly known of old; we refer readers to the curious records of many such scares in Charles Mackay's *Extraordinary Popular Delusions and the Madness of Crowds*, 1852. For example, he details the almost incredible extent of the poison manias that swept Italy and France in the sixteenth and seventeenth centuries, in which people believed themselves victims of a colourless, tasteless, odourless poison called *aqua tofana*, and which could be checked only by a vigorous campaign of execution of alleged poisoners, guilty or innocent.

What is disappointing is that there has been so little research into 'mass hysteria' since Fort in 1932 suggested 'a study of scares, with the idea of showing that they were not altogether hysteria and mass psychology, and that there may have been something to be scared about'.

# Shared visions

People see visions. It is a recurring feature of human experience and one on which rationalism has made little impact. In fact visions seem to be on the increase if our records are anything to go by, as almost weekly we learn of some new sighting of a phantom animal, an unidentified flying object (UFO), or the Blessed Virgin Mary (BVM). A wide range of explanations is available, from psychology and pathology to the occult. Our interest is in visions which are perceived by more than one person, and we are content to leave the explanations to others.

E. Parrish, in *Hallucinations and Illusions*, 1897, discusses a famous incident which began with the death of a ship's cook. Several days later the form of the cook was clearly seen and identified by all on board the ship, limping (he had one leg shorter than the other) across the waters towards them. As the vision drew nearer it suddenly resolved itself into a piece of floating wreckage. Parrish suggests that initially one person, brooding on the loss of a friend, thought he saw the cook and in telling the others planted the suggestion in their minds. This, he says, may be the genesis of all ghosts. We have our doubts — things are not always so conveniently explicable.

A vision was shared by the Abbé Caucanas and thirty of his congregation at Castelnau-de-Guers, France, at Easter 1974 and reported in many papers. The Abbé was rising from kneeling at the altar when he saw 'the face of Our Lord' on the white napkin covering the cib-orium containing the Eucharistic bread. He cried out, and the congregation surged forward to aid him, and they too saw the face. The Abbé said he saw 'the right eye closed, the left open. The nose was bruised and swollen and bore an expression of pain.' Others saw tears flowing, and some a crown of thorns. After fifteen minutes the Abbé lifted the napkin to continue the service and the image disappeared.

Professor E. R. Jaensch (*Eidetic Imagery*, 1930) explained away, in a brief footnote, hundreds of accounts by people who saw statues and paintings come to life. They were persistent images generated in the eye and superimposed on normal vision, he said. Eidetic images. By now we are used to explanations that need explaining themselves and that explain nothing. Taking a panoramic view of strange phenomena we can point to many accounts of groups of people who see previously inanimate objects move or speak, shed tears or bleed. The continuity in such evidence demands our respect. We give them their own sections — see IMAGES THAT WEEP AND BLEED, and IMAGES THAT COME TO LIFE.

To account for mass visions which occur without any apparent element of suggestion, modern writers have proposed some kind of telepathic exchange. An earlier version of this theory, given by Mrs Crowe in *The Night-Side of Nature*, 1854, is that a seer, by touching or otherwise spell-binding other members of a group, can induce them to share his vision. In our FIRE-IMMUNITY section we have noticed the similar role of an officiating magician who creates temporarily the spell of a different order of reality. In *This Baffling World* John

Godwin states his belief that the Indian rope trick is just that – a trick, and suggests how it could be worked as a conjuring illusion. Against this is the experience of two investigating psychologists, described in Andrija Puharich's *Beyond Telepathy*, 1962, who saw the act with hundreds of other witnesses. In its full form a small boy goes up the rope, the magician follows with a knife, and both seem to vanish at the top. Screams are heard, followed by a grisly rain of dismembered parts. The magician comes down with a bloody knife, places the parts in a box, and soon the boy emerges whole and smiling. In some performances witnesses see a dog run off with an arm or leg, and this has to be recovered. The psychologists saw the magician collect the parts of the boy in a basket, go back up the rope and return with the boy whole. When they developed their film, they saw to their astonishment the fakir and boy simply standing impassively by the rope, which was all the time coiled on the floor. The entire sequence had been imagined and conducted in silence. Puharich concludes that the 'hallucination originated with the fakir . . . was telepathically inspired and extended to the several hundred people present'. In 1934 the trick was performed twice in London, and on the second occasion the organizers concealed cameras. When developed, the film revealed the rope on the ground and the boy scuttling for the bushes. Those present were witnessing an event that did not take place in normal reality. In the *Ladies Home Journal* in 1930 William Seabrook described a variation he saw in French West Africa:

'There were two living children close to me. I touched them with my hands. And equally close were the two men with their swords . . . iron, three-dimensional, metal, cold and hard. And this is what I now *saw* with my eyes, but you will understand why I am reluctant to tell of it, and that I do not know what *seeing* means. Each man, holding his sword stiffly upward with his left hand, tossed a child high in the air with his right, then caught it full upon the point. . . . No blood flowed. . . . The crowd screamed now, falling to its knees. Many veiled their eyes with their hands, others fell prostrate. Through the crowd the jugglers marched, each bearing a child aloft, impaled upon his sword, and disappeared into the witchdoctor's enclosure.'

Later Seabrook saw and touched the children, who seemed none the worse for their ordeal. It is a rare illusion that can be paraded arrogantly through a disbelieving crowd.

The best-known examples of mass BVM visions are those at Lourdes (1858) and at Fátima, where in 1917 two little girls had visions of and communion with a radiant lady. This vision, together

*(Below) The fourth stage of the Pontmain vision (see text). Many people gathered, but only five children saw the phenomenon.*

with other such dramatic features as a dancing sun, finally spread to a great crowd of excited Portuguese and was also the occasion of some truly significant prophecies. An equally spectacular event took place in the small French village of Pontmain on the evening of 17 January 1871. Two young brothers became aware of a beautiful lady smiling at them in the sky, hovering about twenty-five feet above a neighbour's house. Their parents and a neighbour could see nothing; but twice again, after work and after supper, the boys described the same vision in the sky, unchanged for an hour or so. We take our details and illustrations from a contemporary account by Abbé Richard, *What Happened at Pontmain*, reprinted 1971. After supper, their excited cries soon attracted a crowd of neighbours, none of whom could see anything. The boys pointed out an equilateral triangle of three bright stars, one above the Lady's head, the others by her elbows. The crowd saw these and nothing else – and, curiously, it is said that these stars were never seen again. As more children arrived they were asked to describe what they saw but were not allowed to confer with the others. Three confirmed exactly the vision of the boys. Then the vision began to change, and the children, now separated by the adults, independently and simultaneously shouted out a joyful commentary. A white banner had unfurled at the Lady's feet and letters successively winked into existence: *M-a-i-s*. . . . Hymns were sung as the children together called out the letters as they appeared. The first sentence went: 'But pray, my children. God will answer your prayers in a short time.' There were frequent interruptions as the children exclaimed on the beauty of the apparition. The second line began: *Mon fils se laisse* . . . (My son lets himself . . .). A nun commented, 'That doesn't make sense,' and urged the children to look carefully: 'It should be *Mon fils se lasse* (My son is wearied . . .).' Several times the children spelled out what they saw, with no mistake: 'No, sister, there is an "I".' Then the sentence completed itself: *Mon fils se laisse toucher*, 'My son lets himself be moved to compassion.' Finally a white vapour obscured the figure from the feet upwards, and slowly the blue oval and stars disappeared. The entire sequence had lasted from 5.30 to 8.45 p.m., in the bitter cold of the evening.

Some visions (see SPECTRAL ARMIES) are portentous. The Pontmain vision occurred the very evening the Prussian advance stopped at Laval not far away, and a few days later an armistice was signed. Similar COINCIDENCES of events, experiences and anomalous phenomena are not confined to prophecy alone, and phenomenalists are inclined to see in them a sign of universal Continuity.

# Strange scenes and phantom cottages

There are many accounts of people who have temporarily visited another world or state of reality and returned to tell their tales. A few examples appear in our sections TELEPORTATION and TAKEN AWAY AND BROUGHT BACK. Others have found another world descending on them suddenly where they stood, so that, like Emanuel Swedenborg walking in the streets of Stockholm, they are 'in vision, seeing groves, rivers, palaces and men'. The stories in the above-mentioned sections involve a disruption of *space*; the stories that follow seem to involve a disruption in *time* as well.

The most famous example of 'phantom scenery' is the Versailles 'adventure' of the Misses Moberly and Jourdain. On 10 August 1901, these two ladies visited the gardens of the Petit Trianon at Versailles, and as they wandered they noticed with some surprise numbers of people in period dress from the days of Marie-Antoinette. They recorded their experiences in a book, *An Adventure*, published in 1911, which was subjected to searching analysis in an attempt to date the period of their 'vision' (see *The Trianon Adventure*, ed. A. O. Gibbons, 1958). The general consensus among investigators is that the ladies looked in on the Trianon at some time between 1770 and 1774. A

feeling of depression and loneliness heralded their trip into the past, and one of the ladies said: 'I began to feel as though I was walking in my sleep; the heavy dreaminess was oppressive.' They were themselves perceived by the people they saw, and twice they asked for and received instructions on how to reach the Petit Trianon; but as far as we know there has been no discovery of any eighteenth-century record of their route being haunted by two eccentrically dressed English ladies. Perhaps Miss Moberly and Miss Jourdain shared telepathically the same trance-vision.

A more modern account is given by Kathleen Wiltshire in her collection of odd experiences (*Ghosts and Legends of the Wiltshire Countryside*, 1973) gleaned from the Women's Institutes of that county. In the 1930s Mrs Edna Hedges, then a young girl, was cycling to visit a friend along Ermine Street, a 'Roman' road, just outside Swindon. A storm began to break, and when she saw a thatched cottage down a small lane off the road, with smoke wafting from its chimney, she decided to ask for shelter. An old man answered the door, tall and sturdy, grey-bearded and wearing a green waistcoat; he beckoned her in. She describes the dark, low-ceilinged rooms and the bright fire inside, and recollects

that she heard no noise at all inside the cottage, even when the storm was at its height. The old man never spoke, but just stood and smiled. Then 'all at once', Mrs Hedges found herself back on the road, continuing her journey. She had no memory whatsoever of leaving the cottage. At her friend's house were some people who had driven up the same road through the storm. They remarked that she must have cycled through the rain, yet she was perfectly dry. On telling her curious story, Mrs Hedges was told there was no such cottage on that stretch, except a derelict, unoccupied for at least fifty years. Some time later, Mrs Hedges went to see for herself, retracing her journey, and found the property dilapidated and the garden a jungle. She says she cannot explain it, but insists it was real and *did* happen.

In *The News*, 7, Janet Bord refers to several sightings of a phantom cottage in a wood near Haytor, Devon, as recorded in Ruth St Leger-Gordon's *Witchcraft and Folklore of Dartmoor*, 1973:

'A newcomer to the district walked along the lane (bordering the wood) one evening and admired a cottage seen through the trees. When she later remarked on this to the owner of the wood, he was rather surprised because there is no cottage there. She went back to look; no cottage was to be seen. Shortly afterwards, the cottage was seen again, this time by someone recently come to live in a new bungalow on the opposite side of the wood. She knew nothing of the earlier sighting. Later, an Ordnance Surveyor visiting the area looked down from a high vantage and saw a cottage he had missed before. There was smoke coming from the chimney and clothes blowing on the line. He walked down to the area but could find no trace of the cottage. He asked a lady, out with her dog, and she said she too had seen the cottage and was unable to locate it. Ruth St Leger-Gordon, having all the details, ascertained that in each case the same cottage was seen on the same spot. A careful search of the site produced no sign of old foundations, so the witnesses were probably not seeing the ghost of a former cottage.'

Our stories here, though, are not so much of magical abductions but of spontaneous dislocations of time and space. Laura Jean Daniels told the columnist Joyce Hagelthorn (*Dearborn Press*, Michigan, 10 May 1973) that after working late one night, walking home through deserted streets, she looked up at the moon. When she looked back at the urban surroundings they had vanished. 'Even the pavement on the sidewalk was gone, and I was walking on a brick path. There were no houses on either side of me, but several hundred feet before me was a thatched roof and cottage . . . there was a heavy scent of roses and honeysuckle in the air. As I

## JOHN SWAIN and his wife Christine will drive 100 miles next weekend— in search of a phantom lake.

The trip will be roughly their 250th in a quest that has gone on for seventeen years.

The mist-shrouded lake the Swains are seeking has a boulder in its centre.

Embedded in the boulder is a sword.

Mr. Swain, a 52-year-old petrol station attendant, his wife and their sons Ted, 28, and Chris, 29, know the mystery lake exists. They've seen it.

They were on holiday when they came across it near Beaulieu Abbey in Hampshire's New Forest.

Ted and Chris were aged eleven and twelve at the time.

Mrs. Swain said yesterday at her home in Ilminster, Somerset:

"We were driving down some little, off-beat lanes on a picnic trip when we saw the lake.

"Then we saw the boulder and the sword about fifty yards from the shore.

"We thought it was some sort of memorial to King Arthur. We were all fascinated by the scene."

That fascination has never diminished.

About once every three weeks for seventeen years the Swains have driven to the New Forest hoping to rediscover their lake.

Mr. Swain said: "I'm certain that what I saw was real.

"We've done everything possible to find the lake. We've made hundreds of inquiries and read countless books . . .

"We're beginning to wonder if we aren't crazy."

One thing the Swains are sure of—their search goes on until they clear up the mystery.

*(Left) The English traditions teem with tales of churches being moved by fairies, spirits, or the devil, seen here making off with Over church, Cheshire. (Above) A phantom lake, 1969. (Below) St Catherine of Siena (d. 1380) felt the baby Jesus in her arms. Can a vision be tangible? (Bottom) The Petit Trianon (see text).*

walked up the brick path and drew closer to the cottage, I could see that there were two people sitting in the garden . . . a man and a woman . . . in very old-fashioned clothes. They were obviously in love . . . they were embracing . . . and I could see the expression on the girl's face.'

As she was wondering how to signal her intrusion, a small dog ran towards her, barking. 'He was quivering all over. The man looked up and called to the dog to stop barking. . . . I somehow realized that he couldn't see me . . . and yet, I could smell the flowers, and feel the gate beneath my hand. While I was trying to make up my mind what to do, I turned to look back the way I had just come . . .

and there was my street! But I could still feel the gate. . . . I turned once again to the cottage . . . it was gone and I was standing right in the middle of my own block, just a few doors from home. The cottage, the lovers, and the wee dog, were gone.' (See Brad Steiger's *Mysteries of Time and Space*, 1974.)

The great biologist, writer and mystery investigator Ivan T. Sanderson claimed to have been transported for a few moments to a medieval French street. He was driving back one night with his wife and an assistant from visiting a remote lake in Haiti when their car bogged down in a pool of mud. They resigned themselves to a long walk. The night was hot, and after many hours trudging over a high, dry plain they were exhausted. In *More Things*, 1969, Sanderson writes: 'Suddenly, on looking up from the dusty ground, I perceived absolutely in the now brilliant moonlight, and *casting shadows appropriate to their positions*, three-storeyed houses of various shapes and sizes lining both sides of the road. . . . [They] hung out over the road which suddenly appeared to be muddy with patches of large cobblestones . . . for some reason I *knew* they were in Paris! It was so vivid, I could draw it.' His wife had stopped and he collided with her. She was gasping and he asked her what the matter was. 'Finally she took my hand and, pointing, described to me *exactly what I was seeing*.' After marvelling at the scene for a little time, they began to feel dizzy: 'We found ourselves swaying back and forth, and began to feel very weak, so I called out to Fred [the assistant], whose white shirt was fast disappearing ahead.' They begged a cigarette from him. 'By the time the flame from his lighter had cleared from my eyes, so had fifteenth-century Paris. . . . My wife also "came back" after looking into the flame. Fred had seen nothing.'

Dartmoor, it seems, is particularly rich in stories of phantom houses. We close with another case from this haunted region, from *The River Dart*, 1951, by Ruth Manning Saunders. Three girls and their father were on a shooting expedition on the moor at Hayford near Buckfastleigh. They were strangers to the area, and the girls got separated from their father and wandered in the darkness until they were quite lost. Suddenly, 'to their joy they saw a light ahead, hurried towards it, and found a roadside cottage. Ruddy firelight danced out from an uncurtained window, warming the night with a friendly glow. The three girls looked through the window and saw an old man and woman sitting crouched over the fire. "We never moved from where we stood", declared the girls afterwards. But, on a sudden, lo, the fire, the old man and woman, and the entire cottage vanished; and night, like a black bag, fell over the place.'

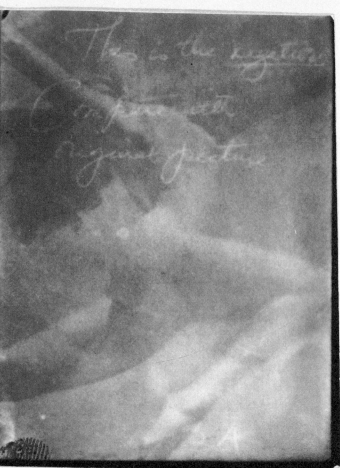

# Images that come to life

At Limpias, Spain, in 1919 hundreds of people, many of them 'scientifically educated persons', swore statements that they had seen 'certain pictures of saints perform miracles, step out of their panels, carry out actions, etc.' Professor E. R. Jaensch, who reports the case briefly in his *Eidetic Imagery*, 1930, attempts to explain this and other visions in terms of eidetic images, sophisticated retinal images that persist in the visual memory and appear superimposed on normal visual images. However, he fails to show how this delicate process, determined by many individual factors, could occur to so many different people at the same time; nor does he take account of the archetypal nature of the vision and its recurrence throughout history to peoples of different cultures. Lucian in AD 155 described seeing the priests in a temple at Hierapolis lifting a statue of Apollo. Suddenly it levitated and soared off into the air as they gazed up from the ground. According to varied sources, when the Araucanians stormed the Chilean town of Concepción in 1600, an image of the Madonna miraculously left the church and appeared in a tree, pelting the invading Indians with stones and clods of earth. In 1609 and the following year there were two visions in a church at Chiavari, Italy, of a statue-

like tableau of the Madonna and Child. In 1906 teachers and pupils at a Jesuit college at Quito, Ecuador, saw a statue of the Madonna open her eyes and change her expression; and several people in the town of Assisi saw a statue of Our Lady of Assisi move and smile in 1948. D. H. Rawcliffe mentions other examples of self-moving images in his *The Psychology of the Occult*, 1952. Pictures were seen to move at Campocavello in 1893, a statue moved its arm and hand at Soriano, Calabria, in 1870, and at Rimini, between 1850 and 1905, paintings were seen to move their eyes and shed tears on at least five occasions (see also IMAGES THAT WEEP AND BLEED).

The idea that statues and paintings can take on a life of their own has its earliest expression in the ancient cosmogonies which tell of the Creator breathing life into the images he has made of human and other forms. There is an archetypal quality about this event which is evident in its survival into our own time, as in the modern examples quoted here; and there is no doubt that the power of this archetype was noticed and made use of by the old magicians. A feature of ancient Jewish magic (said to be continued in modern voodoo rituals) was the 'golem', a clay man, shaped from the virgin earth and brought to life by

the insertion into its mouth of a cabalistic formula, written on parchment, containing the mystical names of God. Sometimes the formula was written on the monster's forehead. In some of the legends which commemorate the old magical practice the golem destroys its creator and runs amuck.

Such stories occur universally, and the ability to create artificial men, whether by magical or mechanical means, is attributed to every ancient civilization. The same art was known to the medieval magicians. Gerbert (Pope Sylvester II), Robert Grosseteste, Albertus Magnus and Roger Bacon are all credited with the manufacture of talking bronze heads which would give advice and answer any questions put to them; and St Francis of Assisi was advised by the crucifix in the church at San Damiano which spoke to him and charged him with his mission. We often hear of animated images that become troublesome (like the PROJECTED THOUGHT-FORM conjured up by Alexandra David-Neel in Tibet) and have to be put down, though often with great difficulty, for golems and other such things develop their own will for life. Albertus Magnus, besides the bronze head, built a tiresome metal man which grew to be such a chatterbox that his student, Thomas

Aquinas, finally smashed it to pieces. Another such anecdote from China is that the wife of the Emperor Ta Chou An was so attracted to an artificial man made by a court artisan that the jealous ruler had it destroyed.

The theme is continued in accounts of visions of the Blessed Virgin Mary in Paris in 1830 and at Lourdes in 1859. On 6 June 1830, Catherine Labouré was woken up at 11.30 p.m. in the Paris seminary of the Sisters of Charity by a voice. A cherub surrounded in light conducted her to the chapel to meet the Virgin in person. The interview lasted two hours. It began when Catherine heard a rustle of silk and looked up to see a radiantly beautiful lady 'seating herself in a chair on the altar steps at the Gospel side – just like St Anne, only it was not the face of St Anne'. The apparition had reproduced the pose and other details of a portrait of St Anne hanging elsewhere in the sanctuary. Catherine thought the vision was of St Anne, and had to be admonished twice before she could accept she was in the presence of the Virgin.

It may be that Catherine *did* see a vision of the portrait of St Anne at first, but the experience soon took off on its own inexorable course. Her second vision occurred on 27 November, and she saw a bright three-dimensional tableau of the Virgin standing on the globe, crowned with stars and surrounded by a glorious light. The Virgin then moved slightly and struck and held a distinctive pose. The whole scene became framed in an oval border on which some words appeared. (These details remind us of the Pontmain vision just over forty years later – see SHARED VISIONS). Slowly the tableau began to revolve around its long vertical axis, and Catherine could see on the back of the oval (!) the symbols of the Sacred Hearts of Jesus and Mary. Catherine was ordered by the vision to arrange for the minting of a medallion that reproduced what she had just seen. It became so popular that many millions were distributed.

Bernadette Soubirous was wearing this 'Miraculous Medal' on 11 February 1858 when she first encountered the BVM in the grotto at Lourdes. Our story becomes even more interesting as we note that according to Bernadette's own testimony, during her sixteenth vision (on 25 March) the Virgin struck a pose as she hovered above the rose bush that Bernadette recognized as that portrayed on her medallion. This was the occasion on which the vision announced, 'I am the Immaculate Conception.' Both Catherine and Bernadette were later canonized, and details of their visions, together with those of six others, can be found in *A Woman Clothed with the Sun*, 1961, edited by John L. Delaney.

Less mystical is a tale included in Samuel Butler's *Ex Voto*. On 3 July

*(Left) From time to time we hear of photographs that change by themselves. In this case, Margaret Fleming (Fate, June 1976) obtained a negative of a strangely distorted 'flying nude' (left) via a psychic experiment (see 'Projection of thought forms'). She made two prints a few days apart, and claims that the image in the second printing had moved, in the negative, to a new position. (Below) Most mythologies include stories of animated images. The painting by Burne-Jones shows St John Gualberto (d. 1073) being embraced, during a prayer, by a giant wooden figure of Christ.*

*(Below) A painting by Gérôme shows Pygmalion, king of Cyprus, who fell in love with a statue of Galatea and was rewarded by Aphrodite, who animated the statue for him.*

1653, a drunk staggered into the Caiaphas chapel at Sacro Monte and was roundly scolded by the stone image of a cockerel on a statue representing St Peter repentant. He was shocked into reforming almost instantly. Butler adds that other people in the chapel were no less astounded than the drunk as the bird flapped its stone wings, repeated its scolding several times, and turning round before returning to immobility.

In an article in the *Flying Saucer Review*, April 1976, Aimé Michel refers to the many records of life-like automata in antiquity and suggests that they are evidence of an advanced ancient technology, possibly of extra-terrestrial origin. Certainly, the earlier the period the more is claimed for its artificers' skill, magical or otherwise. According to the *Asclepius* of Hermes Trismegistus, a book of Egyptian magic, certain statues in the Egyptian temples were so worked and placed that at certain seasons they would become animated by cosmic forces. At the end of the nineteenth century the great scientist Sir Norman Lockyer began to investigate this ancient Egyptian science and discovered that the temples were orientated so that the statue in the sacred heart of the temple would be struck once a year by the rays of the rising or setting sun or of one of the other heavenly bodies. Sadly, his work has received little subsequent attention.

The greatest reputation for animating statues is that of the sorcerer-poet Virgilius of Naples. Among the wonders attributed to him by Gervase of Tilbury and other medieval chroniclers was the fabrication of a brass fly that chased other flies away from Naples. He also made a bronze archer, who guarded a perpetual fire in the city's baths.

It is interesting to note the similarities in the accounts we have from people who have seen pictures or statues come alive. Frequently mentioned are the eerie brightness and unnatural quality of the light at the time of the vision and the inclination of the apparently animated figures to strike formal, conventional poses, as in a tableau or illustrated book. These hologram-type qualities were clearly demonstrated at Pontmain and also in the strange mass vision at Knock (Cnoc), County Mayo. In this small Irish village, on 21 August 1879, many people saw a group of 'shining statues' by the church wall. They took the form of an altar with the Virgin, St Joseph and a bishop. The Virgin turned her arms and eyes to heaven in prayer, St Joseph turned to look at her, and the bishop read from a book. They were about two feet in the air and 'full round as if they had a body and life'. According to the account in J. L. Delaney's book, one witness actually read the print in the book, while another, prostrating herself at the Virgin's feet, clasped only empty space.

# Lightning pictures

Can a flash of lightning transfer an image of the local scenery onto bodies and objects? This question was debated in all seriousness by nineteenth-century scientists and the subject was given a name, Keranography. Yet the issue is still undecided. Cade and Davis in their *Taming of the Thunderbolts*, 1969, say that in some cases lightning victims 'do get peculiar markings on their bodies which give rise to incredible stories of "lightning photographs".' On the other hand, Frank W. Lane in *The Elements Rage* says: 'I am informed, however, that it is established today, that lightning has no photographic properties.'

On 17 June 1896, two labourers were sheltering from a storm in a hut in the south of France when a bolt struck very close to them, knocking them to the ground. A letter to the *Petit Marseille* the next day said: 'the lightning cut open the boots of one man and tore off his trousers; but over and above this, like a tattooer making use of photography, it reproduced admirably on the artisan's body a representation of a pine tree, a poplar and the handle of his watch.' Camille Flammarion wondered if the cabin had acted like a pinhole camera with the flash determining the exposure (*Thunder and Lightning*, 1905) but this does not explain the selection of certain images only from the surrounding scene, nor the imprinting of such images through clothes.

In 1861 Mr C. Tomlinson read a paper on Keranography to the British Association in Manchester, later summarized in the *English Encyclopedia* (article 'Lightning Figures'). He mentioned a little girl who stood before a window during a storm in 1853, and on whose body was found 'the complete image of a maple tree', illuminated outside the window by a brilliant flash. In September 1825, a sailor sitting below the mast of the brigantine *Buon-Servo*, moored in the bay of Armiro, was killed by lightning; a line was seared down his back from neck to hips, and near his groin was etched the perfect image of the horse-shoe nailed to the mast above him. Most dramatic of all: a boy climbed a tree to steal from a bird's nest; the tree was struck by lightning and the boy hurled to the ground; and on his breast was seen 'the image of the tree, with the bird and nest on one branch, appearing very plainly'. This story and twenty-three others can also be found in *Chambers's Journal* for 6 July 1892 – and other collections are given by Flammarion, Steinmetz, and Kretzer.

Andrew Steinmetz, in his enthusiasm for a scientific-sounding theory, ignores the conflicting and significant details in his own evidence to see, in the well-known dendritic patterns of electrical discharges, the complex explanation for the frequent stories of tree-images on the bodies of lightning victims. Undoubtedly the root-and-branch-like patterns of radiating burns left by lightning has given rise to many of these stories – but even if we allow this to dismiss all

our tree-image stories, there remains the considerable residue of incidents involving quite un-treelike images. One consistent detail that cannot be readily explained away is the first-hand observation of the detail and quality of the images in many lightning photographs. Steinmetz himself mentions 'a perfectly engraved image of a cow' on the body of a woman who was tending it when it was struck by lightning (*Sunshine and Showers*, 1867).

Henry F. Kretzer published privately a collection of reports on the antics of lightning, gleaned from American newspapers (*H.F. Kretzer's Lightning Record*, 1895), but since it contained such outrageous gems as the bolt that stripped silver-plating off swords hanging on a wall, perfectly electroplating a cat sleeping on a sofa below, the little volume was not taken seriously. Kretzer relates a tale of two Negroes killed by lightning as they sheltered beneath a tree in Highland Park, Pennsylvania, on 19 July 1892:

'When the clothing was removed from Cassell's body an astounding sight met the undertaker's eyes. Across Cassell's breast was a picture true to nature. The browned oak-leaf of autumn was there. Twined among the foliage were a number of ferns. These too, with the exception that they were brown, were as natural as their model. So plain were the leaves and ferns that even the minutest vein was discernible.'

In about four hours the scene faded into a purple blotch.

We wonder if the phenomenon might not be more significant than any merely mechanistic solution (if one exists) would suggest. In assembling data for this book we are constantly struck by the concurrences between phenomena and their imagery, so that the graphic similarity between lightning and the trees they strike so often begins to hint at more symbolic connections. We take up this theme in our sections on MYSTERIOUS IMAGES and COINCIDENCES.

If we look beyond the inadequate nineteenth-century attempts to rationalize this phenomenon of lightning photography, we find it well recognized in every age. When Vesuvius erupted in 1660, the attendant lightnings were blamed for the appearances of crosses on garments throughout the kingdom of Naples. Isaac Casaubon's *Adversaria* mentions in all earnestness the images of crosses that appeared on the bodies of a congregation in Wells cathedral during a summer storm in 1596. Lightning 'fell' into the church, and although no one was hurt, the terrific violence of the thunder threw many to the floor: 'The wonderful part was this, which afterwards was taken notice of by many, that the marks of a cross were found to be imprinted on the bodies of those then at divine service.' The Rev. G.S. Tyack also

relates this incident in his *Lore and Legend of the English Church*, 1899, quoting Casaubon: 'The Bishop [of Wells] himself found the mark upon him, and others were signed "on the shoulder, the breast, the back, and other parts".' Flammarion adds that the bishop's wife was among those who received the cross stigma. Another incident when crosses appeared on clothes was mentioned even earlier, by Joseph Grünpech in *Speculum naturalis coelestis*, 1508.

One of the most spectacular cases, when lightning struck the high altar in the church of Saint-Sauveur at Ligny, France, on 18 July 1689, is included by most of the encyclopaedists mentioned earlier. Father Lamy, a priest from a neighbouring town, investigated as soon as he had word of the strange effects, and published his report in 1696 in a little booklet that we recommend as a model of observation. The curtains surrounding the altar were blown off their rings, but without breaking the rings or detaching them from the curtain-rail or

ripping the cloth. Various altar cloths were burnt in places, and the main cloth was torn in a huge X-shaped rent. If we are to believe the testimony of the fifty people present, a statue of Christ was levitated and hovered in the air while its stand was shattered. But the incident that aroused the greatest astonishment and terror was the appearance of strange lettering across the main altarcloth. Deciphered when calm was restored, this proved to be the words of a printed text which lay face down on the cloth, but reversed and magnified. Yet this interpretation merely added to the horror when it was found that all the holy words and phrases were missing in this unholy transcription. However, Father Lamy was a match for this, seeing immediately that the omitted words were those printed in red ink on the card and that the lightning had transmitted only the main part of the text printed in black ink. This case was re-examined by Flammarion in *Thunder and Lightning* and found to be a factual report.

Andres Poey, director of the Physico-Meteorological Observatory at Havana, Cuba, published in 1861 his own collection of lightning stories (this book is very rare, and we have seen only references to and quotes from it in our authorities), which proves the variety of the phenomena. At San Vicente, Cuba, on 24 July 1852 the image of a palm-leaf hut and its surrounding was found etched on some dried leaves, and at Sibacoa on the same island in August 1823 lightning imprinted the image of a bent nail on the trunk of a tree. Poey adds that this was an exact but reversed copy of a nail embedded in one of the tree's upper branches.

We end with an aspect of our subject that, as far as we know, has never been researched: the imprinting of images *beneath* the skin. In 1812, at Combe Hay, Somerset, six sheep were struck dead by lightning in fields near a wood of oak and nut trees. When they were skinned, 'a facsimile of part of the adjacent landscape' was found on the inside of the skins. This was reported by James Shaw to the *Journal of the Meteorological Society*, March 1857. This oddity is matched across the years by the rabbit shot by Jasper Barrett near his Jefferson, South Carolina, home in February 1971. While it was being prepared for supper his wife and a friend saw the outline in black of a woman's face on the skinned flesh of one foreleg. It was about an inch across with a rosebud mouth, curly hair and long lashes, reminding its viewers of the fashions of the 1920s. Curtis Fuller, reporting the story in *Fate*, October 1971, said that within a week of the story appearing in the *Charlotte Observer*, four thousand people had trekked to see it, and for several days extra police were detailed to control the crowds.

*(Left) The branching pattern left by lightning explains some 'lightning photographs' but not all. (Below) This ghostly face at the window of an Alabama courtroom is said to be an image of an imprisoned Negro who stared out during a storm in 1878 and was photographed by a lightning flash onto the glass. (Above) Flammarion tells of people fixed in a rigid death tableau by lightning, sometimes with an image of the local scene engraved on their skin.*

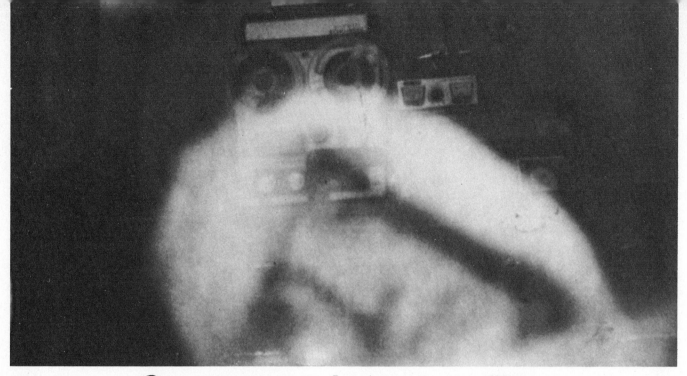

# Spontaneous images on film

In our MYSTERIOUS IMAGES section we give a few cases where figurative or symbolic designs have appeared on, and sometimes in, people, animals and objects. Other cases in which similar effects have been attributed to the action of lightning are mentioned in our LIGHTNING PICTURES section. A modern version of this artistic phenomenon is the appearance of extraneous imagery or unaccountable optical effects on photographs. It is interesting to note that photography and spiritualism developed over the same period, and that it was only a matter of forty years between Nicéphore Niepce's first photograph in 1822 and the publication of the first 'spirit photograph' by William H. Mumler, an engraver and amateur photographer from Boston, Massachusetts. Sadly, Mumler's rather crude effort proved to be the first in a long line of hoaxes. We omit here all but a few references to the vast numbers of apparently genuine 'spirit photographs' to concentrate on more contemporary evidence in which, either the circumstances and controls are better known, or, even more interesting, the phenomenon has occurred outside the context of a 'seance'.

The 'spirit' hypothesis has been overshadowed by the notion that imagery is plucked or projected from the minds of the participants and imprinted in some telekinetic fashion onto the photographic material. This process has occasionally been demonstrated, providing authentic proofs under controlled conditions, as in the case of Ted Serios (see PROJECTED THOUGHT-FORMS); but to date only a very small number of people are known to be able to control it, and in

most of these cases the control is admitted to be erratic and transient (Serios's power to influence film seems to have faded away after 1967). What interests us here is the occurrence of spontaneous imagery in photographs among people who claim no special powers. Cases are reported from time to time in newspapers, and experience has shown that these form only the tip of the iceberg. Peter Haining writes that he made several appeals for 'ghost photographs' during the preparation of his *Ghosts: The Illustrated History*, 1975, and was astonished at the high response. Yet again it seems that phenomena once thought to be the exclusive province of religious devotion and mysticism prove to be more widespread.

One of the earliest and best-documented incidents happened in 1920, when Dr G.L. Johnson, who among other impressive qualifications was a Fellow of the Royal Photographic Society, took a party of investigators to visit a photographic medium in Crewe, William Hope. In his *The Great Problem: Does Man Survive?*, 1928, Dr Johnson says that he took with him a bundle of photographic plates, bought at random from several suppliers in London. At no time was Mr Hope allowed to approach the members of the party, but they photographed him with several different cameras. When the plates were developed they showed a profusion of faces (of people alive and dead), clouds of 'ectoplasm', flower-like shapes and written messages. A sealed box of plates was held to Mr Hope's head and, when later developed, the two centre plates revealed more writing (the adjacent plates remained unexposed). Sir Arthur

Conan Doyle's *The Case for Spirit Photography*, 1922, was largely a study of Hope's 'Crewe Circle'.

A dramatic modern case was investigated from 1972 onwards by Dr Berthold E. Schwarz and reported at length in *Flying Saucer Review*, 20–4 and 21–1. The central figure was Mrs Stella Lansing of Massachusetts, who had previous UFO experiences and was now finding a great variety of anomalies on her cine-films. Many hundreds of feet of 8mm and Super-8 film, shot at different places and times with different cameras and makes of film, showed clock-like arrangements of lenticular, UFO-type shapes that rotated and flashed; other effects were curious foggings, faces and faint, distorted views of familiar landscapes. Sometimes she said she had hunches and 'just had to film', and on other occasions the intrusions were only discovered when the film came back from processing. Dr Schwarz, a highly respected psychiatric consultant, was aware of the thought-projection theory, and was constantly alert for clues in Mrs Lansing's behaviour, experience and life-style that might have some connection with the effects. As Eisenbud found with Ted Serios, there were no overt signs of such 'synchronistic' links, and certainly nothing on the scale demonstrated by, say, Gemma Galgani, whose STIGMATA included bleeding 'scourge-marks' identical in design and location to those on her favourite crucifix. However, both Eisenbud and Schwarz believe that the complex and subtle web of circumstance and details of personal significance yields synchronistic events more often and in more ways than we might generally suppose.

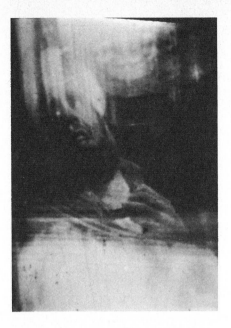

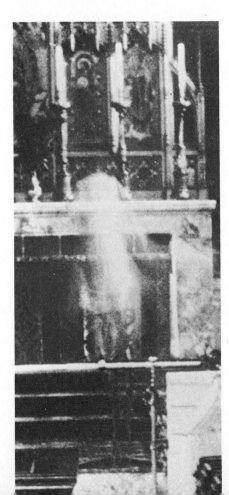

*(Left) The Veilleux brothers (see text) kept finding strange, unwanted images on their photographs – here a Rudolph-Valentino-type face appears tilted in front of a shot of their tape-recorder. (Above) Stella Lansing (see text) tried to film her favourite TV show, but when the film came back from processing she found collages of distorted objects superimposed on the domestic views, in the middle of which was this bearded, turbaned figure holding a reed or a flute. (Below) Could a similar process account for many alleged photographs of ghosts, like this one, taken by a solicitor in St Nicholas' Church, Arundel, Sussex, which shows a phantom priest before the altar?*

During the decline in Serios's talents, Eisenbud learned of the strange photographs produced by two brothers, Richard and Fred Veilleux, of Waterville, Maine. They cautiously revealed that they had begun experimenting with a ouija board in 1966, which later revealed to them when and where to take their pictures. Their first 'assignment' was on 1 August 1967, by the gravestone of a little girl in the cemetery where both brothers worked as stonemasons. The photograph showed a small girl standing beside the headstone, and she was easily identified, having lived in the neighbourhood until her murder some years before. Photographs taken by the brothers (and by their wives) of members of the family, usually seated at the kitchen table, would be blotted out by faces, scenes or white shapes. Other effects, similar to Mrs Lansing's, seem to be complex montages of some sort and definitely not double exposures. Eisenbud experimented with the brothers and obtained several authentic proofs. One photograph mentioned in his report to *Fate* (January and February 1976 issues) contained two faces superimposed over two ordinary doors; they were later identified as a young and an old portrait of a US Marshal, Jeff D. Milton. At first it was thought that both portraits had been taken from Hunter and Rose's *Album of Gunfighters* in which they are placed side by side, and the brothers' effect seemed an obvious fake until it was discovered that one of the authors of the book, Rose, was in the habit of retouching his published photographs to protect copyright, and the Veilleux version was not the same as the book's. Eisenbud embarked on a search of all the known photographs of Marshal Milton but failed to discover any original for the Veilleux picture. This strange manipulation shows up in another of the brothers' efforts with an Australian rock-painting.

In surveying the pictorial evidence in this category generally, one cannot fail to notice the preponderance of faces, a fact that may prove to be significant. Schwarz quotes the work of Jan Ehrenwald on the relationship between psi-effects and the body-image (i.e. our idea of ourselves), and one speculation is that these images might be spontaneous affirmations of issues and beliefs central to our being, or, as Schwarz expresses it, an automatic 'extension of ego-function and a psychokinetic manifestation' (*Flying Saucer Review*, 20–6). Perhaps in this context faces are symbolic of identity, as in a photograph where Mrs Lansing's face is blotted out by that of her husband's deceased maiden aunt, and in another where a beauty-spot-like 'facial lesion' appears on her cheek. Many other examples from the history of the subject could be found. Also we hear from time to time of people who are the opposite of photogenic; people who always find their faces marked or obscured in their photographic portraits. In his *Mysteries of Time and Space*, 1974, Brad Steiger published a photograph taken by a colleague on a Polaroid camera. The subject, a woman, claimed she could not be photographed, and she was right. The camera was functioning perfectly before and after, but in the print of her she is obscured by a white cloud. In other cases this defect is a distinctive mark on the face, reminding us of the old belief that the mark which the Lord put on Cain (Genesis 4:15) reappears on his descendents. In the Lansing case Schwarz had consulted the famous telepath, magician and investigator, Joseph Dunninger, who examined Mrs Lansing's photographs and believed them genuine. Between them they arranged an experiment in which Dunninger attempted to project the numerals '57' on to his daughter's forehead. On Schwarz's polaroid print they found to their surprise a dark spot just off centre on her forehead, rather like the *tilaka* of the Hindus (*Flying Saucer Review*, 20–6).

A robed figure is another image that frequently appears spontaneously on photographs. Common types are phantom monks, ladies in grey, and Christ-like figures in the sky (see also ODD CLOUDS). In 1972 Schwarz published a report on the experience of the wife of the famous UFO contactee, Howard Menger (*Flying Saucer Review*, 18–4). She claimed she was not religiously devout, but once, during the terminal illness of her son, she switched off the TV and was astonished to see a coloured image of Christ remaining on the screen – although the set was black and white! In another of Schwarz's investigations (*Flying Saucer Review*, 21–3, 4) two friends of the central figure, Mrs M., both took photographs. On one appeared a 'white-robed man' and on the other 'Christ in white robes'. Incidentally, Steiger's book shows a photograph of a hand that appeared on an unplugged television set on Christmas Eve, 1968!

Some of the effects produced by spontaneous photography are rather frightening. Haining in his book reproduces a Polaroid photograph of a dog taken by Sam Watkins of Virginia, in which the dog is replaced by three views of his younger brother, Bill. As Haining points out, it is impossible to triple-expose Polaroid film; but the sinister aspect of the thing is that Bill was killed by a car a few days later, as he stood in the same pose as the one in the photograph. These effects hint darkly at a universal reciprocity between mind and matter, and raise important questions, not just about the nature of ghosts and UFOs, but about the nature of evidence and of reality itself.

# Mysterious images

'After the death of Dean Vaughan, of Llandaff, there suddenly appeared on a wall of the Llandaff cathedral, a large blotch of dampness, or minute fungi, formed into a life-like outline of the Dean's face.' (*Notes and Queries*, 8 February 1902.) Folklore is fabulously rich in such tales of images – from the scorch-mark left by the devil in the north door of Blythburgh church, Suffolk (see BLACK DOGS), to the grave in Pekin, Illinois, of a man hanged for the murder of his sister, over which nothing will grow; the resulting bare patch is said to be an excellent likeness in outline of the woman's face (*Gentry Journal*, 30 April 1897).

Reports of spontaneous images seem to go in waves. On 12 March 1872, crosses appeared on windows in Baden-Baden, Germany. Authorities ordered them washed off, but they proved resistant, even to acids. Two days later at Rastadt more crosses appeared, followed shortly by death's heads. The same happened at Boulley, after which the appearances became epidemic, as crosses, eagles, skulls, bands of colours and other religious and political symbols broke out on windowpanes across the countryside. The authorities were alarmed because feelings were still high after the recent Franco-Prussian war. A squad of Prussian soldiers smashed windows of one house because people saw in them a group of French Zouaves and their banners. According to the *Religio-Philosophical Journal*, 29 March 1873, the Zouaves could still be seen waving their flags in the fragments of shattered glass, defiant to the last.

From this date, Fort noted, reports of images in window glass were regularly featured in the American press right up to 1890. It could not be said that the American public was merely elaborating on the European events, because sporadic outbreaks had been reported in America since at least 1870; and besides, events of this kind were recorded long before the advent of photography.

Another series began with 'A faithful and unmistakable likeness of the late Dean Liddell, who died in 1898', which appeared on a wall of Christ Church, Oxford, in mid-1923. Three years later, *TP's and Cassell's Weekly*, 11 September 1926, reported that it was still there: 'One does not need to call into play any imaginative faculty to reconstruct the head. It is set perfectly straight upon the wall as it might have been drawn by the hand of a master artist. Yet it is not etched: neither is it sketched nor sculptured, but it is there plain for all eyes to see.'

Later in that same year of 1926, reports of images came from Bristol and from Uphill, Somerset; and in the old Abbey at Bath an image of a soldier with a pack was clearly seen in a discoloured patch on one of the pillars close to a monument to the Somerset Regiment. Local theosophists, reported the *Bath Weekly Chronicle*, identified it as a thought image created by pious visitors.

Critics of such reports point out that the eye has a natural tendency to see images in accidental patterns, and that these images often reflect intense emotional states. This is no doubt true – the process is used to advantage in

psychoanalysis and in art – but we are more concerned with coherent images which do not rely on 'suggestion' or peculiar mental states for their interpretation, but which, to the contrary, unmistakably depict some recognizable symbol or cipher. Examples include the egg laid in Arkansas with the numeral '6' on one end (London *Daily Mail*, 14 December 1973), and the kitten born in Nice, France, with the date '1921' distinctly marked in grey fur on the white of its belly (London *Daily Express*, 14 May 1921).

We have mentioned in our INVISIBLE ASSAILANTS section the strange case of Eleonore Zugun, on whose arm the word 'Dracu' appeared in front of witnesses (London *Evening Standard*, 1 October 1926). Then there was the even more demonstrative case of a young French girl whose responses to questions took the form of words and pictures that appeared on her body (*Daily Express*, 17 November 1913). Similarly, the modern stigmatic, Marie-Julie Jahenny, of the Breton village of La Fraudais, bore, in addition to her other spontaneous marks of distinction, a flower, a cross and the words '*O Crux Ave*'. Dr Imbert-Gourbeyre followed her case for over twenty years, throughout which the marks remained visible. In his *La Stigmatisation*, 1894, he explains in terms of tiny beads of clotted blood forcing their way through the epidermis to lie just below the surface – but the interesting question, how the blood became organized into coherent images, is avoided completely.

If this organizing force were to exist, and to respond to sentient control, and to be capable of intervening in physical processes, its effects would be not unlike those of our data. All knowledge is founded on experience and first-hand testimony, yet the modern world-view is so deep-rooted in most of us that we would rather doubt our sanity than question scientific authority. So what then are we to make of the experience of a pilgrim who visited the Italian stigmatic, Palma Matarelli, in April 1872, and is quoted in Father Thurston's *Physical Phenomena of Mysticism*? A white cloth had been given to the stigmatic to wipe off the blood that trickled from punctures in her forehead: 'This wiping left upon the linen not simple blood-stains, but emblems clearly outlined, representing inflamed hearts, nails and swords. This is truly a marvel and I saw it with my own eyes.'

It is timing that often gives the appearances of marks or pictures the added dimension of being in some mysterious way related to a social context. For instance, in the first half of December 1680, Rome was excited by a 'strange and wonderful' comet that became visible near the ecliptic against the constellations of Libra and Virgo. At

*(Left) In Rembrandt's painting the portentous writing is seen on the wall on the night of Belshazzar's feast, when he was killed by Darius and the invading Persians (Daniel 5). (Top) The scales of this butterfly fish spell out in Arabic 'There is no God but God.' (Middle) The comet egg of 1680 (see text).*

8 a.m. on 11 December, Rome buzzed with extra news: 'A prodigious egge was laid by a young pullet, with a perfect comet in it, and as many stars, and in the same form as the enclosed figure shows.' The account in the *Loyal Protestant and True Domestic Intelligencer*, 2 April 1681, says quite clearly that the image was not on the shell, but 'within the egge, most clearly exprest'. The COINCIDENCE of a cometary visitation, the public expectation, and the miraculous egg sounds so fantastic that even the *Loyal Protestant* in that credulous age is moved to invite you to believe it or not as you wish.

Our last item is singular by any standards: the day it rained Virgins. The *English Mechanic*, 12 June 1908, reprinted from French sources the eye-witness account by the Abbé Gueniot of the church at Remiremont. On 26 May 1907, a severe storm swept over the Vosges area of France. Large hailstones fell profusely. The Abbé was reading in his presbytery (the object of his attention, oddly enough, was a treatise on glacial formation) when a neighbour urgently called him to see the 'miracle'. There was a message in the hailstones. The Abbé went to inspect, and, by his own account, found very distinctly on the front of the hailstones, which were slightly convex in the centre, the bust of a woman with a robe turned up at the bottom like a priest's cope: 'I should perhaps describe it still more exactly by saying that it was like the Virgin of the Hermits. The outlines of the image were slightly hollow, as though they had been formed with a punch, but were very boldly drawn.'

Gueniot noticed that the hailstones were almost regular spheres, with what looked like a seam, as if they were moulded. 'The imprint on the two I examined was so regular that it can hardly be due to chance.' The logical hypothesis of human manufacture was also rejected, because of the vast quantity of image-bearing hailstones over the whole area of the fall, and the many observations of them falling. The Bishop of Sainte-Dié convened an enquiry, at which scientists heard 107 other witnesses, who vouched for the event (*English Mechanic*, 3 July 1908), although opinions on its cause varied.

This fall had other peculiar characteristics: it was confined to a strip of land three-quarters of a mile wide and several miles long; and although many of the hailstones fell with sufficient force to do considerable damage to crops and greenhouses, many others were seen to fall without much force at all, seeming 'to have fallen from a height of but a few yards'. Since there was no evidence of imposture, this accords very well with the strange falls and flights recorded in our other sections. The Abbé Gueniot had his own very satisfactory explanation for the descent of hailstones bearing the image of the Virgin of the Hermits. A week earlier it had been the day of the Virgin's feast, but no feast had been held: 'The town council of Remiremont, for profound reasons which I need not discuss, forbade the magnificent procession which was in preparation; but on the following Sunday at the same hour, the artillery of heaven caused a vertical procession which no one could forbid.'

*(Left) A trick of the light, producing in a tree a shining Madonna-like figure, caused excitement at Metz, France. (Below left) Dean Liddell of Oxford, shortly before his death in 1898. (Below right) Years later in 1923 his image was observed in damp stains on the cathedral wall.*

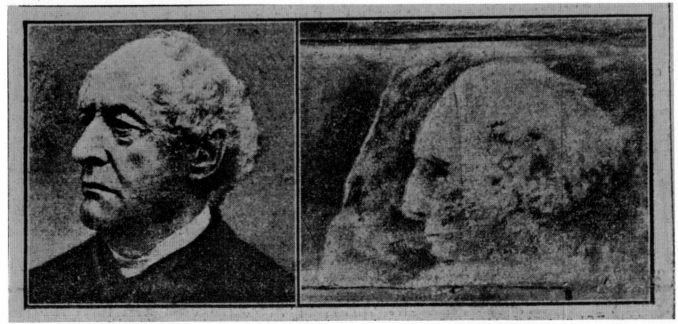

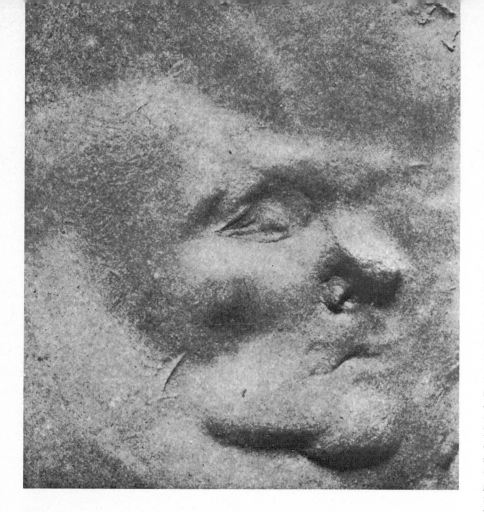

# Projected thought-forms

The idea of a reciprocal relationship between the subjective world of thoughts and ideas and the 'real' world of objective events and objects is a chestnut of great antiquity, argued, pro or con, by every school of philosophy. It can be seen operating in all forms of magic and ritual, and is the basis of all artistic and literary metaphors. As above, so below; uniting all opposites. Throughout the philosophy of all times recurs the belief that events and objects may be as ephemeral as thoughts, while thoughts can occasionally become concrete and objective 'realities'.

In the great rise of modern science such a notion is heresy, yet the echoes of it have persisted. The latest findings from both paraphysics and sub-atomic physics are prompting a belated recognition and respect for ancient truth as more and more authentic proofs are obtained of the transmutation of matter and the apparent suspension of the known laws of space, time, matter and energy. We are told that an electron can travel between two points in space without physically traversing the distance between them, just as objects in the larger world of man have been observed to disappear and reappear elsewhere (see MATERIALIZATION AND

FLIGHT OF OBJECTS). When solid objects spontaneously change their structure, colour or motion, these effects might be logical consequences of the inexplicable randomness that Heisenberg showed to exist in the motions of the sub-atomic particles.

The discovery of telekinetic forces has been the main motivation behind the experiments of Dr J. B. Rhine at Duke University, who began research into what is now called psychokinesis in the 1930s. Psychokinesis, or PK, is the enigmatic process more popularly described as 'mind over matter', and in 1945, Dr Rhine announced that he had conclusive evidence of PK effects in influencing the way dice (tumbled in a machine) fell. Rhine divides the subject into PK influences on 'moving targets', like the dice; 'living targets' which might imply anything from LEVITATION AND SPONTANEOUS FLIGHT to influencing the growth of plants; and 'static targets' which largely include the 'thought-ography' associated with Ted Serios (see illustration).

The projection of an image onto sealed film, apparently by PK or some other paranormal means, gives results that are more accessible to analysis. It is interesting to note that with Serios and

the small number of others who can repeat this effect, their 'hits' are far outnumbered by 'wild' images and sometimes complete disruption of normal optical processes 'overexposing' the film. The ability to affect, consciously or unconsciously, unexposed film may be more widespread than most people realize, to judge from the number of accounts we can find of 'wild images' turning up on photographs taken by ordinary people (see SPONTANEOUS IMAGES ON FILM).

We are particularly interested in cases where a desired effect has been achieved purely through the exercise of imagination. In 1935, Mrs Gertrude Smith of York, Pennsylvania, discovered she could mentally coax her hens to lay eggs bearing images. The *York Gazette and Daily*, 4 April 1940, quoted her as saying: 'I would stand near the hen yard and visualize sunflower-petals along with my initials. In a few days my father came into the house all excited and said: "Here is the sunflower egg". The pattern of a sunflower was incised into the shell on the flattened part.' She soon obtained more patterned eggs, one of them marked with the reversed letters of her initials: 'When I broke one open, the design appeared raised on the inner surface of the shell.' A later edition of the *Gazette and Daily* testified to the genuineness of the patterned eggs and referred to a sworn deposition by other witnesses. Mrs Smith said she tried visualizing an egg with a triangular cross-section, and when one arrived she became so frightened by her power that she never tried again.

In many of our sections we tell of objects or images that appeared in response to conscious or unconscious demand, and observe their synchronous nature (see COINCIDENCES). Mrs Crowe gives an example in *The Night Side of Nature*, 1854, of a girl who dreamt she was offered two roses, one red and one white, and chose the red one. She woke with a pain in her arm, on which by degrees 'there arose the perfect figure of a rose, perfect in form and colour. It was rather raised above the skin'. It took a fortnight to fade away. The case of Mrs L. Forbes, of Thornton Heath, near London, was often quoted by Dr Nandor Fodor to support his opinion that poltergeists are genuine psychological phenomena, or as he put it, 'bundles of projected repressions'. One night in 1938 Mrs Forbes dreamt of being pulled in two directions by her dead father and her husband. Her father then drew a cross on her left breast with a finger. In the morning Mrs Forbes discovered on that site an inflamed mark. An examination by a doctor disclosed a previously unsuspected cancer in that position, necessitating an operation. (See STIGMATA and MYSTERIOUS IMAGES for discussion of similar cases.)

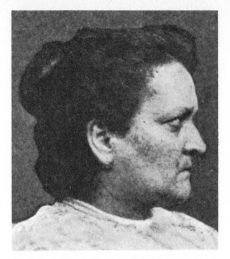

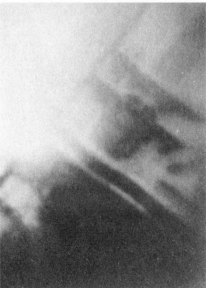

*(Left and above) Eusapia Palladino, at the height of her powers in the 1890s, could impress her features into putty in sealed containers, supposedly by an effort of will. (Below) In the 1960s, Dr Jule Eisenbud studied the comparable claims of Ted Serios to project mental images onto sealed film. Eisenbud found no evidence of trickery during his long investigation (see his* The World of Ted Serios, *1968). An example of a 'target' (below), and (bottom) Serios's result. (Right) Krishna multiplies himself to make love to the thirty-three Gopis.*

The whimsical character of PK projection (or whatever it is) comes over in a series of disturbances that occurred in the house of Dr E. E. Phelps, a Presbyterian minister of Stratford, Connecticut, in March 1850. The *New Haven Journal and Courier*, 19 April 1850, gives the testimony of a friend and witness, Dr Webster: 'When the Phelps family returned from church, they found the furniture strewn about the rooms, and curious figures constructed of clothing arranged in one of them, constituting a sort of tableau, depicting a scene of worship. There were eleven figures, arranged in life-like attitudes. All but one were female figures; all were in postures of extreme devotion, some with their foreheads nearly touching the floor; others kneeling about the room with open Bibles before them, *which indicated different passages sanctioning the phenomena then going on* [our italics]. In the centre of the group there was a figure suspended as though flying through the air.' Later other figures were found, the clothing they were made from coming from all parts of the house, unseen, despite a close watch. One figure, made from Mrs Phelps' dress, looked so convincing that their young son was moved to say: 'Be still, Ma is saying prayers.' A good account can be found in E. W. Capron's *Modern Spiritualism: Its Facts and Fanaticisms*, 1855, drawn from Dr Phelps' own records. Weird though this scene is, it is not unique. In his *Poltergeist over England*, Harry Price quotes a story of similar clothing-figures during the haunting at Ringcroft, Galloway, in 1695, from a contemporary pamphlet.

To judge from the many stories of 'mind over matter' both from daily experience and mythology, the only limit may be the human imagination itself. Both Dr W. Y. Evans-Wentz and that remarkable woman Alexandra David-Neel, highly credible scholars and explorers of Tibet, spoke of the power of the *dubthab* rite there by which adepts could materialize a human apparition, called a *tulpa* – a power claimed by many kinds of occultists and magicians. David-Neel attempted to manufacture a *tulpa* of her own, using the prescribed meditation and visualizing exercises. How she succeeded is told in chapter 8 of her *Magic and Mystery in Tibet*. This was no subjective illusion, for the little monk-like figure she dreamt up was seen on many occasions by others. She tells how the *tulpa* slipped away from her control and began to perform independently of her will; and reflecting her fears, the *tulpa*'s placid features became sly, mocking and malignant. It had to be firmly de-materialized by an exhausting reversal of the whole process.

As with most of the phenomena in our sections, the spontaneous outbreaks outshine those feeble performances which take place under a freak human will, and both pale before the dazzling, controlled displays of power put on by the true mystics. In his life of Milarepa, Evans-Wentz says that the great sage, while dying at the Red Rock, projected a great number of *tulpas* of himself; such was his power and skill that many of his followers in places far apart thought they encountered Milarepa himself. Similar tales are told of Jesus after his resurrection, and of many saintly men (e.g. Padre Pio), that they were seen in several places at the same time (see TELEPORTATION for the transatlantic bilocation of Mary of Agreda).

# Cities and islands in the sky

If we were to have the, by all accounts not uncommon experience of seeing a city in the sky, a city embellished with the most noble architectural effects, white marble towers, domes, etc.; if we were lucky enough to see such a thing, we might be sufficiently curious as to its actual nature to look for an explanation. From the list of explanations authoritatively offered over the centuries we could select one of the following causes for our vision: that it was (i) a holy city like the New Jerusalem, 'coming down from ... heaven, prepared as a bride adorned for her husband' (Revelation 21:2), seen by St John on Patmos in the second century AD; (ii) a reflection, due to some undetermined atmospheric function, of an actual city elsewhere (but we wonder why cities should project themselves so much more frequently than the landscapes in between them); (iii) a city of the blessed dead such as is occasionally seen particularly off the coasts of Celtic realms; (iv) a peculiar effect of cloud and mist; (v) an actual flying city like Laputa in Swift's *Gulliver's Travels*; (vi) a delusion of drink or religious excitement.

Before (or perhaps instead of) investigating causes we document the phenomenon.

An image in the sky 'giving the impression of distant land with wonderful white buildings' was seen from the island of Sanday in the Orkneys in 1840; it was seen again in 1857 when it lasted for about three hours. E.W. Marwick, who quotes these records in *The Folklore of Orkney and Shetland*, adds that the phenomenon is not uncommon in the North. Local people explain it as being the crystal and pearl city of the mys-

terious Fin Folk, occasionally revealed to mortal eyes; or it may be the intermittently manifest isle of Hether Blether, whose quasi-location is west of the actual sacred island of Eynhallow. Mr Marwick explains it as a mirage but does not suggest what it is a mirage of.

Roderick O'Flaherty, writing in 1684, describes a phantom island that often appears off the west coast of Ireland. He gives several possible explanations; that it is the island of O Brasil, known to cartographers but to nobody else; that it is the terrestrial paradise kept hidden by special ordinance of God; that it is a fabrication of evil spirits or merely an illusion of the clouds. Which of these speculations is to be preferred, says O'Flaherty wisely, 'is more than our judgments can sound out'.

W.G. Wood-Martin in 1902 records several appearances of O or Hy Brasil. It was seen off Sligo in 1885, and after a previous sighting a correspondent wrote:

'I myself, upward of half a century ago, saw a wonderful mirage resembling that recently described as having been visible off our Tireragh coast (county of Sligo); and had I been looking on the Bay for the first time, nothing could have persuaded me but that I was gazing at a veritable city – a large handsome one too, trees, houses, spires, castellated buildings, etc.'

Wood-Martin explains that such cities are reflections of real cities somewhere else, and he offers as analogy the claims of sailors in Dublin Bay that they can sometimes see Mount Snowdon 'looming' a hundred miles away. But looking out to sea from the west coast of Ireland the nearest known city in that

direction that could loom would be New York, whose distinctive architecture is never a reported feature of the west Irish city vision.

On 18 July 1820 Captain Scoresby of the ship *Baffin* pointed his telescope at the unexplored shore of West Greenland and spied 'an extensive ancient city abounding with the ruins of castles, obelisks, churches and monuments, with other large and conspicuous buildings'. He drew some of these features. Sir David Brewster put the drawings together into a panorama, which is reproduced in his book, *Natural Magic*. But in his engraving the architectural features are reverting to natural rock forms and have not the 'distinctness of reality', as Captain Scoresby said they had.

One of the attractions of Alaska is that its local sky is peculiarly receptive of images of the city of Bristol in England. Fort in *New Lands* lists several reports of the appearance of Bristol over Alaska and quotes the tradition that this city is there visible every year between 21 June and 10 July. It, or something like it, is said to have been regularly seen by the Alaskan Indians before white settlement. In 1887 the famous pioneer Willoughby saw and photographed this aerial city, or so it was claimed, but his print looks so like the city of Bristol that many people have supposed it to be a photograph of material Bristol rather than its Alaskan phantom. Yet there is ample evidence that some remarkable city or other is at times apparent in the Alaskan skies. In the *New York Times*, 31 October 1889, Mr L.B. French reported seeing quite plainly in the sky near Mount Fairweather, Alaska, 'houses, well defined streets and trees. Here and there rose tall spires over huge buildings, which appeared to be ancient mosques or cathedrals. . . . It did not look like a modern city – more like an ancient European city'. Fort quotes another correspondent from the Yukon who in June 1897 had seen a great city in the sky. Members of his party speculated on whether it most resembled Toronto, Montreal or Peking, but concluded that it was more like 'some ancient city in the past'.

The archaic and splendid features often attributed to aerial cities, even when viewed in non-religious contexts, link them, phenomenally speaking, with the ideal cities of mystic vision, such as St John's pearly city of Jerusalem. An example of this class from Flammarion's *L'Atmosphère* is the 'vast and beautiful city, adorned with monuments, domes and steeples' seen by the traveller Grellois between Ghelma and Bône in North Africa. He knew of no earthly city resembling it. However the tendency of most modern viewers is to seek a local origin for their vision. Thus in the case quoted by Fort from the *New York Sun*, 6 March 1890, of a large unknown city seen at 4 p.m. over Ashland, Ohio, although some declared it to be the New Jerusalem, the majority were divided between Mansfield, thirty miles, and Sandusky, sixty miles away, as its original. The incident produced a typical Forteanism: 'May have been a revelation of heaven, and for all I know heaven may resemble Sandusky, and those of us who have no desire to go to Sandusky may ponder that point.'

To emphasize the recurrence of the 'city' phenomenon we select from Fort's collection in *New Lands* the apparition of Edinburgh, so-called, seen over Liverpool, 27 September 1846; the snow-covered, icicle-hung, inhabited village which appeared over Pomerania on 10 October 1881, and was said to resemble a settlement on the island of Bornholm a

hundred miles away; and the series of phantom cities, islands and other scenes which were reported from Sweden between 1881 and 1888. From the classic phantom-city land of Ireland: an aristocratic town of mansions set in shrubberies behind white palings seen over Youghal, Cork, in June 1801, and two other visions of a walled town viewed earlier from the same city in 1796 and 1797; at Ballyconneely on the west coast a phantom city of assorted houses in

*(Left) St John's vision of the New Jersualem as a city floating down from the sky.*

*(Above) The flying city of Laputa appeared to Swift's Gulliver in a form which has since become popular with UFO and SF illustrators.*

*(Below) A photograph of the mirage of Bristol, taken in Alaska (see text).*

different styles of architecture was on view for three hours on 2 August 1908.

Those whose favoured explanation for phantom cities is the Swiftian 'Laputa' one, that they are actual cities, detached, mobile and airborne, meet objections that any such bodies would be reported by astronomers or radar stations by pointing out that they are indeed so reported. The UFO literature is full of examples of sighted or radar-detected objects, many of apparently vast size, all of unknown nature, and many earlier observations of such things are to be found in Fort's collections.

The phenomenon of a recurrent landscape, most often a city or island, appearing annually or seasonally in a particular area of sky, is one which we do not think has been fully covered by any explanation yet devised. We suggest that the tradition of an enchanted land or island of the dead, described so frequently in Celtic folklore and the mythologies of many other races, is partly derived from actual visions of such a landscape. Its regular appearance at certain times may have given the old Druid priests the opportunity of predicting a vision of paradise, or of crediting themselves with its invocation. Legend attributes to them the habit of creating such grandiose phantasmagoria. A survival of ancient practice may lurk in the incident quoted by Hunt from Gilbert's *Parochial History of Cornwall*:

'The editor remembers a female relation of a former vicar of St Erth who, instructed by a dream, prepared decoctions of various herbs, and, repairing to the Land's End, poured them into the sea, with certain incantations, expecting to see the Lionesse country rise immediately out of the water, having all its inhabitants alive, notwithstanding their long submersion. But,
"Perchance some form was unobserved, Perchance in prayer or faith she swerved,"
No country appeared.'

# Phantom ships

Phantom ships at sea are one thing; and ever since the early morning of 11 July 1881, when King George V as a young naval officer sighted the *Flying Dutchman* in the South Atlantic, we have been respectful of this phenomenon. Ships sailing through the clouds are, we suppose, a degree more wonderful – that is, if one unexplained phenomenon can be judged more wonderful than any other; but when they have crews on board, we can not but feel that the event is more sensational than, say, a shower of frogs.

Ships in the sky are as old as history and repeat themselves in today's newspaper. They are the prime material of the UFO literature which has proliferated so richly, in company with the phenomenon, since the 1950s; and current interest in the subject has led to the disinterment of numerous such items in old histories. Thus in the *Flying Saucer Review*, May–June 1971, is resurrected a report from 1743 from a farmer near Holyhead in Anglesea, who saw a packet-boat sailing through the clouds 1500 feet overhead. He estimated its displacement as about 90 tons. Its keel was clearly visible, proving that it was no mirage of a ship at sea.

There is a reference in ancient Irish annals to 'fantastical ships' seen in 1161, sailing against the wind in Galway harbour. W. G. Wood-Martin, quoting this in *The Elder Faiths of Ireland* (1–216), gives another instance 'on a serene evening in the autumn of 1798', when hundreds of people on a hill at Croaghpatrick, Mayo, saw an aerial navy. It was, explains Wood-Martin, 'produced by the reflection of the fleet of Admiral Warren which was then in pursuit of a French squadron off the west coast of Ireland.' He further explains that the Galway ships of 1161 must have been a reflection of Northern war-galleys.

Long before any known airship there was a belief in airships. Agobard, Archbishop of Lyons in the ninth century, was confronted with a crowd of local people escorting four prisoners who, they said, had been caught landing from an airship. They requested the Archbishop's leave to stone them. Agobard refused, not believing the airship story, and later reported (we quote him from G. G. Coulton's *Medieval Panorama*) that the locals were so unreasonable as to 'believe and assert that there is a certain region called Magonia, whence ships come in the clouds: the which bear away the fruits of the earth . . . to that same country'.

The popular histories of Cornwall and Brittany contain many references to ships which are seen to sail across land, particularly on certain anniversaries, at times preceding storms or at the death of a notable person. The Land's End district of Cornwall was once famous for such apparitions, of which several are recorded in W. Bottrell's *Traditions and Hearthside Stories of West Cornwall*. The actual paths over which these ships navigate are sometimes noted; and we suspect that certain old roads were originally laid to follow the traditional route of some such regular local phenomenon as a phantom ship. In about 1835 Robert Hunt, author of *Popular Romances of the West of England*, spoke to a man who had seen the wondrous ship of Porthcurno, also described by Bottrell, which 'would drive into Parcurno against wind and tide; oft-times she came in the dark of evening and, without stopping at the Cove, took her course over the old caunce towards Chapel-Curno; thence she sailed away, her keel just skimming the ground, or many yards above it, as she passed over hill and dale till she arrived at Chygwidden'. The ship would then vanish at a rock, beneath which a hoard of coins was discovered.

On the arms of the Duke of Argyll, Chief of the Clan Campbell, is a vessel described heraldically as 'a lymphad or ancient galley, sails furled, flags and pennants flying gules, and oars in action sable'. At the death of a senior Campbell, this ship appears on Loch Fyne by Inveraray, Scotland. Lord Halifax in his *Ghost Book* says he was told by the Duke that just after the death of his father, Lord Archibald Campbell, in 1913, the galley had appeared with its usual crew of three men and had followed its regular course over the Loch to a certain spot on the shore, whence it proceeded overland to the sanctuary of St Columba. A curious detail is that on this occasion it was seen not only by local people but also by a visiting Englishman who called out, 'Look at that funny airship!'

A similar apparition was seen on 26 June 1959 over New Guinea. The case, first reported in the Sydney *Sun-Herald* and later widely canvassed in UFO literature, is an interesting one because of the number and sobriety of the witnesses (Father Gill and the entire staff and inmates of the Anglican Mission in Papua) and because it is another instance of a well-documented modern event for which there is much precedent in early records and folklore. The ship which hovered over the Mission was circular with a superstructure 'like the bridge of a boat'. Its crew of four leant over the rails, and when Father Gill and his flock waved to them, they waved back.

'The Great Airship Flap of 1897' is the name now given to the most remarkable phenomenon that ever defied explanation. The events of this saga are so bizarre as to seem incredible, yet if we are to give credence to any historical records of the very recent past, we can scarcely withhold it from the mass of contemporary statements to the effect that throughout the nineteenth century, particularly during its last decade, the skies of North America were infested by a large miscellany of 'impossible' airships.

In Charles Fort's *New Lands* is the first compilation of some of the many scattered reports of mysterious lights and airships in 1896 and 1897; and Fort was the first to make the revolutionary suggestion that the phenomenon might well be attributed to visitors from another world. Recently a great many more newspaper reports of the time have been unearthed by UFO researchers and quoted in such books as John Keel's *UFOs Operation Trojan Horse*, 1970, and Clark and Coleman's *The Unidentified*, 1975. April 1897 was the peak of the 'flap'. There were airship reports from all over America, the majority from the Midwest and Texas. A cigar-shaped winged object, with a canopy or superstructure and brightly lit with coloured lights, passed over Iowa, Michigan, Washington and many other states. Thousands of people saw it over Chicago. There were absurd but respectably attested reports of landings, messages received and occupants encountered, varying from dwarfish Orientals to tall, bearded white men; and there were hoaxes and strange rumours of secret airship inventors. There were at the time no known dirigible airships flying in America, yet on 19 April 1897 the *Dallas Morning News* reported the crash of an airship at Aurora, Texas, together with the remarkable statement that the dead pilot was 'not an inhabitant of this world', and that 'Mr J. T. Weems, the US Signal Service officer at this place and an authority on astronomy, gives it as his opinion that he was a native of the planet Mars.' There are still old people at Aurora who remember the incident. A recent proposal to reopen the grave and examine the 'Martian' was defeated by residents' objections.

Of all the newspaper reports of 1897 airship activities the one that most amazes us is the following from the *Houston Daily Post*, 28 April:

'Merkal, Texas, April 26. Some parties returning from church last night noticed a heavy object dragging along with a rope attached. They followed it until in crossing the railroad it caught on a rail. On looking up they saw what they supposed was the airship. It was not near enough to get an idea of the dimensions. A light could be seen protruding from several windows; one bright light in front like the headlight of a locomotive. After some ten minutes a man was seen descending the rope; he came near enough to be plainly seen. He wore a light blue sailor suit, was small in size. He stopped when he discovered parties at the anchor and cut the ropes below

him and sailed off in a northeast direction. The anchor is now on exhibition at the blacksmith shop of Elliott and Miller and is attracting the attention of hundreds of people.'

Loren E. Gross, another patient scholar of the 'airship flaps', suggests in his *Charles Fort, the Fortean Society and UFOs*, 1976, that we should try to see the Aurora and Merkal cases against the popular imaginings of the time. This was the period, Gross points out, when Percival Lowell's telescopic surveys of Mars from his giant new telescope on a mountain near Flagstaff, Arizona, were receiving much attention in the press, and creating a boom in amateur astronomy. Another factor must have been the serialization that spring of H. G. Wells' *War of the Worlds* in *Cosmopolitan* magazine. Not surprisingly there was much talk of 'men from Mars'. On 7 March 1897, the *Salt Lake Tribune*, Utah, published an article referring to beliefs in 'cloud ships' under the title 'A Sea above the Clouds – Extraordinary Superstition once prevalent in England'.

Thus at least twelve days *before* the anchor-incident at Merkal we find that a newspaper in another state had told the story of a much earlier anchored 'cloudship'. This occurred in Bristol at the beginning of the thirteenth century and is recorded in the *Otia Imperialia* of Gervase of Tilbury. People coming out of a church after Mass heard a cry in the air and saw a 'cloud-ship' overhead with its anchor and cable caught on a tombstone. A sky-sailor descended the cable to free it, but was detained by the people and drowned in the gross atmosphere of earth. The crew of the airship then cut the cable and made off. This story has yet another precedent. In *Fate* magazine, March 1958, is printed a translation from another thirteenth-century manuscript, the Norse-Irish *Speculum regale*, describing how in about AD 956 a sky-ship's anchor caught on the porch of St Kinarus's church in the borough of

Cloera. Again one of the sailors descended the rope, but this time the bishop deterred the people from seizing him, and he sailed off unharmed with the rest of the crew, leaving the anchor as a souvenir of their visit.

*(Left) The ship of Porthcurno (see text), engraved by Joseph Blight. (Top) The Flying Dutchman. (Above) Traditional images, such as the crescent moon as the boat of souls, are repeated in phenomenal reality. (Below) One of Adamski's photographs of a 'mothership' with attendant UFOs.*

# Spectral armies and sky battles

Phantom soldiers in battle array marching over the land or in the sky: this is a spectacle which cries out for an explanation. Nor does it cry out in vain. In times when traditional mythology was an active force, it was well known throughout northern Europe that the gods and heroes of Valhalla were occasionally to be seen fighting in the sky, and no Breton peasant would have been surprised at the vision of King Arthur and his retinue passing overhead on their way to battle or the chase. The recurrent phenomenon of phantom armies could everywhere be explained in terms of local myths. As these lost their power, other explanations were developed. The apparition of an army in the sky was interpreted as the portent of a battle to come or the spectre of an ancient one, or a mirage reflecting real soldiers somewhere on earth, or a function of second sight, or a meteorological freak, a psychological projection, or extraterrestrials on manoeuvres. We think there may be something in each of these explanations, but rather than judge between them we follow our set policy of emphasizing the phenomenon itself above its possible causes.

If there be any value in the unanimous testimony of gentlemen of credit down the ages, the phenomenal reality of spectral armies is well established. St Augustine records a case in *The City of God*. During the Roman civil wars a noisy battle between 'evil spirits' was seen and heard taking place on a plain in Campania, so realistically that the saint tells of footprints of men and horses afterwards observed on the ground. This event shortly preceded an actual battle which took place on the same site. Note the explanation, typical of the time, in terms of spirits and portents.

When fairies are believed in, they of course provide the explanation of 'phantom soldiers'. W. G. Wood-Martin in *The Elder Faiths of Ireland* records an instance in 1797 of an army of 'fairies'

marching across the bog between Maryborough and Stradybally. They were observed at the unghostly hour of midday. In 1836 another phantom army was seen on the hills at Ballyfriar, and there is a case like St Augustine's of a fairy battle which left physical traces on the ground. In 1800 two little armies were reported to be fighting from the ditches on each side of a road in Kilkenny, and afterwards bushes were found crushed, trees broken, and there was blood on the grass.

Apparitions of unearthly battles were recorded quite frequently during the sixteenth century and were linked by several historians with the outbreaks of millenarian fervour at that time, such as the Anabaptists' rising at Münster in 1525. Ronald Holmes in *Witchcraft in British History* cites other instances from seventeenth-century Scotland which he relates to the religious revivals of the Covenanters. According to a contemporary record, on Clydeside in the summer of 1686 there were 'showers of bonnets, hats, guns and swords, which covered the trees and the ground; companies of men in arms marching in order upon the water-side . . .'. Similar rains and phantom armies seen in Scotland towards the end of the eighteenth century coincided with John Wesley's warnings about the diabolical reality of such things. Mr Holmes blames them, not implausibly, on mass hysteria, but this psychological explanation does not account for the many cases of phantom armies seen during times of no particular religious excitement and by people not subject to it.

The year 1642 was a good one for phantom battles and for pamphlets on them. One such, printed in London and to be seen at the British Library, tells all in its title: *A Signe from Heaven, or a Fearful and Terrible Noise heard in the Ayre at Aldborow* [Aldeburgh] *in the County of Suffolke, on Thursday, the 4th day of August, at 5 of the clocke in the*

*afternoone – wherein was heard the beating of Drums, the discharging of Muskets and great Ordnance for the space of an houre or more. . . .* The title goes on to claim as witnesses 'many men of good worth' who will undertake to testify to leading Members of the House of Commons and to exhibit a stone of great weight which fell from the sky during the uproar.

Another contemporary pamphlet describes *A great Wonder in Heaven, shewing the late Apparitions and Prodigious Noyse of War and Battels, seene on Edge-Hill, neere Keinton, in Northamptonshire, 1642.* On four successive Saturday and Sunday nights, visitors to the battlefield of Edgehill (near Kineton, Warwickshire) were treated to a repeat performance of the recent Civil War contest. Gentlemen of credit were dispatched by the King at Oxford to investigate. They personally witnessed the phenomenon and swore statements to that effect.

A recent sighting of a phantom army, which was given some publicity at the time, was reported by a gentleman of credit, well known to one of us as such, who swears it is a true account. In November 1956, our friend Peter Zinovieff and his half-brother, Patrick Skipwith, were camping in the Cuillin Mountains of Skye. At about three o'clock one morning Peter heard strange noises, opened the tent flap and saw 'dozens of kilted Highlanders charging across the stony ground'. He woke Patrick who also saw them. Both were very frightened. The next evening, after a day's walking and rock bashing (Peter was then a geology student at Oxford), they pitched the tent further up the mountains and sat up with coffee to see if the spectres would return. Nothing happened and they fell asleep. At 4 a.m. they were awakened by the same noise and again with terror saw the Highlanders, but 'retreating, stumbling across the boulders, looking half dead'. At first

66

light they ran down to the Sligachan Hotel, and later that day they told their story to a local man, Mr Ian Campbell. He said they were not the first to see the same thing and explained the Highland soldiers as phantoms 'either from the thirteenth century or the '45 Rebellion'.

The age of enlightenment brought the theory of mirages, or rather the word 'mirage', to account for spectral armies. Sir David Brewster applied this reasonable explanation to a wide range of unreasonable phenomena – in itself an irrational proceeding – in his *Natural Magic* of 1832. One of the best attested 'phantom army' sightings was on 23 June 1744, on the mountain of Souterfell in the Cumberland Lake District. At about seven in the evening Daniel Stricket, servant to John Wren of Wilton Hall, saw many troops of soldiers riding up and over the mountain. Mr Wren, summoned, also saw them, and so did 'every person at every cottage within the distance of a mile, the number of persons who saw them amounting to about twenty-six'. Brewster explains that they must have been reflections of real troopers on the other side of the mountain. But there were no soldiers then in the district, nor was there a road on the far side of the mountain; so Brewster explains further, incredibly: 'But if there was then no road along which they could be marching, it is highly probable that they were troops exercising among the hills in secret, previous to the breaking out of the rebellion in 1745'. Charles Fort, referring to this case, remarks on the amazing prescience of these troops, and he adds typically: 'There has never been an explanation that did not itself have to be explained.'

Fort in *New Lands* goes on to assail the explainers with volleys of phantom soldiers, giving references mostly from contemporary reports.

In 1785, at Ujest, Silesia, soldiers were seen marching through the sky at the same time as the military funeral of General von Cosel was being held. Some time later, the funeral was long over and the phantom soldiers were seen again.

On 3 May 1848, at Vienne, in Dauphiné, an army in the sky was seen by twenty witnesses; on 30 December 1850, phantom soldiers in the sky near the Banmouth; on 22 January 1854, phantom soldiers over Buderich; on 8 October 1812, the same at Ripley, Yorkshire; from September to October 1881, white-robed figures in the sky over Virginia, platoons of 'angels' in white robes and helmets marching above Delaware, and similar reports from Maryland, all summarized in *Scientific American* that year. For several hours a day on three consecutive days from about 1 August 1888, infantry divisions led by a chief with a flaming sword marched across the sky near Varasdin, Croatia. The event was recorded in *L'Astronomie* with the comment that investigation had failed to discover any corresponding terrestrial soldiers in the region; nor, had such soldiers been found, would their presence explain this repeated, localized apparition.

We have many more reports from all ages of the spectral army phenomenon, but no space here even to mention them. Mrs Crowe in *The Night Side of Nature* gives some excellent cases of this remarkably persistent phenomenon, including a full report of the 1881 Ripley incident referred to above and details of the sighting near Lanark, Scotland, in 1686, when only one man in a crowd failed to see the phantom regiments apparent to all the others. Suddenly, with terror, he too saw them, and Mrs Crowe suggests that he may have temporarily received the second sight from a seer standing by him. This excellent authoress rejects the mirage theory on the grounds that there is often no possible original image to be reflected, particularly in the cases when the phantom soldiers' uniforms are of another age. She speaks in terms of spirits, spirit-seers and impressions of ancient events occasionally reforming as apparitions.

(Above) On 29 September 1914 the London Evening News *published a short story by Arthur Machen called* The Bowmen. *It was inspired by newspaper reports the previous month of the harrowing retreat from Mons, in Belgium, in which the British army, despite overwhelming German forces, managed to retire in good order and hold the line. Machen's story was about the intercession of St George with a spectral army on behalf of the British. It became very popular and was much reprinted, appearing the following year as a little book, to which Machen attached an Introduction, claiming that his story had been responsible for the crop of reports and rumours that angels had indeed appeared over the field of battle. This claim was hotly contested. Harold Begbie immediately wrote a book,* On the Side of the Angels: an Answer to 'The Bowmen', *in which he abused Machen for his 'amazing effrontery' in pretending that it was his story which was being imitated by the 'angel' reports. Begbie quoted many accounts from individual soldiers of the visions they and their comrades had seen at Mons, accounts which were given to witnesses before Machen wrote his story. Machen, he said, had naively supposed himself to be the inspirer of the legend, whereas he had merely 'picked up' unconsciously something that was in the air at the time. Begbie's informants claimed to have seen a wide range of visions, including knights, bowmen, saints, glowing angels, mysterious clouds (hiding them from the enemy) and phantom armies. A Lieutenant-Colonel wrote to Machen that on the night of 27 August 1914, during the retreat, he and all his brigade had seen ghostly squadrons of cavalry riding alongside their line of march.*
(Opposite) The wild hunt or fairy cavalcade, two names for a phenomenon which has repeated itself over the centuries. (Left) in Good Newes to Christendome, 1620, *is the record of a spectacle, seen by thousands, in the sky above Mohammed's tomb, of a radiant female with sword and book putting to flight a Moslem army. The vision lasted 21 days.*

(Above) Noah's Ark on Mount Ararat, by Hieronymus Bosch. (Below) A photograph of Mount Ararat, showing 'the outline of the Ark', was printed in the Daily Telegraph, 13 September 1965.

# Arkeology

We would not like to say that anything is impossible, but few things seem to us less likely than that Noah's Ark should still be where the Flood left it up on Mount Ararat. They told us at school that the Old Testament story was a myth or allegory, and at the time we believed them. After all, the legend of a great flood that destroyed all but one family is a universal one, from as far afield as Mexico and South America, and Ararat is not the only mountain reputed to be the Ark's last resting place. Mount Nisir in Mesopotamia is named in the early Babylonian account, and Mount Judi to the south is the site favoured by the Syrians and Moslems. There could of course have been many floods and many arks, one for all these mountains, and it is also possible that the Biblical story is wrong in one detail, that Noah's command was not just a single vessel but a flotilla.

The first known ascent of Mount Ararat was made by Friedrich Parrot in 1829. He was not looking for the Ark, nor did he spot it, but he has his place in the history of arkeology for breaking the old taboo which prevented the local inhabitants from climbing the mountain, thus opening the way for later expeditions.

In 1876 Lord Bryce discovered on a rocky ledge some 13,000 feet up the slopes of Ararat a piece of shaped wood about four feet long, possibly gopher wood. Could it be a spar from the Ark? Lord Bryce cut off a small piece as a souvenir.

In 1892 Archdeacon Nouri, a dignitary of the Chaldaean Church, went off to Armenia in search of the Ark. On 25 April he approached the summit of Ararat, and there it was! The *English Mechanic* of 14 October 1892 described his feelings, as with five or six companions he contemplated from various angles the great wooden vessel. He 'was almost overcome. The sight of the ark, thus verifying the truth of the Scriptures, in which I had before had no doubt, but which, for the sake of those who do not believe, I was glad, filled me with gratitude'.

Nouri's discovery was evidently not the first Ark sighting, for in the cathedral of the monastery at Echmiadzin, the seat of the Armenian Patriarch near the foot of Ararat, is a small fragment of wood, the relic of an earlier arkeological expedition by a monk at the time of St Gregory the Enlightener. He is said to have made several attempts to climb the mountain, but each time, after ascending a little way, he fell into a deep sleep and found himself teleported back to the monastery. Finally he was told in a vision that the summit of Ararat, where the Ark lay, was forbidden territory, but that as a reward for his persistence he would be given a piece of its timbers. This piece, duly received, is the monastery's greatest treasure. At the time of the monk's expedition the survival of the Ark was a well established tradition. As early as 275 BC a Babylonian historian, whose record was preserved by later Greek writers, stated that the ark of Xisuthros was still to be seen in the Kurdish mountains of Armenia, and 'the people scrape off the bitumen, and carry it away, and make use of it by way of an alexipharmic and amulet'.

The coming of the aeroplane was a great stimulus to arkeology. There was a sighting in 1916 when a Russian pilot, V. Roskovitsky, reported a large vessel lying on the upper slopes of Ararat. The Tsar dispatched an expedition, and the object was found and identified as the Ark. Unfortunately the report was lost during the Russian Revolution the following year. These things happen in arkeology. An article in the US magazine *Christian Herald*, August 1975, retails the following story, that of the Armenian and the lost newspaper cutting. The Armenian, who died in America in 1920, told people that in 1856, when he was a young man living near Ararat, 'three foreign atheists' had hired him and his father to guide them up the mountain on an anti-arkeological expedition to disprove the Ark's existence. To their fury they found it. They tried to destroy it, but in vain, for it was too large, so they made their guides join them in an oath to say no more of the matter. The lost newspaper item, which several people claim to have seen but no one has yet produced, reported the death-bed confession of a British scientist confirming the Armenian's story.

Another unlucky piece of evidence was the six large, clear photographs taken in the summer of 1953 from a helicopter less than a hundred feet above Mount Ararat by an American oil worker, George Jefferson Greene. They showed the outline of the Ark, so it

appeared, half buried in rocks and ice on the edge of a cliff. Greene tried but without success to raise an expedition, and since his death in 1962 the photographs have vanished.

The period between the end of the Second World War and 1974, when the Turks put a stop to further Ararat expeditions on grounds of national security, was the great age of arkeology. In the summer of 1949 two parties set off to find the Ark. Following a divine revelation, Dr Smith, a retired missionary of North Carolina, raised funds and proceeded to Ararat with three companions. These funds, reported *Le Monde*, 24 September 1949, 'were easily found, since certain enthusiasts had no hesitation in selling their peaceful businesses in order to join the explorers'. The Ark, however, was not found. But on 31 August 1949 *France-Soir* printed exciting news from the other expedition under the headline 'We have seen Noah's Ark . . . but not on Mount Ararat.' The find had been made on Mount Judi of an impressive craft 500 feet long, 80 feet wide and 50 feet high, together with some bones of marine animals and, not far away, Noah's burial place. The explorers, two Turkish journalists, also mentioned the local legend that the Ark sometimes appears like a ghost ship beneath a covering of mud. We are not quite sure from the account whether it was the actual Ark that was spotted or its phantom apparition.

Most recent arkeological expeditions have been based on the hotel in Dogubayazit, a Kurdish town beneath Ararat, whose proprietor, Farhettin Kolan, is an arkeological expert and acts as a mountain guide. He saw the great Riquer expedition of 1952, the successful Navarra attempt of 1955 and the seven unsuccessful ones by John Libi up to 1969. Poor Libi, a San Franciscan who saw the exact site of the Ark in a dream, retired frustrated at the age of 73 after an adventurous arkeological career which included the experience of being chased by a stone-throwing bear, a phenomenon unique in our records. Another familiar face on the Ararat scene is Eryl Cummings, 'the grand old man of arkeology', who has made thirty-one ascents since 1961.

The most successful arkeologist to date is Fernand Navarra, whose book was published in French in 1956 and in English in 1974 under the title *Noah's Ark : I Touched it!* From beneath a glacier and a frozen lake high on Ararat Navarra excavated a number of planks and a hewn L-shaped beam and in 1969 he guided a party mounted by an American organization, Search, which discovered more such timbers and brought back samples. These were declared by experts using the radiocarbon method to be some 1,400 years old, though other experts at laboratories in

Bordeaux and Madrid thought that this result was due to the samples becoming contaminated with extraneous carbon-14 and produced the more Biblical date of about 3000 BC.

Within recent years such arkeological breakthroughs have become regular events, each new discovery upstaging the last. Mr George Vandeman, a director of the Archaeological Research Foundation of New York, was reported (*Antiquity*, 1966, 5) as stating that worked wood recovered by an Anglo-American expedition to Ararat was part of a large boat. Hundreds more tons of the same timber still lay buried under the ice, but so hard that electric saws had been broken trying to cut it. Mr Vandeman estimated the size of the boat to be about two-thirds that of the *Queen Mary*, very much the size of Noah's Ark as given in the Bible. Then we have the excellent satellite photograph here reproduced from the London *Daily Telegraph* on 13 September 1965, and a comment from Senator Frank Moss of the US Senate Space Committee, 'It's about the right size and shape for the Ark.' The last we heard was in the summer of 1974, just before the Turks closed the area, with no less than eight Ark-hunting expeditions in the field. The most vociferous of the rival leaders, Tom Crotser, a veteran of four previous Ararat ascents, was quoted in the *San Francisco Examiner* of 29 June 1974: 'Man, there's 70,000 tons of gopher wood up there.' The pieces already secured had, he claimed, been shown by carbon dating to be between four and five thousand years old.

Judging by its post-diluvian history, Noah's Ark has an existence like that of the Loch Ness Monster or the Abominable Snowman, phenomenal rather than physical. As is usual with such things there are legends, sightings and ambiguous relics and photographs, all of which fall short of scientific proof. Yet people continue to dream of Noah's Ark and some go in search of it, and it responds with dream-like evidences of itself which never quite achieve hard reality.

An attraction of the subject for phenomenalists is that it illustrates one of our themes, the tendency of experiments to justify the experimenter. On Archdeacon Nouri's ascent of Ararat and subsequent discovery of the Ark, Charles Fort made the appropriate comment: 'I accept that anybody who is convinced that there are relics upon Mt. Ararat, has only to climb up Mt. Ararat, and he must find something that can be said to be part of Noah's Ark, petrified perhaps. If someone else should be convinced that a mistake has been made, and that the mountain is really Pike's Peak, he has only to climb Pike's Peak and prove that the most virtuous of all lands was once the Holy Land.'

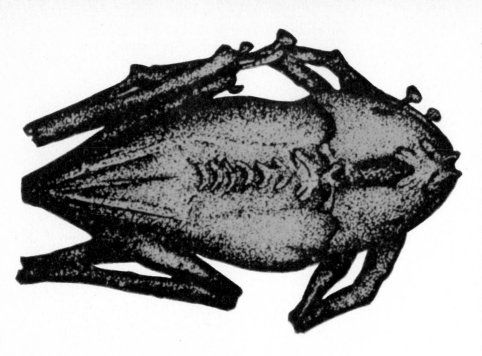

# Toad in the hole

In the Great Exhibition of London in 1862 the eastern annexe contained a curious and controversial exhibit: a lump of coal with a clearly defined frog-shaped depression, together with the body of the frog which had been found within the cavity at a colliery in Newport, Monmouthshire. *The Times* carried an irate letter from a Captain Buckland, accusing the directors of the Exhibition of 'gross imposition' and calling for the frog and its coal to be 'expelled'. He continued that it was utterly impossible for a frog or toad to bear the heat and pressure necessary to form coal at depths of over 300 feet, to say nothing of the millions of years during which it must have lived so enclosed. As authorities for this, he cited the 'settled opinion' of his father, the Dean of Westminster, and a note passed to him by Professor Owen of the British Museum.

In 1825 the legendary ability of toads to live encased in rock was tested by another Buckland, Dr Frank, author of *Curiosities of Nature*. He made twelve cells in two stone blocks, one of limestone, one of sandstone, placed a toad in each, sealed them firmly with a sheet of glass, putty, and a slate covering, and buried them three feet down in his garden. A year later the toads in sandstone were found to be long dead. Most of the toads in limestone were alive – two had even put on weight – but this was ascribed to a crack in the glass, possibly admitting small insects, etc. He tried again, but all the toads died. A correspondent in *The Times*, 23 September 1862, mentioned the work of a M. Seguin in France, who encased twenty toads in a block of plaster of paris and found after twelve years that four were still alive. We note, from actual stories of

finding encased toads, a curious detail: they are found in cavities which fit them perfectly, like moulds, as though the material itself had been in a plastic state when the toad entered it.

William Howitt, in his *History of the Supernatural*, 1863, wrote: 'Now all naturalists . . . know that toads and frogs – like tortoises, serpents, dormice and the whole tribe of insects that bury themselves in the earth, or conceal themselves in secret places where they live through the winter without food – sink themselves into the ground, or in the mud at the bottom of ponds, to pass the winter.' Indeed, this is alluded to by such classical authorities as Jerome Cardan and Izaak Walton as the reason for the mysterious appearances of frogs after a rain (see SHOWERS OF FROGS AND FISHES); they supposed the fresh water fertilized or reconstituted the seeds or slime into their former shapes. Howitt continues:

'Some years ago, at Farnsfield in Nottinghamshire, I saw a ditch undergoing a thorough digging out. . . . At the bottom of more than a foot's depth of mud as stiff as butter, on the firm earth below it, lay a regular stratum of frogs. It was a wonderful sight! Scores of frogs speedily woke up and hopped away to seek fresh quarters. If these frogs could live six months in this nearly solid casing of viscous mud, why not six or any number of years?'

In time mud would metamorphose into rock. The question should have been, is it possible for encased frogs to survive the pressures and geological spans of time needed to form the rocks they have been found in?

The outburst from Captain Buckland in *The Times* brought to light other

witnesses of toads being found in lumps of coal and other rocks, and we reproduce some accounts here. A paragraph in the *Stamford Mercury*, of Lincolnshire, 31 October 1862, is doubly interesting, because it tells of a toad found seven foot down in stone bedrock, while *The Times* correspondence was still going on – a coincidence that intrigues us greatly. Workmen were excavating a new cellar to a house in Spittlegate, Stamford, and found the toad in its cavity. The report concludes: 'No fact can be more fully or certainly established by human evidence . . . let the sceptics on this subject say what they will.' One correspondent told of a toad being found in a marble block used in the fireplace of Chillingham Castle, reminding us that William Howitt himself knew of a stone ball that had topped a gate-post of a mansion for hundreds of years. One day it fell and broke on the ground, revealing a live toad in its heart. The journals of Gilbert White also record the finding of a stoned toad on 25 May 1776.

The earliest first-hand story known to us, recorded in the *Annual Register* for 1761, is that of Ambroise Paré, chief surgeon to Henry III of France (1574–89): 'Being at my seat near the village of Meudon, and overlooking a quarryman whom I had set to break some very large and hard stones, in the middle of one we found a huge toad, full of life and without any visible aperture by which it could get there. . . . The labourer told me it was not the first time he had met with a toad and the like creatures within huge blocks of stone.'

Not so common in modern reports are the findings of animals other than frogs and toads. The variety discovered by our forebears was much more exciting, and the edition of *Annual Register* referred to above cites examples of snakes, crabs and lobsters, besides the usual toads and frogs, from the writings of Baptist Fulgosa, Francis Bacon, Agricola and Horstius. It also records the astonishing though apparently well-known information that the stones used to pave Toulon harbour were often broken to reveal 'shellfish of exquisite taste'; and that in the hard stones quarried at Ancona on the Adriatic were to be found 'small shellfish, quite alive and very palatable'.

The phenomenon can be extended to creatures found in other material than stones and rocks. Dr Robert Plot's *Natural History of Staffordshire*, 1686, refers to the finding of toads inside trees as well as stones. Similarly, the *Mémoires* of the French Academy of Sciences for 1719 report that 'in the foot of an elm, of the bigness of a pretty corpulent man, 3 or 4 foot above the root and exactly in the centre, has been found a live toad, middle-sized but lean and filling up the whole vacant space.' The writer could only imagine that some spawn became

*(Left and above) A mummified frog that exploded from a piece of coal. (Top, centre) One of several letters to* The Times *with contemporary accounts of toads in stones, in response to Captain Buckland's indignant demand for the expulsion of an embedded toad from the Great Exhibition (see text). (Right) Photograph of a live toad found embedded in coal by W. J. Clarke in Rugby. It had no mouth or rectum. It lived for five weeks.*

lodged in the young tree, 'by some very singular accident', and that the toad grew within the tree, living on its sap. It scuttled away as soon as the trunk was split open enough for it to fall out, so its limbs had certainly not atrophied from its supposed lifetime confinement. The incident was referred to some years later when the *Mémoires*, 1731, reported: 'M. Seigne of Nantes lays before the Academy a fact of the very same nature, except that instead of an elm, it was an oak and larger than the elm, which still heightens the wonder.'

We would also like to mention the occasional fall of animals from the sky encased in ice. For instance, at Bovington, Mississippi, a gopher turtle, measuring six by eight inches, entirely coated in ice, fell during a hailstorm as recorded in *Monthly Weather Review*, May 1894; and the same journal for June 1882 tells that the foreman of the Novelty Iron Works at Dubuque, Iowa, observed the melting of two hailstones from a storm on 16 June, which revealed 'small living frogs'. (See also FALLS OF CREATURES AND ORGANIC MATTER.)

In one of his letters (quoted by Howitt) the Rev. Richard Cobbold spoke of attending a lecture by the celebrated geologist, Dr E. D. Clarke, at Caius College, Cambridge, in February 1818. Dr Clarke had been present at the digging of a friend's chalk-pit, in the hope of finding fossils. He was happy when workmen hit a layer of fossil echina and newts at 45 fathoms. To his astonishment three intact creatures were broken out of a lump of chalk-stone. He placed them on a sheet of paper in the sunlight, and all were again astonished when they began to move. Two of them died later and were shown at the lecture; the third, when placed in water, 'skipped

and twisted about, as well as if it had never been torpid', so actively in fact that it escaped. Dr Clarke and his friend set about collecting specimens of all the species of newts in the area, but none resembled the recently revived ones: 'They are of an entirely extinct species, never before known,' wrote Cobbold. 'Dr Clarke took great delight in mentioning this.'

Readers who are not put off by that last story are invited to try this one, perhaps the damnedest piece in this whole book. In France, early in 1856, workmen were blasting a tunnel through solid stone as part of the Saint-Dizier to Nancy railway. While they were breaking a large boulder, a monstrous form emerged from a cavity in it, shook its wings feebly and died with a hoarse cry. It was about the size of a large goose, with a hideous head and sharp teeth. Its four long legs were joined by a membrane and terminated in long and crooked talons; its body was a livid black; its skin thick and oily. This living fossil was taken to the town of Gray, where a naturalist, 'versed in palaeontology, immediately recognized it as belonging to the genus [sic] *Pterodactylus anas*'. The stone was 'lias' (Jurassic limestone), which accords with the era of these creatures, and the rock cavity formed an 'exact hollow mould of its body, which indicates that it was completely enveloped with the sedimentary deposit'. Our source is the *Illustrated London News*, 9 February 1856, which quoted the original account in the *Presse grayloise* – and, knowing the way embarrassing evidence has of getting 'lost', we would be surprised if any other record exists. Somehow that defiant death-rattle seems an appropriate answer to Captain Buckland and his cronies.

# The hollow earth

We have collected innumerable reports, evidences, legends, superstitions or whatever, all indicating that our earth is hollow and that there is a living world within it. The thesis has been proved by many writers, and we are as respectful towards their proofs as we are to any other heresy or to any scientific orthodoxy. But we are less interested in the proof than in the antiquity and recurrence of the hollow earth belief and in the active phenomena with which this belief is associated.

Are there or were there ever creatures, human or otherwise, living just below the surface of this earth, perhaps in communication with even greater depths? Many ancient civilizations were based on the belief that such creatures existed as guardians of treasures and profound secrets which an experienced magician could make them reveal. Initiation into the Mysteries involved the candidate's descent into a chamber deep within the earth, where his encounters with the subterranean inhabitants, as monstrously alarming as any in a H. P. Lovecraft novel, left him either mad or a inspired prophet or both. The creatures of the underground kingdom, Tartaros or Hades, were conceived as a mixture of dead souls and elemental spirits, and their world had many points of contact with life on the surface. If there is any truth in the ancient myths and histories, there must once have been considerable traffic between the lower world and the upper. People moved from one to the other. We recall, for example, that according to the old Irish histories there was once a battle between the Milesians and the magically skilled native race, the Tuatha De Danaan, for possession of the country. Finally it was split between them, the victorious Milesians taking the upper half and banishing the older race to the country below the surface. There they merged with the fairies, and in that guise have been familiar apparitions to every Irish generation (see LITTLE FOLK).

Descents into the dominions beneath the earth and encounters with creatures from its depths are familiar items in universal folklore. And when we look for physical evidence to support these accounts we stumble across the greatest and most suppressed archaeological secret: the existence of vast, inexplicable tunnel systems, part artificial, part natural, beneath the surface of a great part of the earth. All over Britain and Ireland are records, legends and relics of underground ways running between the ancient and sacred places of every district. Baring-Gould's *Cliff Castles and Cave*

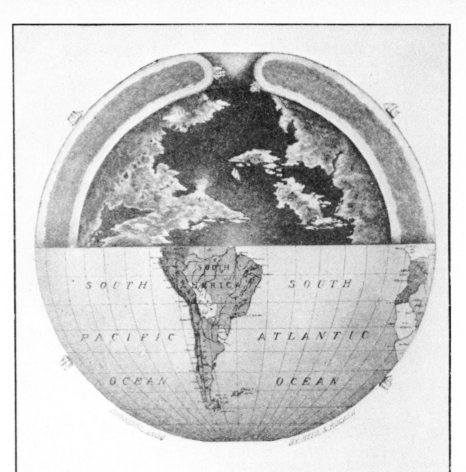

## GLOBE SHOWING SECTION OF THE EARTH'S INTERIOR

The earth is hollow. The poles so long sought are but phantoms. There are openings at the northern and southern extremities. In the interior are vast continents, oceans, mountains and rivers. Vegetable and animal life are evident in this new world, and it is probably peopled by races yet unknown to the dwellers upon the earth's exterior.

THE AUTHOR.

*Dwellings of Europe* has amazing records of the extensive cave and tunnel structures beneath France and other countries. Like the tunnels much used during the recent Vietnam war, those of Europe were resorted to as refuge by the local people in troubled times. Their earlier, mystical purpose was in connection with the invocation of creatures or spirits from the lower world. In Harold Bayley's *Archaic England*, 1919, are reports from early travellers of great tunnels stretching under much of Africa, including one beneath a river called Kaoma, 'so

lengthy that it took the caravan from sunrise to noon to pass through'. As we write, July 1976, there is news of a military-backed expedition setting off for the Andes in South America with the double object of investigating the riddle of the 'technologically impossible' ancient stone cities in the high mountains and exploring the vast network of mysterious tunnels, said to run throughout the entire Andes range. If we wanted to prove the existence of a living world beneath our own, we would have no difficulty in pointing to the entrances to the underworld and no lack of historical evidence of contacts between men and subterraneans.

To re-establish the ancient theory of the hollow earth was the purpose for which William Reed in 1906 wrote *The Phantom of the Poles*. 'I claim', he began, 'that the earth is not only hollow, but that all, or nearly all, of the explorers have spent much of their time past the turning-point, and have had a look into the interior of the earth.' At each of the Poles, so Reed sought to prove, there is a large, round-lipped hole, into which all polar explorers inadvertently sail. Many of these, including Peary, Franklin, Nansen and Hall, penetrated quite deeply into the world of the interior, and Reed found much evidence in their writings to support his theory. Accounts of the atmosphere growing warmer as the Poles are approached, of verdant polar territories abounding with animals, of floating timber and vegetation far from any known source; these he combined with noted instances of compass irregularities and displays of the Northern Lights (which he thought were reflections of light from within the earth) to prove the existence of the inner world. Later writers have lent their enthusiasm to his cause. Much has been made of the strange aerial expedition of Admiral Byrd to the Antarctic in 1956, during which it was announced on the radio (13 January, 1956) that the party had penetrated to a land 2,300 miles *beyond* the South Pole. After another flight the Admiral stated enigmatically: 'I'd like to see that land beyond the [North] Pole. That area beyond the Pole is the Centre of the Great Unknown.'

Ray Palmer, editor of the American magazine *Flying Saucers*, has done much to advance the hollow earth theory, showing that the interior is a more likely source of mysterious lights and UFOs than outer space. That grand old UFOlogist, Brinsley Le Poer Trench, has recently taken up the idea, and in *Secret of the Ages: UFOs from Inside the Earth* he invokes creative paranoia, suggesting that many of our phenomena, such as THE SURREY PUMA and other mystery creatures, come from within the earth, and hinting at evidence that the intra-terrestrials may already be plotting a military operation against our world of the surface.

There is much we admire in the hollow earth theory, but in this modern age, with satellites, surely . . . yet we do not underestimate the power of military secrecy, and there is no doubt that much was suppressed in the official reports of Admiral Byrd's strange flights. More seriously, there is an established phenomenal connection between faults and rifts in the earth's crust and apparitions of monsters, phantoms and mysterious lights. Loch Ness is on the geological crack across Scotland; and the Monster

of Bolinas Swamp in California lives right on the fault line running north from San Francisco, the territory also of the hairy Bigfoot. Several articles have appeared in the *Flying Saucer Review* pointing out the attraction for UFOs of areas of geological faults. We find significance in this clustering of phantoms round clefts and caverns, traditional gates to the underworld. Perhaps they are indeed passing in and out. If we suppose, as many cranks and great men before us have supposed, that there is life

in a subterranean world which occasionally interpenetrates with our own, many of the strange phenomena in this book begin to seem more reasonable. And we remind those who are too timid to admit the possibility of a hollow earth of the sturdy answer William Reed gave when he asked himself the question: what proof have we that the earth is *not* hollow?

'Not one iota, positive or circumstantial. On the contrary, everything points to its being hollow.'

*A page from William Reed's* Phantom of the Poles, *1906. (Above) The subterranean kobolds, familiar to miners everywhere, excavate a fossil* Ichthyosaurus; *Jules Verne's adventurers in a similar scene find a mushroom forest on the way to the Centre of the Earth. (Below) An ESSA-7 satellite picture of the North Pole claimed by UFOs-from-the-Earth's-interior advocates to clearly show the hole there. When we obtained this picture the National Oceanic and Atmosphere Administration took pains to point out that there is no hole – the dark area being the combined effect of the planet's tilt in the sun's light and a photo-mosaic technique compiled over 24 hours. That, say the hollow-earthers, is their story.*

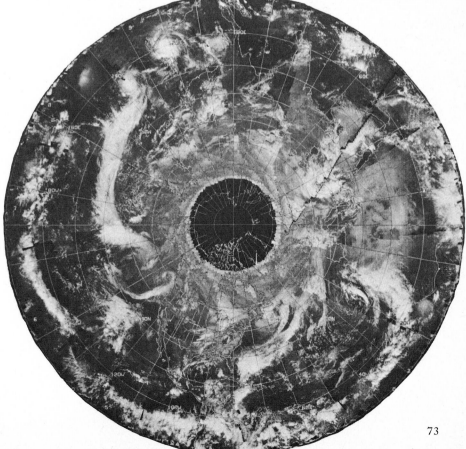

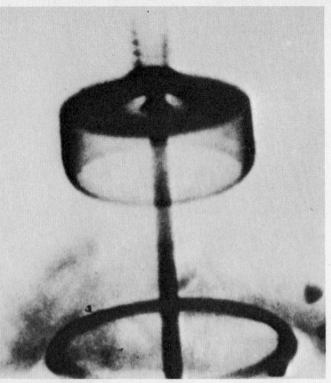

# Anomalous fossils

'When I came to fossils,' wrote Fort, 'dark cynicisms arise.' The geological record, he pointed out, is a prime example of circular reasoning in science; fossils being dated from their surrounding strata, and the strata from the fossils found in them. The matter is not helped by the bitter controversies of recent years over the anomalies and errors in such scientifically respected dating techniques as the carbon-14 and thermoluminescence tests. In his summary of the present knowledge of the chronology of human evolution, based on these and other methods of dating ('Man Emerging', *New Scientist*, 1 and 8 July 1976), Dr Stuart Fleming admits that there is a gap between 9000 BC and 400,000 BC within which it is impossible to give accurate dates to relics because of the limitations of the dating methods. Yet despite the impossibility of any really positive proof, academic orthodoxy firmly upholds the cosmogonic myth that we have ascended to our present enlightened, civilized state through uninterrupted development from savage, superstitious beasts, our ancestors. This view is in opposition to the older and universal theory of human history as a decline from the primeval 'Golden Age' and discounts the Platonic belief that civilizations rise and fall in cycles with intervening cataclysms.

What interests us here are the evidences of a human presence and technology on this earth long before the evolutionists would have us believe it was possible. Some of these evidences

have been actively suppressed and deliberately ignored; some have quietly and mysteriously disappeared from museum stores and records; some might still be on display somewhere patronizingly labelled in ignorance as a 'Ritual Object' or somesuch.

We are referring to, among other things, apparently human footprints in sandstone laid down in the Carboniferous period, between 225 and 280 million years ago. That is about 200 to 250 million years before our ape-ancestors split from the mainstream of monkey evolution (i.e., a mere 30 million years ago, according to Dr Fleming) – if it really did happen that way! The *American Journal of Science*, 3–139, details the discovery of a series of human footprints found in sandstone near Carson, Nevada, in 1882. Three years later tracks, easily identified as human, were found in sandstone near Berea, Kentucky, according to the *American Antiquarian*, 7–39. There are other discoveries, any one of which, if accepted, could collapse the geological order of the ages overnight, bringing with it the Darwinian edifice.

Even more heretical – it seems that many of these fossil tracks, while distinctly human in appearance, are giant in size. According to a US Department of the Interior booklet, *The Story of the Great White Sands*, a government trapper, in 1932, found a line of thirteen prints in the gypsum rock of White Sands, New Mexico. They were about 22 inches long by 8 to 10 inches wide. In

1896, the *American Anthropologist* described some 14½-inch human prints found in West Virginia. Brad Steiger gives other examples in his *Mysteries of Time and Space*, 1974, including what appears to be a fossil imprint of a shoe, showing a well-cut and double-stitched leather sole, found in 1927 at Fisher Canyon, Nevada. The rock was identified by a geologist as Triassic limestone (laid down 160 to 195 million years ago). This sort of data has been eagerly collected by a group of 'Bible scientists' who call themselves 'Creationists'. Two of their groups, the Films for Christ Association and the *Bible Science Newsletter*, have mounted at least one expedition to retrieve a set of prints from the bed of the Paluxy River in Texas. They are in Palaeozoic strata (Carboniferous?) and show the tracks of a human being and a three-toed dinosaur crossing each other, one of the human prints squashing the edge of a dinosaur print. Indeed the large size of some of the fossil tracks, and their shape, seem very similar to the prints associated with our modern mystery anthropoid monsters (see THE GREAT AMERICAN MONSTER and UNREASONABLE FOOTPRINTS).

Then there are the artifacts. *The Times*, 24 December 1851, tells of a miner returning from California with a block of auriferous quartz which he accidentally dropped. It split open to reveal a straight cut iron nail, firmly embedded near its centre. According to a note in the *Report of the British Association*, 1845, Sir David Brewster once

*(Above) This trilobite crushed beneath a sandalled heel, was discovered by a fossil-hunter at Antelope Springs, Utah, who split open a slab to find the tableau fossilized in its interior. The trilobite was said to have been alive when it was squashed – which puts the incident some 300 million years before the advent of dinosaurs!*

*(Above) A photograph of a coin, dated 1397, found embedded in Carboniferous coal, from* Strand Magazine *21-477 (1901). (Left) in 1961, gem-hunters in California found a shell-encrusted nodule estimated to be 500,000 years old. After a diamond saw broke in splitting it, it was X-rayed.* INFO Journal *4 (1969) compared the fossilized artifact to a modern sparking plug. (Below) The* American Journal of Science and Arts, *19-2 (1831), carried a letter describing the cutting of a marble block from quarry near Philadelphia in 1829. After slicing off a thick slab the quarrymen found, deep within the rock, this small (1½″ × ⅝″) indentation with two raised characters.*

announced to a meeting the finding of a two-inch nail half embedded in a lump of solid limestone from a Scottish quarry. A notice of a gold thread found in a stone from eight feet down in Berwickshire appeared in *The Times*, 22 June 1844. A lady cracking lumps of coal to fill her scuttle, says the *Morrisonville Times*, of Illinois, 11 June 1891, was surprised to find two halves of one lump linked by a small chain, the ends of which were still embedded solidly in the coal which bore a clear imprint of chain. The *Scientific American*, 5 June 1852, contained a plea for help in solving a puzzle. Quarrymen blasted out fifteen feet of puddingstone on Meeting House Hill, Dorchester, Massachusetts, and found in the rubble the two halves of a metallic bell-shaped vessel. It is described as about 4½ inches high and made of some alloy, like composition metal, inlaid with silver in an intricate floral design. The quarrymen were in no doubt that it had come from deep within the rock. The best the editor of *Scientific American* could come up with was to suggest that it might have been made by 'Tubal Cain, the first inhabitant of Dorchester'. In his *Secret Treasure*, 1931, A. Hyatt Verrill gives two incidents where coins have been found inside masses of flint, one in Chute Forest near Stonehenge, and the other in a gravel pit at Westerham in Kent.

In 1786–88 coins, tools, stumps of columns and other worked stones were found in a quarry in Aix-en-Provence, France, fifty feet down below eleven beds of compact limestone. An anonymous writer in the *American Journal of Science*, 1–144, quotes from 'the *Mineralogy* of Count Bourbon' the details of this astonishing find. Among these tools from another age was a wooden board, one inch thick and 7–8 feet long, now turned into a 'very fine and agreeably coloured agate'. The Count noticed with astonishment that the utensils, board and stoneworkings followed the same pattern used by his men (even the board was worn in the same manner, being rounded and wavy at the edges). An ancient and a modern technology had duplicated each other on the same site; predictable, perhaps, and yet, as the Count remarks, one of them 'preceded the formation of this stone'.

There are several different theories to account for artifacts which have been found out of their proper time or place. Quite possibly there have been civilizations in the remote, unknown past, but to postulate technological civilizations hundreds of millions of years back in time on the basis of a single nail, thread or pot is as irrational as, say, Sir Richard Owen inventing the absurdly cross-legged *Labyrinthodon* to explain fossil tracks which had 'thumbs' pointing outwards! We would need much more evidence – even if we widened our acceptances to imagine the hypothetical civilization to be non-human (e.g. reptilian). Another idea arises out of Fort's speculations on FALLS and MISSILES FROM THE UPPER REGIONS, and on the mysterious force of TELEPORTATION, which transports objects through solid matter: that the same forces might transport occasional objects back in time to when the sedimentary strata were laid down.

We have another idea, equally preposterous and therefore no less worthy of consideration – the spontaneous generation of these anomalous buried objects *in situ*, within the womb of the earth. Consider our section TOAD IN THE HOLE, on living animals found in the hearts of rocks. Can one seriously imagine that these animals appeared on earth before their due time to become encased in mud and compressed into rock and to survive across millions of years against all biological reason? Is this any less incredible than spontaneous creation or teleportation? The medieval naturalists often debated whether there was a 'shaping force' (*vis plastica*) that formed fossils in the earth. Some thought it a divine trick to test men's faith. But the basic nature of fossils has been well known since the Greek philosophers, so that Michael Valentini's belief that stones copulated and bore young in the earth was to his eighteenth-century colleagues deplorable backsliding. Nevertheless the *vis plastica* theory has had strong adherents including Kepler, Avicenna and Aristotle, and though regularly refuted it persists in dreams and popular traditions, as in the dream-theme of finding coins or other 'lucky' objects in unexpected, hidden places.

In his *Synchronicity*, Jung suggested that Kepler's notion of an earth-soul, an *anima telluris*, was the forerunner of his own theory of synchronicity. The forces which harmonize the myriad independent yet interrelated systems of life and matter on the living planet are essentially the same as those which order the contents of the mind. The mind and the earth are wombs in which things are brought into being. Among the dreams which Jung uses to illustrate how these two great spheres of existence interpenetrate is one in which the dreamer finds human heads in low relief on slabs lodged in Triassic rock. In another dream an earth-coloured gnome leads the dreamer into a deep cave where he finds columns of hard 'lignite', shaped into life-like human busts. They extend far back into the living rock 'and must therefore have come into existence without the aid of man'. If some synchronistic process can so unite mind and matter as to impress visible images onto a film or body (see PROJECTED THOUGHT-FORMS), perhaps there is an analogous force which projects forms into the earth.

# Unreasonable footprints

On the morning of 9 February 1855 the inhabitants of the South Devon towns of Topsham, Lympstone, Exmouth, Teignmouth and Dawlish awoke to find themselves in the centre of what *The Times* a week later called an 'Extraordinary Occurrence'. The report took the form of a letter, from which the following extract summarizes what happened:

'It appears that on Thursday night last there was a very heavy fall of snow in the neighbourhood of Exeter and the south of Devon. On the following morning the inhabitants of the above towns were surprised at discovering the tracks of some strange and mysterious animal, endowed with the power of ubiquity, as the footprints were to be seen in all kinds of inaccessible places – on the tops of houses and narrow walls, in gardens and courtyards enclosed by high walls and palings, as well as in open fields. There was hardly a garden in Lympstone where the footprints were not observed.

'The track appeared more like that of a biped than a quadruped, and the steps were generally eight inches in advance of each other. The impressions of the feet closely resembled that of a donkey's shoe.'

A lively correspondence on the mystery developed in *The Times* and spread to the *Illustrated London News*, in the course of which further interesting details came to light. The 'devil's footprints' had been found to stretch for a distance of over a hundred miles. At one point they had jumped over the two-mile wide estuary of the River Exe, continuing on one side where they had left off on the other. Nothing had impeded their progress or broken their even spacing of $8\frac{1}{2}$ inches. They were found on each side of a haystack, which was untouched, and on each side of a 14-foot wall. A curious feature of the prints was that they were placed one in front of the other rather than as in a normal animal trail.

Happily for those of us who enjoy explanations, the event happened during the high season of scientific rationalism, and a fine crop was raised in answer to the mystery. They included otters, leaping rats, a rope trailing from a balloon, and the devil (this one was strong locally). Professor Owen, the explainer of the *Daedalus* sea-serpent (he said it was a seal), weighed in authoritatively with his verdict – badgers. All the explanations were convincing, and all of them accounted for something, but none of them accounted for everything, such as the haystack, the 14-foot wall, the prints on the house-tops, their even spacing and linear arrangement.

The mystery remains, but it is not unique, merely one of many such. *Notes and Queries*, 9–6–225, quotes a Japanese history, the *Kokon Chomonshu* of the thirteenth century: 'In the year 929 the Imperial palace was found one morning full of demon's tracks as big as an ox's and coloured red and blue.' Two incidents can be found in the *Chronicon anglicanum* composed by Abbot Ralph of Coggeshall in the early thirteenth century. In the first, monstrous, pointed, hoof-like tracks appeared on the ground the day after a fierce electrical storm on 29 July 1205; and in the second, which took place at York in the reign of Richard I, 'there appeared in certain grassy flat ground human footprints of extraordinary length; and everywhere the footprints were impressed the grass remained as if scorched by fire.'

A correspondent in Heidelberg, on hearing of the Devon prints, wrote to the *Illustrated London News*, 14 March 1855, that similar tracks could be seen every year in sand and snow on a hill on the Polish border; and in his account in *Oddities*, 1965, of the Devon incident, R. T. Gould mentions the entry for May 1846 in Captain Sir James Ross's record of his Antarctic explorations, describing how on the sub-Antarctic island of Kerguelen a party found hoof-like prints in the snow, stretching for some distance, although there was no animal on the island to account for them.

In Dr E. L. Dingwall's *Tomorrow*, 1957, is a modern account of a man named Wilson who visited a secluded beach on the west coat of Devon in October 1950. He was the first person to walk on the cliff-enclosed beach after the tide had left the sand quite smooth, and was therefore surprised to see a series of hoof-like prints which began under a perpendicular cliff and led in a straight line to the sea. They were not cloven, but evenly spaced at six feet apart, and deeper than his own – a giant, heavy stride compared to the mincing 'devil's footprints' left in Devon snows nearly a century previously. Wilson also noticed that each print was not impressed, but appeared to be 'cut out of the sand'. Dingwall adds that similar tracks were reported on New Jersey beaches in 1908, 'marks like the hooves of a pony in thick snow, and again we have the story of how tracks led up to wire fences and continued on the other side'. They were attributed to the 'Jersey Devil', a mystery animal of the region, that had been known from the previous century and was still generating sightings as late as 1930. Twin-lobed, crescentic tracks,

THE mysterious appearance of two huge parallel furrows scarring the earth of a small valley high in the Alps above Nice is puzzling French scientists.

For nobody can explain how they came to be in a place which is completely inaccessible to car or tractor. What are they? What caused them? Experts at the Ministry of Defence are examining photographs of the furrows in an attempt to find the answer.

The photographs, taken by police officers, show a startling scene. The furrows start near a crag, and gouge their way across the valley in a huge curving arc 70 yards long.

### Helicopter?

The man who took the photographs, police commandant Henri Pelet, said: "With two police constables I examined the valley and measured the furrows. Each one was seven inches wide and they were exactly six feet apart along their entire length. Perhaps the most amazing thing is that each furrow was ten inches deep.

Could the marks, perhaps, have been caused by an army helicopter which landed there during a mountain patrol?

"Theoretically," said the commandant, "a helicopter could land there. It would be very risky. It is, however, very unlikely. For the furrows could not have been made by wheels and there are no tyre tracks in the valley. In any case the army has confirmed that they have no reports of any of their helicopters landing in that area."

The furrows were discovered by 60-year-old shepherd Louis Mathias who each year takes his flock of 500 sheep high into the Alps to escape the Mediterranean sun which dries up the lowland grazing pastures.

"The furrows were certainly not there last year," he said. "I could not understand it at all. It looked as if something mechanical had been there. But I knew no tractor or car could have been driven to the spot."

Commandant Pelet confirmed that the valley could be reached only by foot. "When I set off to investigate the tracks" he said, "we drove for an hour by Jeep and then had to walk for three hours to get to the valley."

The commandant had acted on standing instructions from Paris police headquarters that all reports of phenomena must be investigated.

And his report contains one more puzzle for the scientists. For there is a paragraph indicating that "small boulders, rocks and pebbles in the path if the furrows seem to have been almost pulverised."

### No saucers

There have been suggestions that the marks could have been caused by a flying saucer landing in the valley. The commandant said: "These sort of marks might be caused by strange visitors. But I'm sure they were not in this case.

"I have been checking around and there have been no reports of sightings of mysterious flying objects anywhere near the area."

similar to but smaller and more irregularly spaced than the Devon tracks of 1855, were reported from Belgium in 1945, and investigated by Russell (see *Great World Mysteries*, 1957).

One of the most interesting theories about the tracks comes from the personal experience of the explorer James Alan Rennie, during a venture into Northern Canada in 1924. He and his mate, a French Canadian dog-skinner, while crossing a frozen lake, came across a set of large, bear-like, two-toed tracks, spaced equally in a single line. Their unnaturalness 'reduced my companion to gibbering terror'; the poor man asserted that they were made by Windygo, the Canadian version of Bigfoot (THE GREAT AMERICAN MONSTER). Later Rennie returned across the same lake, and in bright sunshine caught sight of something that chilled him to the bone. He was half a mile from the shore, and saw the tracks 'appearing miraculously before my eyes . . . in "line-astern"' with no animal, no sign of any life at all, to account for them, just 'those tracks springing into being as they came inexorably towards me. I stood stock still, filled with reasonless panic. The tracks were being made within 50 yards of me – 20 – 10 – then smack! I shouted aloud as a large blob of water hit me in the face. I swung round brushing the water from my eyes and saw the tracks continuing across the lake' (*Romantic Strathspey*, 1956).

Fort pointed out that many reports could be found of strange creatures and monsters seen after earthquakes or volcanic eruptions – or, we might add, remembering Abbot Ralph, after electrical storms. The *Philosophical Transactions* 50–500, reports that after the quake of 15 July 1757 marks like hoofprints were found on a patch of sand 100 yards square at Penzance, Cornwall – they were not crescentic but 'little cones surmounted by basins of equal diameter'. A correspondent to the *New Zealand Herald*, 13 October 1886, writes of visiting the area desolated by an eruption of the volcano Rotomahana, and finding in the mud and ashes the footprints of a horse-like animal. He also refers to a story among the Maoris of a stag-like creature, unfamiliar to them, having been seen in the new wilderness. On 20 November 1970 the London *Daily Mirror* reported that seven giant footprints, 4 feet long, 6 inches deep and 4 yards apart, had been found in a crater 10,000 feet up the volcano Etna in Sicily. They were being examined by scientists, but typically that was the last ever heard of them.

We have records from the Scottish Highlands of strange tracks and of strange animals; yet, the two are rarely matched. *The Times*, 14 March 1840, reported that, for the second winter running, foal-like tracks, but 'of considerable size', were discovered ranging for twelve miles in the glens of Orchy, Lyon and Lochay, south of the fairy-haunted Rannoch Moor. One of the legendary creatures of this district is especially interesting, the *Fachan*, with 'one hand out of its chest, one leg out of its haunch, and one eye out of its head',

hopping out in forays from its home in Glen Etive, a few miles north-west of Rannoch Moor. There is a similar beast in Brazil, known as Pe de garrafa or Bottle-foot, because it leaves a single line of deeply impressed prints suggestive of the bottom of a bottle. In Bernard Heuvelmans's *On The Track of Unknown Animals* is a hunter's description of it, given in 1954, which confirms its humanoid appearance and single leg. Heuvelmans reminds us that the medieval geographies were frequently illuminated with delightful drawings of Sciapods (one-legged humanoids) sleeping in the shade of their oversized feet. One of the few accounts that link a mythic image to physical evidence is in medieval record, the *Chronicon de Melrose*, for August 1065. Again in a storm, and at York, an enormous image of the Devil on a black horse charged through the sky to the sea: 'The tracks of this horse were seen, of enormous size, imprinted on a mountain at the city of Scandeburch [Scarborough]. Here, on top of several ditches, men found, stamped in the earth, prints made by the monster, where he had violently stamped with his feet.'

Yet another piece of the puzzle comes from the giants' stamping grounds in Scotland. Otta F. Swire tells in *The Highlands and Their Legends*, 1963, how she and her husband were motoring from Cluanie to Glengarry, near the southern end of Loch Ness, across a virgin blanket of snow when they saw on a small frozen lochan, not footprints but 'marks as of cartwheels, clear and unmistakable in the new-fallen snow. Curious, we stopped and got out to see where they led. No sign or track of any living thing was to be seen . . . and there was no trace of footmark, wheel mark or sledge mark in the snow on the loch shore, either where the wheel marks began on the snow-covered ice or where they ended, or indeed anywhere else.'

Despite inquiries they learned nothing more until some months later when an informant mentioned the 'Devil's Coach': 'He drives over the moors in the winter and his wheel marks are often seen on lonely frozen lochs, but never a sign on land, nor a sign of the horses that draw his coach.'

Like many of our other categories, both the tracks and their interpretations have changed over the years; UFOs and laser beams have recently been suggested as the cause of the Devon 1855 prints. Any unilateral approach to the mystery brings out frustrating paradoxes. Mrs Swire put it thus: 'I have been told that there are no hoof marks because the Devil's horses are spirits whereas his coach, used to carry mortals, must have earthly substance; but if this is so, why do the wheels leave tracks only on ice? And whom does he carry off? And why?'

We are equally perplexed.

# Phenomenal highways

We have written of phantoms and fireballs, of mystery animals, strange lights, black dogs and fairies, all of them participants in the intermediate state of reality we call phenomenal. In terms of the hard reality recognized by science their existence can not be proved. It is evident only in its symptoms, and by analysing these symptoms we detect patterns. Haunted tracks for example. We wonder why so many of our phenomena are associated with certain spots and certain routes. Do the alternative realities of our records have an alternative highway system?

Mystical paths: a neglected subject, yet one which has plentiful data. Reports of an elemental force which passes regularly on particular straight routes through the country, sometimes with destructive or ominous results, are universal. It may or may not be visible, but when it is, it is usually conventionalized in one of the forms listed above. A good example to illustrate the phenomenon is the Wild Troop of Rodenstein in Germany. This disagreeable force steers a straight course between the two lofty castles of Rodenstein and Schnellert, blasting all in its path. Up to the middle of the eighteenth century the dates of this phenomenon were recorded by the local authorities. In Crowe's *The Night Side of Nature*, 1854, it is said that in about 1850 a traveller, Mr Wirth, inspected the local court records and found the last entered note of its occurrence in June 1764. However, it apparently went on long after the authorities had lost interest, for Mr Wirth was shown ruined houses as evidence of a recent passage by the Wild Troop.

Like everyone else we are impressed by official records, and to find the best we turn as always to China. The mystical pathways of China are the subject of an entire science called *feng-shui*, which in imperial times was directed by a government bureau, the Board of Rites. The practitioners of *feng-shui* see the landscape in terms of opposing and harmonizing influences (*yin/yang*) which generate an omnidirectional vital force called *ling*. This force tends to follow the descending ridges of mountains and other edifices which rise towards heaven from the earth; and it may be collected or dispersed, increased or diminished at any site by the nature of the artifact built there.

*Feng-shui* was an integral part of Chinese life, and the Board of Rites sought to secure the best cosmological benefits by strictly regulating the siting and architecture of houses, temples, roads, tombs and so on, harmonizing, according to Taoist theory, the influences of heaven and earth. (For the most complete modern study of *feng-shui* see Stephan Feuchtwang's *Anthropological Analysis of Chinese Geomancy*, 1973). These cosmic benefits were even thought to accrue to families who had houses or tombs at favourable sites. In his chapter on *feng-shui* in *The Religious System of China*, 1892, De Groot records the disinterment, by the Board of Rites, of a student whose body was illegally buried on a most favoured site reserved in principle for members of the imperial family.

An intriguing aspect of *feng-shui* is its abhorrence of straight lines, which were thought to generate disastrous and evil 'winds'. Where straight paths were unavoidable, in streets, courtyards and formal approaches, they were obstructed at each end by 'spirit screens' or by specially sited bends and corners. There are good reasons for believing, as Steve Moore suggests in *The Ley Hunter*, No. 72, that these evil influences were associated with destructive ghosts and 'poltergeists', which traditionally could only travel in straight lines. Indeed it is a Chinese practice to ward such demons off by hanging mirrors opposite open doors and windows and to paste drawings of the guardian spirits and Taoist charms on the doors themselves.

From China we turn to Ireland and discover traces of the same science as the Chinese *feng-shui*, though in a state of terminal decadence. On this, as phenomenalists, we make our position clear. Similarities in universal traditions do not come about, as the nineteenth-century anthropologists endlessly argued, through invasions and migrations (though since there is something of everything in everything else there is some truth in all these theories) but through common experience. Nor are fairy stories just dramatizations of elements in the human psyche (though there is some of this in them too) but are based on observations of phenomenal reality which is everywhere much the same. So we suppose that the tradition of 'spirit paths' all over the world arose from actual experience of phenomena associated with certain tracks and lines of country.

Evans-Wentz in *The Fairy Faith in Celtic Countries* has something to say on the fairy paths of Ireland and Brittany, which run in straight lines between the ancient hilltop forts which are the fairies' citadels. On certain days of the year people avoid these paths for fear of interrupting a fairy procession, and for the same reason they are never built on. An Irish seer told Evans-Wentz that fairy paths are seasonal channels of terrestrial 'magnetic' energy. No explanation is given for the visible part of the phenomenon, the fairies themselves.

Some incidents connected with fairy paths are related by Dermot MacManus in his book of modern Irish fairy lore,

*The Middle Kingdom*, 1972. They illustrate the evil consequences of building houses on these paths and are of great interest when compared with the similar Chinese tradition. In 1935 Michael O'Hagan inadvertently blocked a fairy path through building a westward extension to his house into an open field which lay in direct line between two ancient hill forts. His five children all fell ill, one almost to death, and the doctor was professionally baffled. A visit to a wise woman, versed in local mystical topography, revealed how the matter stood; the new building was pulled down and the children straightway recovered. MacManus gives other quite recent examples of Irish people being influenced in their choice of a building site by considerations of the fairies and their ways.

The same phenomenon behind the mystical paths of Ireland, an elemental force, active at certain seasons and best avoided, is conventionalized in England in terms of BLACK DOGS. Most books of local folklore refer to black dog tracks, which have the same mystical properties as our other examples. In one of the best collections of black dog legends, Patricia Dale-Green's *Dog*, is an account of a phantom creature that rushes at midnight through a Devonshire village along a road from the church, demolishing a corner of the schoolhouse – or seeming to demolish it; because, though falling masonry is heard, no actual damage is done. We have another reference to the phantom dog's habit of

destroying buildings in its path, at Lyme Regis, Dorset, where it is said to have knocked down the corner of an inn called the Black Dog. This makes us wonder whether the inn was called after an existing phantom or the phantom was attracted by the name.

In Scotland, says A. A. MacGregor's *Ghost Book*, the phantom black dog is called *cu sith* and travels in straight lines along customary routes. The sight of it is ominous, often followed by death. A recent case illustrating this connection between phantoms, their tracks and hidden dangers is given by Tongue and Briggs in *Somerset Folklore*. A straight track on the north Somerset coast is referred to as Death Mile because haunted by a black dog that means death to whoever sees it. In 1960 a man to whom it appeared died within a year, and so also did a young girl who saw it, though her companion who did not see the dog was unaffected. Another reference to the dangers of spirit paths is in *Fate* magazine of October 1972, quoting a first-hand account from a Honolulu publication by a native author, Napua Poire. She reminisces about an adventure when she was a little girl. One evening she found herself alone in a forbidden part of the island on a spirit path, and stood there rigid with terror as the marching footsteps of an invisible procession drew nearer. It was almost upon her when she felt a hand push her out of the path. Her parents later explained that she had been on a path reserved for the wandering spirits called

the 'night marchers', and it was the kindly shove of an ancestor spirit that had saved her from death.

Ever since the publication in 1958 of Aimé Michel's *Flying Saucers and the Straight Line Mystery* the idea of a connection between strange objects in the sky and hypothetical lines of magnetic or gravitational variation has haunted the imaginations of UFO theorists. A New Zealand writer, Bruce Cathie, offered proof of the matter in a book of mathematical reasoning, *Harmonic 33*, but for lack of precise data on the observed paths of UFOs any connection between aerial and geological phenomena is difficult to establish. Our numerate friend Robert Forrest claims to have disproved it altogether. Proofs and disproofs cancel each other out, and as always we are left with only one certainty, the phenomena from which every theory is derived. Our subject here has been the observed connection, dating from very early times and continuing into the present, between phantom forms, mystery lights, certain old tracks, ancient sacred centres, channels within the earth's magnetic field, geological irregularities and a seasonally recurrent force or energy wave which can be dangerous or fatal to human life. Only when science is unified, when geologists, dowsers, archaeologists, ghost hunters, UFO spotters and anyone else with an axe to grind unite to study phenomena which transcend the field of any one discipline: only then will this subject receive the attention it cries out for.

# Odd clouds

Today clouds may be eulogized in song as 'ice cream castles in the air' or not given a second thought; but to the ancients they were a perfect symbol of the phenomenal universe. The *Prajna Paramita*, a Buddhist hymn of the first century AD, insists that the forms we take for everyday reality are transient, and the true nature of reality is more like the ceaseless shape-changing of clouds and dream-images – a view consistently supported by all forms of mystical experience. We begin our look at the phenomenon of odd clouds with an incident from the log of the barque *Lady of the Lake* to be found in the *Journal of the Royal Meteorological Society*, 1–157. On 22 March 1870 the captain and crew saw a 'remarkable cloud' that remained stationary against the wind until it was lost in the evening darkness. They described it as a stable, circular form with an internal semicircle divided radially into four, from which extended a long 'tail' which curved back towards the 'body'. This massive fluffy tadpole of a cloud challenged everything they knew about the behaviour and constitution of clouds, but being practical sailors, they were content merely to note the details and avoid speculation.

Many of the strange apparitions classified as UFOs are described as cloud-like, reminding us of earlier reports of 'cloud ships' such as those which were known to the French country people at the time of Agobard, Archbishop of Lyons in the ninth century (see PHANTOM SHIPS). Photographs of UFOs commonly show objects which look half solid and half nebulous, like ghosts appearing or vanishing. A typical sighting which merges UFOs with meteorological effects was reported in the *Flying Saucer Review*, 9–4. In November 1958 Dr and Mrs M. Moore were in their car near the border of North and South Dakota. The sky was cloudless except for a 'silvery, cigar-shaped object, like a giant windsock', which accelerated out of view leaving behind it a trail of strange purple clouds.

Another link between UFOs and our present phenomenon is indicated in *New Report on Flying Saucers* by Lloyd Mallan, a reporter from *True* magazine. He describes an interview with Allen Noonan, who believed that this planet was hollow and that he was in touch with 'Galactic Command' who maintained UFO bases within. Mallan was told by Noonan that two UFOs might appear in the cloudless sky outside their hotel window, so he loaded his camera with infra-red film and waited. Ten minutes later, 'two saucer-shaped clouds had formed in trail between some buildings across the way'. Mallan felt sure they were conventional lenticular clouds, but was astonished that they should have appeared when and where Noonan had predicted. We can only observe that cloud-summoning and cloud-busting have always been among the powers claimed by shamans and magicians. Similar performances were recorded in ancient China, and repeated among the North American Indians and the 'magnetizers' of nineteenth-century Europe (see illustration) and in the experiments of Wilhelm Reich.

Cloud, mist and vapour are basic elements in mystery. In *Human Animals*, Frank Hamel gives many instances of fogs that aided the transformation of witches into animals and birds or that concealed them with cloaks of invisibility. The world over, supernatural beings and sages are said to use clouds as vehicles or messengers. Indeed, one of the continuities in our data is that metamorphoses are often indicated or accompanied by mists or clouds. Most phantoms have this quality; thus, a BLACK DOG legend from Dorset, quoted by Patricia Dale-Green, says the beast will grow larger if it is watched, eventually swelling into a large cloud and vanishing. Several forms of the 'transition-cloud' exist in the spiritualist cosmology, such as the soul likened to a vapour rising from the body at the moment of death, and the clouds of ectoplasm from which materialize faces, hands, and so on. Ghosts too have a mist-like structure, and interestingly there are many accounts of ghostly human forms with parts of their anatomy (traditionally those lost or damaged in a violent death) hidden or replaced by a local cloudy mass.

Many religious apparitions and SHARED VISIONS begin or end with a small, curious cloud. On 16 October 1964, Mrs Rosa Quattrini (known as Mama Rosa) was talking to a neighbour in an orchard at San Damiano, Italy, when both noticed a peculiar cloud forming in the air among the branches of a damson tree. Then it floated over to a pear tree where it seemed to solidify into a female form, resplendent with beams of light, a crown on her head and a flower in each hand. This was the first of many appearances of the Virgin to Mama Rosa, and only she ever saw the radiant lady on these occasions. In contrast, the entire congregation of a service in Warsaw, in 1801, saw the shining Virgin Mary appear from a cloud. In PHANTOM MUSIC AND VOICES we tell of the day when 'demons' interrupted the services of St Clement Hofbauer. Later the same day, as Zsolt Aradi tells it in his *Book of Miracles*, 1957, while St Clement prayed before the altar of St Joseph, 'hundreds of people saw a cloud forming above the altar, then enveloping the figure of the saint, who disappeared from their sight. In his place [they] saw a celestial vision.

*(Left) A spectacular luminous lenticular cloud looms like a UFO over Mount St Helens, Washington. (Right) This photo taken during a bombing mission in the Korean War seems to show a giant Christ figure in the clouds.*
*(Below) The 19th-century 'magnetizer', Ricard, claimed to be able to conjure up clouds with his gestures.*

*(Below) A painting by Masolino di Panicale of 'The miracle of the snows', showing the foundation of the Santa Maria Maggiore church. Strange clouds formed overhead, and with divine draughtsmanship dropped a 'point snowfall' to delineate the groundplan.*

A woman of great beauty, with radiant features, appeared and smiled at the worshippers, who only a few hours ago had been frightened by the prodigies of the devil.'

People who see apparitions in clouds are inclined to accept them as messengers and feel they are being communicated with. Medieval chronicles abound with this kind of celestial vision during strange meteorological events, and people continue to this day to see figures among the clouds (see our sections on CITIES, PHANTOM SHIPS and SPECTRAL ARMIES in the sky). One curious case from the last century was recorded in a pamphlet, *Wonderful Phenomena*, by Curtis Eli, from statements collected by Addison A. Sawin. On 3 October 1843, Charles Cooper, labouring in a field near Warwick, heard a low rumbling in the sky and looked up to see a strange, solitary cloud beneath which hung, or hovered, three 'perfectly white' figures, calling to him with 'loud and mournful noises'. He thought they were angels; and Sawin, a spiritualist, naturally saw in it 'the glorious hope of the resurrection'. What is more interesting to us is that the other witnesses, some nearly six miles away and some in an adjacent field, all agree on the 'remarkable cloud' though not all of them saw the 'angels' or heard the sounds.

Sometimes we hear of clouds appearing in answer to an unspoken need. Harold T. Wilkins, in his *Strange Mysteries of Time and Space*, 1958, quotes a British naval officer's story about the Allied invasion of North Africa. He said the sea was dead calm and the entire fleet was completely exposed, an easy target for German bombers. Before long, as though in response to their nakedness, an 'immense black cloud' formed, staying directly over the armada for ten consecutive days. The officer said: 'I was not alone in thinking that Providence set the cloud there.' A similar story is told of clouds that 'miraculously' veiled the retreat of the British army at Mons, August 1914 (see SPECTRAL ARMIES).

Tales of encounters with UFOs and their 'occupants' sometimes involve terrifying vapours that paralyse, blind and suffocate. We have many data on clouds behaving malevolently – some bursting into flames, some luminous or magnetic, some which 'bounce' along and others which hiss or broadcast series of loud explosions, and many other frightening and inexplicable pranks.

We have noticed in our sections on things which fall from the skies that some of these falls originate in odd clouds. In *Strange World*, 1964, Frank Edwards relates the story of Ed Mootz tending his Cincinnati, Ohio, garden on 22 July 1955, when it rained a blood-like oily liquid. Mootz saw this grisly rain falling from a small red, pink and green solitary cloud that appeared to be rolling along about 1000 feet overhead. Drops that fell on his skin began to sting him. He went inside to wash, and when he returned the cloud was gone. Strangely, it was not reported elsewhere. The next day the trees and grass were dead; everywhere the red rain had fallen was now brown, shrivelled and dying. According to Edwards the incident was never explained, despite investigations. Similarly, we recall that in the case of the shower of 'blood and muscle' on the tobacco-field at Lebanon, Tennessee (mentioned in FALLS OF CREATURES AND ORGANIC MATTER), a red cloud was noticed flying directly over the field.

Clearly then, there are clouds which are only were-clouds. There is no way, in our conventional knowledge of clouds, to account for the 'ball of fog' that swooped down with a hiss onto a car in Minnesota. According to the *Eagle Bend News*, 25 May 1961, the car was left unbearably hot and pitted with tiny holes. Nor for the report by a postman in Thailand, quoted in the *San Francisco Chronicle*, 23 April 1962, that he saw a red and green fog crumble into little pieces which he thoughtfully collected.

# Phantom music and voices

L. Boilly 1824.

In any tome on hallucinations are references to phantom music and disembodied voices, discussed in terms of mental and nervous aberrations. The following example of 'fallacious perception' by a patient is quoted by Edmund Parrish in *Hallucinations and Illusions*, 1897: 'Every tree which I approach, even in windless weather, seems to whisper and utter words and sentences . . . the carts and carriages rattle and sound in a mysterious way and creak out anecdotes . . . the swine grunt names and stories, and hens seem to scold and reproach me, and even the geese cackle quotations.' In the sounds of nature, however produced, men have always heard the music and poetry of other worlds. To reduce the phenomenon to clinical terms is to damn at a swipe all that is intuitive and mystical in human nature.

Voices seem to manifest both internally and externally, though we are aware that, ontologically, this distinction itself may be an illusion. Of the internal kind we could cite the famous cases of Martin Luther, Ignatius Loyola, Benvenuto Cellini and even Sigmund Freud. Socrates had a *daemon*, a voice that warned him of actions likely to offend the gods. Some voices torment the listener, and others urge on to action, as in the cases of St Joan (who heard the Archangel Michael and Saints Catherine and Margaret), St Francis of Assisi (who heard a voice from a crucifix bidding him to 'rebuild my church'), or George Fox (who founded the Quaker

movement at a similar prompting). The phenomenon continues today and is claimed by many UFO percipients to be a telepathic contact with beings from other worlds or dimensions than ours.

Of the 'exteriorized' voices, there can be no greater claims than those which concern the commands of the gods that thunder down from above in the Bible and in universal mythology. Before this materialist age people were more sensitive to communications from nature, and objects and animals could speak like men if the spirit moved them. Herodotus said (*Histories*, 2–54) he was told by the priestesses of the Dodonian oracle of Zeus that the sacred grove containing the famous whispering oak was revealed by a talking bird that alighted in its branches. Wood from this tree was said to have been set into the keel of the *Argo*, by Athena, giving the ship the vocal power to warn Jason of danger ahead. Disembodied voices are still associated with portents, especially warnings of the death of a friend or relative, and are so astonishingly common that even Flammarion's great three-volume compilation, *Death and its Mystery*, 1922, could not exhaust the fund of anecdotes.

We are interested in the sounds and voices which often accompany 'poltergeist' activity. They have a very strange quality; sometimes faint, sometimes so abnormally loud that they are more like shock-waves of great force. Consider the fantastic story of Calvados Castle in France, which suffered an astonishing

range of phenomena from October 1867. They were still continuing when reports were published in the *Annales des sciences psychiques* in 1893. Among the frequent levitations and perambulations of the furniture, the vanishing of Lourdes medals and other holy charms used in a continuous exorcism, doors and windows opening by themselves, and the pulling off of bedclothes, were a variety of sounds. These ranged from creaks, groans and footsteps to organ music being repeated in the air for hours after one of the occupants had ceased playing. The castle constantly shook under heavy blows 'so strong that objects suspended on the wall rattled in their places. . . . To acquire some idea of their violence, one must imagine a wall collapsing, or a horse, or cannonballs thrown against a door.' At times the whole building shook violently 'from top to bottom', yet there was little damage, and the noises could only be heard inside the castle.

These effects are typical of poltergeist sounds, the characteristics of which are exaggeration and imitation. Alfred Monin's biography of the Curé of Ars, St John Vianney, says he was particularly persecuted by this kind of phenomenon. At times his courtyard would ring with the noise of a great army, camping, marching or charging. In the winter of 1824–25, the Curé could not sleep for the noise 'of a large flock of sheep passing over his head', and whenever he entered a lower room of his house all could hear sounds as though 'a large escaped horse' pranced around him invisibly, rising into the air and slamming down onto the floor with all hoofs. Though the Curé was known to be an ascetic, he was followed by a demonic voice which mocked him for indulging in 'luxury', yelling: 'Vianney, Vianney, you truffle-eater, you! Are you still alive; haven't you died yet? I'll get you!' A similar vocal persecution is described by Evelyn Waugh in *The Ordeal of Gilbert Pinfold*.

One of the strangest loquacious entities in our records took up temporary lodgings with the Dagg family of Clarendon, Quebec, in 1889. According to *Light*, December 1889, an investigator named Percy Woodcock visited the family on 15 November, and was taken by the adopted daughter of the house, Dinah, to a shed where previously she had seen a strange man. Nervously she called out: 'Are you there, mister?' Imagine Woodcock's astonishment when from the middle of the empty shed, about four feet away, came the clearly audible voice of an old man. It cursed them both in deep gruff tones, using language that Woodcock would not record or that *Light* could not print, and saying: 'I'm the devil. I'll have you in my clutches. I'll break your neck.' Woodcock and Mr Dagg talked to the voice for several hours during which it admitted causing the mysterious fires (see FIERY PERSECUTIONS) and TELEPORTATION of household objects (see MATERIALIZATION AND FLIGHT OF OBJECTS), and apologized for the inconvenience it had caused. During the interrogation the foul and obscene language subsided, and the voice promised to leave the following Sunday night.

When the news spread, people came from miles around. On the Sunday the voice was on good behaviour though at times rather tactless. It answered questions and seemed to display an intimate knowledge of anyone who entered the house, often proclaiming aloud embarrassing details of their lives that they would rather have kept private. On being congratulated about his change of character the voice said: 'I am not the person who used the filthy language. I am an angel from heaven sent to chase him away.' The transformation was not yet complete, for the entity occasionally lost its temper in a volley of blasphemy, but by Sunday evening it was joining the crowds in singing hymns in such a 'beautiful flute-like voice' that it was now implored to stay. The next day the Dagg children announced that it had finally left them. They described how a 'beautiful man', resplendently dressed in shining clothes, had hugged them and bid them goodbye. They sang a final hymn together (the 'angel' playing a small harp-like instrument) and as the children watched they saw a light, 'red like a fire', blaze at his feet, rising to surround him as he ascended, singing sweetly, into Heaven. Fort's typically laconic footnote to his account of the story: 'It sang a hymn and departed.'

Some of these voice phenomena must have been quite impressive. A poltergeist case recorded by Dr Reid Clanny, *A Faithful Record ... of Mary Jobson*, 1841, features 'exquisite music', heard by many witnesses independently, followed by a voice of 'angelic sweetness' quoting from the scriptures. In deliberating upon the canonization of St Clement Hofbauer, the Church accepted evidence of diabolical interference with his mission. In 1801, his sermon to a crowded church in Warsaw was frequently interrupted by the cries of a phantom baby. When he continued voices broke out in the air all over the church, crying that it was on fire. Flames and smoke were seen everywhere, even from the street, and minutes later, after panic subsided, these were found to be as ethereal as the voices.

Phantom music is a favourite ingredient in ghost and fairy stories. It is not just a fiction: here are two modern accounts. An empty office in Peter Street, Manchester, is haunted by thin piping tunes heard by many people in the building. A letter to the *Manchester Evening News*, 24 October 1968, suggests it was the same phantom flautist heard in the same office block two years previously. (Interestingly, Plato, in the *Critias*, speaks of victims being haunted by interminable reedy tunes.) A weird strumming from a piano gave over a hundred impromptu concerts in a house in Humber Avenue, Coventry, Warwickshire. According to Bill Duncan, the occupier, quoted in the London *News of the World*, 13 January 1974: 'It sounds as though someone is plucking the strings. . . . It doesn't sound anything like modern music.'

*(Left) Tartini composed his 'Devil's Trill' sonata after hearing an obsessive tune in a dream. (Below) Noises and weird music are typical effects of poltergeist infestations. This illustration is of the famous 'Drummer of Tedworth', Wiltshire, in 1661. (Right) In many traditions demonic musicians play irresistible music which continues until the dancers drop or die.*

# Accidents to iconoclasts

Some archaeologists proceed to a cheerful old age. Yet, on the evidence of history, their profession would seem a dangerous one. That so many old stones and buried treasures have survived the centuries intact is certainly due to the popular belief that no good will come to him who disturbs them.

Records of the misfortunes of graverobbers, vandals and iconoclasts are legion and universal; and their ill luck is often inherited by later owners of relics sacrilegiously obtained. There is, for example, a notorious Egyptian coffin lid – or fragment of a coffin lid – in the British Museum. Its adventures are given in Arthur Weigall's *Tutankhamen*, as told to him by a previous owner, Mr Douglas Murray:

'He purchased the coffin some time in the [1860s], and no sooner had he done so than he lost his arm, owing to the explosion of his gun. The ship in which the coffin was sent home was wrecked, and so was the cab in which it was driven from the docks; the house in which it was deposited was burnt down; and the photographer who made a picture of it shot himself. A lady who had some connection with it suffered great family losses, and was wrecked at sea shortly

afterwards. . . . The list of accidents and misfortunes charged to the spirit which is connected with this coffin is now of enormous length.'

Also of great length is the list of accidents to rustic mound-thieves and stone-killers – and they continue to this day. Some quite recent examples are given in the last chapter of *The Secret Country* by Colin and Janet Bord, 1976. Many others have been recorded in S. Menefee's articles in *Folklore* (1975 and 1976) and in L. V. Grinsell's *Folklore of Prehistoric Monuments*, 1976.

People who disturb megalithic sites, even to the extent of measuring them or counting their stones, are liable to be themselves disturbed by meteorological or other portents. On 12 August 1740, John Wood, architect of Bath, proposed to take a plan of Stanton Drew stone circles in Somerset, whose stones are said to be wedding guests petrified by the devil. He was opposed:

'No one, say the country people about Stanton Drew, was ever able to reckon the number of these metamorphosised [*sic*] stones or to take a draft of them, though several have attempted to do so, and proceeded until they were either

struck dead upon the spot, or with such illness as soon carried them off.'

Nevertheless he persisted, 'and as a great storm accidentally arose just after, and blew down part of a great tree near the body of the work, the people were then thoroughly satisfied that I had disturbed the guardian spirits of the metamorphosised stones, and from thence great pains were taken to convince me of the impiety of what I was about.' (John Wood, *A Description of Bath*.)

Wood repeated his impiety by taking a plan of Stonehenge with the same results, a violent storm which drove him to shelter in a nearby hut.

Some years later, Dr William Borlase excavated a 'giant's grave' in the Scilly Isles. That night a hurricane destroyed the islanders' crops of corn and potatoes – a direct consequence, so they claimed, of the Doctor's archaeology. The incident is described in Halliwell's *Rambles in Western Cornwall*, 1861.

It is well known that no one in Ireland will, or would, take timber from a rath, which is a sacred enclosure or fairy grove. The railway companies in their early days found many such impediments on their chosen lines, and the

# Girl's death in legend of curse

## FROM OUR CORRESPONDENT—New York, Dec. 14

Miss Evalyn McLean, former joint heiress to the Hope diamond and its reputed curse, was found dead last night at her home in a suburb of Dallas, Texas, where she lived alone. A post mortem examination showed no indication of violence; an analysis of stomach contents is to be made.

Neighbours broke into the house after seeing no activity for several days, and found the body, dressed in blue jeans and sweater, on a bed.

Miss McLean, 25, a former Dallas debutante, quiet-living, was the granddaughter of the late Evalyn Walsh McLean, who said that she paid $40,000 (then £8,000) for the Hope diamond about 60 years ago.

She left it jointly to her six grandchildren when she died in 1947. A dealer bought it from the estate in 1949 and gave it to the Smithsonian Institution in Washington. The grandchildren were never allowed to touch it.

The Hope diamond turned up in London in 1812 and got its name

**Evalyn McLean : Dead in house.**

from Henry Thomas Hope, an English banker who bought it in 1830. The story is that the 44½-carat stone was ripped from the forehead of an Indian idol, and came into the

hands of a French traveller who was later torn to death by a pack of rabid dogs.

Louis XIV of France is said to have given it to Mme. de Montespan as a mark of royal favour, which she lost soon after.

Louis XVI, the legend says, gave it to Marie Antoinette and it disappeared when they were executed in 1793.

As far as Mrs. Evalyn Walsh McLean was concerned, her first son was killed in a car accident, her husband died in a mental home, and a daughter died of an overdose of sleeping pills in 1946.

The Hope family is said to have fallen on evil days after buying the diamond, and the catalogue of owners in the 16 years before Mrs. McLean includes Jacques Colet, who killed himself, Prince Ivan Kanitovitsky, who was murdered, Sultan Abdul Hamid of Turkey, who was dethroned, and a mistress who was murdered; and Simon Montharides, whose carriage was dragged over a cliff by a shying horse killing himself, his wife and their child.

same inconvenience is still occasionally suffered by road-making contractors. At the other end of the world the Japanese refrain from cutting trees on Mount Miwa or at any other rural sanctuary. The innumerable instances of disasters visited on people who offend sacred timber begin with that in AD 661 (noted in Jean Herbert's *Shinto*) of the Empress Saimei, who felled a sacred grove to build a palace: which palace was immediately destroyed by the elements, together with its Grand Treasurer and many of the court. A young Samurai, seeing good timber lying waste, took the logs to build his own palace – with the same results.

To the delight of local wiseacres at the time – and of wiseacres generally ever since – the Puritan during the interregnum of Cromwell who chopped down one of the two stems of the sacred Glastonbury thorn, the tree which sprang from St Joseph of Arimathaea's staff and blossomed every Christmas morning; this Puritan received a splinter in his eye which prevented him from continuing work on the second stem.

Dr Robert Plot, the old historian of Oxfordshire, records with relish the misfortunes of Cromwell's commissioners who took up quarters in the King's apartments at Woodstock Palace on 13 October 1649 and warmed themselves by burning the locally revered King's Oak. They seem thus to have invoked all the most unpleasant classes of phenomena described in these sections. A BLACK DOG rushed through the rooms upsetting chairs, phantom footsteps were heard, papers were torn and scattered and ink spilt. The logs of the King's Oak were mysteriously hurled around. On 20 October the commissioners were attacked in their beds, and from then on were continually buffeted by INVISIBLE ASSAILANTS. Windows were broken by volleys of stones and – something we have never heard of before in this connection – horses' bones. For all this Dr Plot blames 'immaterial beings'. The last straw was when the commissioners, having plotted to set aside some of the estate for themselves, having drawn up an agreement to that effect and hidden it in a pot beneath the roots of an orange tree, found the earth in the pot burning with a blue, sulphurous flame; upon which they fled.

Of all such curses, coincidences, strokes of ill luck or whatever they may be, the most famous is the Curse, or supposed Curse, of the Pharaohs, which started its career of entertaining the public and mortifying the Egyptologists on 6 April 1923 with the death of Lord Carnarvon shortly after his expedition had forced open the funerary chamber in the tomb of Tutankhamen. Arthur Weigall, who was present at the opening, describes in his essay *The Tomb of Tutankhamen* the frivolous atmosphere

of the occasion. On Carnarvon boasting that he would give a concert down in the tomb, Weigall was inspired to remark, 'If he goes down in that spirit, I give him six weeks to live.' That was on 16 February. Carnarvon's death, attributed to a mosquito bite, was soon followed by that of Mr A. C. Mace, one of the leading excavators; and then, to the delighted applause of the press ('ninth victim, . . . tenth, . . . twentieth victim', etc.), the other members of the Tutankhamen party began to die off, several in mysterious or tragic circumstances. Weigall (unknown fever) was claimed as the twenty-first victim, following Carnarvon's half-brother (suicide during temporary insanity), and old Lady Carnarvon (insect bite again), until by 1930 only one of the original tomb-invaders was left alive – their director, Howard Carter.

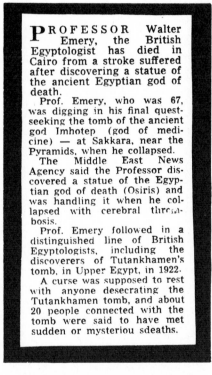

PROFESSOR Walter Emery, the British Egyptologist has died in Cairo from a stroke suffered after discovering a statue of the ancient Egyptian god of death.

Prof. Emery, who was 67, was digging in his final quest-seeking the tomb of the ancient god Imhotep (god of medicine) — at Sakkara, near the Pyramids, when he collapsed.

The Middle East News Agency said the Professor discovered a statue of the Egyptian god of death (Osiris) and was handling it when he collapsed with cerebral thrombosis.

Prof. Emery followed in a distinguished line of British Egyptologists, including the discoverers of Tutankhamen's tomb, in Upper Egypt, in 1922.

A curse was supposed to rest with anyone desecrating the Tutankhamen tomb, and about 20 people connected with the tomb were said to have met sudden or mysteriou sdeaths.

*(Left) A curse is commonly associated with gems looted from strange idols. (Above) A modern example (1971) of the reported link between tomb-defilement and sudden death. (Below) Tutankhamen's mask was said to have a blemish corresponding to the mark of Lord Carnarvon's fatal mosquito bite.*

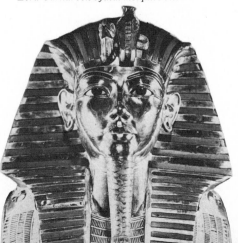

The belief that the 'Curse of the Pharaohs' accounted for Lord Carnarvon is naturally unpopular with archaeologists, yet it is a fact that before he opened Tutankhamen's tomb Carnarvon received clear warning that if he did so he would soon die. The warning came in a letter from Count Hamon, the famous mystic, better known as Cheiro. With the letter, written on 30 November 1922, was a message Cheiro had received by automatic writing. It read:

LORD CARNARVON NOT TO ENTER TOMB. DISOBEY AT PERIL. IF IGNORED WOULD SUFFER SICKNESS; NOT RECOVER; DEATH WOULD CLAIM HIM IN EGYPT.

This message worried Carnarvon and he sought advice from another noted seer of the time, Velma. She inspected his palm and saw the probability of his early death in circumstances connected with the occult. A few weeks later he visited her again and she declared that his hand looked even more ominous than before. Lord Carnarvon considered withdrawing from the Egyptian enterprise, but things had gone too far, and he bravely decided to 'challenge the psychic powers of the ages' – his own phrase.

With his usual significant inconsequentiality, Charles Fort's only comment on the Carnarvon affair was to quote from some London newspapers of the time (*Daily Mail*, 2 April 1923; *Daily News*, 3 April): 'Upon Lord Carnarvon's estate near Newbury, Hampshire, a naked man was running wild, often seen, but never caught. He was first seen upon March 17th. Upon March 17th Lord Carnarvon fell ill, and he died upon April 5th. About April 5th, the wild man of Newbury ceased to be reported.'

Another of the WILD PEOPLE, this time an atavistic Orcadean, was the portent of tragedy in the household of an Orkney farmer, whose son-in-law guaranteed the truth of every detail in his account published in *Old Lore Miscellany of Orkney, Shetland, Caithness and Sutherland*, July 1911. The farmer was in the process of excavating a large old mound on his land when he was approached by a wild man, its guardian, old and grey-whiskered, 'dressed in an old, grey, tattered suit of clothes, patched in every conceivable manner, with an old bonnet in his hand, and old shoes of horse or cowhide tied on with strips of skin on his feet'. This apparition warned the farmer that, should he persist in his attack on the mound, he would lose six cattle and there would be six funerals from his house. The six cattle actually died as predicted, and six deaths followed in the farmer's household. The writer of the account was present at the fourth death, when he was told the story.

# Stones that move and grow

'As steady as a rock' would have meant nothing to the ancient Celts, in whose world rocks and boulders were living, growing, locomotive creatures, some endowed with the homing instincts of a carrier pigeon, others providing vehicles on sea or in the air for travelling Druid magi, others given to prophetic utterances. Nor to this day are they as steady as they are reputed to be. We have modern records of stones falling from the sky, moving along the ground and propelling themselves, or being propelled by mysterious agencies, through the air.

To settle once and for all the dispute as to whether stones move by themselves, the answer is they do, and we display a photograph to prove it. This rock is one of a tribe that live and move on a three-mile-long dry lake bed called the Racetrack Playa in Death Valley, California. No one has ever seen them move, and no one knows how they do it. Explanations include references to lunar influence, earth magnetism, UFOs and sunspots. A scientist who has been investigating the mystery since 1968, Dr Sharp, favours a combination of wind and rain as motive forces, but one difficulty is that the rocks, varying from small pebbles to half-ton boulders, move in different directions, and they slide rather than roll as they would tend to do if blown by the wind. One large rock, measured and tracked by Dr Sharp, has recently moved 212 feet.

There are countless traditions of stones which have a decided preference for one particular spot and will make their own way back there if removed. Among examples claimed is the King's Stone, one of a megalithic group, the Rollright Stones, in Oxfordshire, which are also said to take themselves off for a drink at the local brook on a certain day each year. In T.H. Ravenhill's *The Rollright Stones* is the story of how the Lord of the Manor of Rollright fared when he took the King's Stone to make a bridge on his estate (see INVISIBLE BARRIERS for more on this effect). First, it was found beyond the strength of a team of horses to drag it away. Others were harnessed, and yet others, and finally the stone was moved. Strange events followed, ominous sounds in the Manor House, disturbances, enough to make it seem wise to put the stone back. This time the first horse harnessed to it galloped uphill, drawing the stone with ease back to its proper position.

Exactly the same story, with the detail of the one horse easily returning the stone which it had taken many to remove, was told to Robert Graham, author of *The Carved Stones of Islay*, 1895, by a native of that remote Scottish island.

Such tales are common, as also is the related class of incidents where stones, assembled for building a church, have mysteriously moved from the site chosen by the builders to another spot, where the church had eventually to be built. Examples can be found in any book of church lore and local traditions; but from such sources we are rarely given precise dates and witnesses' accounts, and so the incidents partake of the vague incredibility of folklore, considered perhaps as of psychological origin. We are pleased therefore to be able to quote a modern instance, recorded at the time, of a stone that was disturbed and the circumstances leading to its replacement. We think it may illuminate some of the earlier cases.

We have a cutting from the London *Sunday Pictorial*, 9 October 1944: 'Bulldozer Frees Poltergeist'. The bulldozer belonged to the US Army, and was used to widen a road in the village of Great Leighs, Essex. In doing so it removed a large boulder which was said to be pinning down the evil spirit of a former local, the witch of Scrapfaggot Green. Whether or not this actually released a spirit, it must certainly have seemed that way to the people of Great Leighs, as the whole village was seized with poltergeist fever. The church bells began to ring without ringers, the church clock went haywire, sheep were found missing from walled fields, heavy poles and agricultural accessories were tossed about, and great stones appeared where before no stones had been. The *Sunday Pictorial* sent a reporter who was mystified. The great ghost-hunter Harry Price was called in, and the sequel is given in his book, *Poltergeist over Britain*. He advised that, since everyone believed the disturbances to have followed from the moving of the stone, the best thing would be to put it back just as it was. This was done formally, with a midnight ceremony, on 11 October 1944, and from that time the troubles of Great Leigh were over.

Stones which hurtle or float through the air are often features in the sort of disturbances attributed by neo-animists to the 'poltergeist'. Showers of stones attacking the house, breaking through windows and landing at the feet of a Rumanian peasant girl, Eleonore Zugun, were the first symptoms of the disturbances which plagued her and her family for many years, starting in 1925 when she was twelve. The continual repetition of these attacks, and the general instability of objects in her environment, made things so uncomfortable at home that her parents at one time sent her to a lunatic asylum. Once when the family was at dinner a round stone, still wet from the brook outside, crashed through the window. A priest was called, who attempted to lay the stone by marking it with a cross and throwing it back out. A short interval, and the same stone as marked re-entered as violently as before. Harry Price, in whose *Poltergeist over Britain* the case is described, compares this incident with a similar one in 1887, where a large, round, wet pebble from a stream smashed through a window of the mill house near Appleby, Westmorland, disturbing its occupant's dinner hour and beginning a long series of destructive but unaccountable assaults on fittings and furniture.

*(Left) One of the mysteriously moving rocks in Death Valley, California. (Above) Our most recent case of stones that move. (Below) Near Fernagh Old Church, County Kerry, Ireland, is a stonied and venerated rock-mother. The stones within the hollows were said to defy permanent removal, to return home of their own accord and to cause grief to whoever disturbed them. There is a ubiquitous belief that such rocks generate little ones. (Bottom) In St Levan's churchyard, Cornwall, is a rock whose cleft is said to be growing. A local legend predicts that the end of the world will come when a donkey with panniers can pass through it.*

Not all volatile stones are violent; some are more gently directed and float or *fall slowly*. A charming case was fully reported in *The Times*, 18 January 1843. At Livet in France two young girls were out picking up leaves when stones of different colours showered down on them, slowly and harmlessly. They called their parents, took them to the spot, and the stones fell on them too. Respectable witnesses were summoned, priests, doctors, and all were gently and colourfully stoned. It only happened at one spot, and only when the girls were there. After a few days it stopped.

'Who built thousands of piles of stones in a Cotswold field?' asked the London *Sunday Express*, 4 May 1975. Mr Peter Lipiatt, of Widden Hill Farm, Horton, near Chipping Sodbury, Gloucestershire, asked the question when he found the thousands of little stone heaps ('it would have taken a human being a lifetime to build them') all over his barley field. It was Mr Lipiatt's principle not to be superstitious, so the thing must have been done by birds or animals. The appropriate authorities were consulted. Said the expert at the Zoological Museum, Tring, Hertfordshire: 'No British bird does this sort of thing. Most decidedly not.' From the British Museum (Natural History), Kensington, London, came the statement, 'The only British mammal that does make small piles of stones is the Boy Scout.' From the Boy Scout Association: 'I think you can rule out Scouts in this case.' Local sages remain baffled by the phenomenon which in former years would have been met by the explanation that the stones grew there.

As to whether stones do actually grow and produce young ones, as has been widely believed since at least the time of the Roman historian Pliny, the received modern belief is that they do not. We take no sides in the dispute, nor are we quite convinced by either of the contradictory assertions, rustic or scientific, however forcefully expressed. In East Anglia the stones described as growing are the flinty conglomerates locally called pudding stones. In *Notes and Queries*, 8th series, 7–485, Mr Isaac Taylor tells how he was taken to see a breeding stone in the parish of South Weald, Essex. It was a boulder with a cavity holding a small pebble, which, he was informed, had been born from the parent stone, and if it were removed another would grow in its place.

It was once proposed to put the matter of growing stones to the test. A Suffolk farmer told the vicar that as often as he cleaned his fields of flints they grew back again. Nonsense, the vicar told him. If he were to put a flint on the mantelpiece and watch it, he would find it did not grow. The farmer rejected the test on the grounds that if a potato were put there it would not grow either.

# Strange deaths
# and lightning fatalities

Some readers may think we accept every old wives' tale; but not so. We do not accept, for instance, that lightning never strikes the same spot twice. It does, and there are curiosities. Consider the following. In 1899 lightning struck a man dead in his back yard in Taranto, Italy. Thirty years later his son was killed on the same spot and in the same manner. Then on 8 October 1949 Rolla Primarda, the grandson of the first man and son of the second, was killed in the same back yard – struck by lightning. Our source is *Fate*, March 1950; and from the same magazine, April/May 1952, comes another case of strange behaviour by lightning which makes us wonder whether the elements may possess senses of humour and aesthetics or respond to these senses located in the universe at large. The case concerns the late Major Summerford. This brave officer was wounded in Flanders in 1918, not by the

enemy but by a flash of lightning which knocked him off his horse and left him paralyzed from the waist down. He was invalided out of the army, retired to Vancouver and took up fishing. In 1924 he was by a river with three fellow anglers when lightning hit the tree beneath which he was sitting and paralyzed his right side. Within two years he had more or less recovered from these shocks and was able to take walks in the Vancouver park, where, in the summer of 1930, during a sudden storm he was again struck by lightning. This time he was permanently paralyzed and died two years later. Even then he had not finished his career as an involuntary lightning conductor. In June 1934 there was a storm over Vancouver. Lightning struck the cemetery and shattered a tombstone. It was Major Summerford's. Yet his record of lightning-proneness is by no means unique. A ranger in

Shenandoah National Park, Virginia, Mr Roy C. Sullivan, earned a place in the *Guinness Book of Records* as the only man to have survived four attacks by lightning. He was struck in the years 1942, 1969, 1970 and 1972. On the last occasion his hair caught fire, and after that he carried a five gallon can of water in his car as a precaution. Then in the *Washington Star-News*, 2 August 1973, it was reported that Mr Sullivan had again, for the fifth time, been struck by lightning and had again survived.

If certain people have an affinity with lightning, so have certain spots. The Electrical Research Association has maps showing 'lightning nests' where strikes are most frequent, and both thunderbolts and fireballs are more common in some places than others. Again, as so often in studying the history of our phenomena, we are led to suspect that the mysterious properties of lightning were more clearly recognized in the distant past than they are now, and that perhaps they were made use of. Fort suggested that primitive communities may have valued for practical reasons the gifts of people who naturally attract lightning, fires and the levitation effect. Tribal shamans are often marked out for their careers by being struck by lightning or by involuntary levitation. In *Shamanism* Eliade gives an instance of an Eskimo shaman who received his gifts after being hit by a fireball. The connection between lightning invocation (or the calling down of fire from heaven) and the monuments of prehistoric science is a most interesting subject. Such mystical fiery operations as are attributed to the priests of Baal were performed at certain traditionally sacred spots, probably at natural 'lightning nests'. Some of the Shinto sanctuaries in Japan are at places where lightning has struck, and such places were fenced off and held sacred by many people including the Etruscans and Romans. In Britain the evidence of dowsers is that some stone circles, notably the Rollright Stones in Oxfordshire, are on sites where meteorites or thunderbolts have fallen, and there are relics of an ancient elemental science in the traditional use of the megalithic instruments called 'thunder stones' for invocation of storms.

We postulate two modes of ancient ceremonial magic: one, peaceful, for calling down lightning to release the nitrogen contents in the soil and fertilize the fields; and another, warlike, for hurling fireballs and thunderbolts at the enemy. The right person; the right place and time; a lightning flash. In 1949 Charles Sappal of Riverview, Florida, was struck by lightning which knocked a bottle from his hand. On 22 June 1950 he was at the same spot. Again lightning flashed, this time killing him.

Lightning bolts from a clear sky, or deaths from no apparent cause. In the

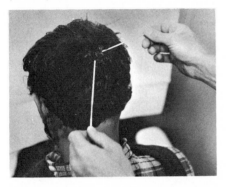

(Left) The death of the Russian physicist, Richmann, in 1753, when a lightning bolt hit his apparatus. (Above) The monument in Devizes to the Instant Karma of Ruth Pierce (see text).

*Monthly Weather Review*, 28 and 29, 1900, is a case of two men standing in a field struck dead from a cloudless sky. Many others are on record. From *Ciel et terre* Fort quotes the incident in 1893 when nineteen soldiers marching near Bourges in France were struck by 'an unknown force'. They were knocked to the ground and some were killed. It was stated at the inquest that the weather had been fine, with no thunder around. Another Fortean gleaning from *Ciel et terre*: lightning from a clear sky struck and killed a man on the summit of Mount San Gorgonio, California. Two days later it happened again and a man was killed on the summit of Mount Whitney some 180 miles away.

This last case reminds us of Elijah and the fiery chariot that removed him from the mountain top, and of the Brazilian space-age magicians, Manoel Cruz and Miguel Viana. On 17 August 1966 these two, experimenters in electronics as related to UFOs and cosmic communications, walked up Vintem Hill at Nitteroi near Rio de Janeiro. It was a hot afternoon, but they took with them raincoats and lead masks with no eyeholes. That evening a glowing disc was seen to swoop and hover over Vintem Hill, and on its summit next morning the

two men were found dead. They were unmarked, and no cause of death has ever been established. The only clue, a scrap of paper, handwritten: '4.30 p.m. Be at the determined place. 6.30 p.m. Swallow capsule. After the effect protect the face with metal and wait for the signal to show itself.' There was a UFO 'flap' on at the time, and 'Murder by UFO' was the popular and official verdict. But this modern tendency to attribute mysterious events to UFOs merely rephrases the ancient belief that the elements respond to human invocation and form in their behaviour significant or intelligent patterns. Perhaps in their own allusive, subtle language fireballs, lightning, UFOs and suchlike phenomena are communicating a meaning.

Lightning records abound with coincidences. Consider, for example Pliny's story of a monster which devastated a city in ancient Etruria. The Etruscan augurs called down lightning to kill it. The name of the monster was Volta, the same as the great electrician many centuries later!

Bolts from the blue are, of course, the traditional media of divine retribution, and if, as is said of them, the ancient magicians were able to work the effect for their own ends, there are equally good records of people who, without seriously intending to, have brought it upon themselves. 'May God strike me dead' is a terrible oath. We tried it ourselves as children, but perhaps it needs a guilty conscience to be properly

effective. The dramatic case of Ruth Pierce is recorded on a stone monument in the Market Square of Devizes, Wiltshire. On 25 January 1753, Ruth and three other women joined together to buy a sack of wheat in the market. Each was to contribute equally to the cost, but Ruth kept back some of her money and then swore she had paid in full, adding that 'she wished she might drop dead if she had not. She rashly repeated this awful wish, when, to the consternation of the surrounding multitude, she instantly fell down and expired, having the money concealed in her hand'. The inscription states that the Mayor and Corporation of Devizes hope by means of the permanent monument to 'transmit to future times the record of an awful event . . . hoping that such a record may serve as a salutary warning against the danger of impiously invoking the Divine vengeance'.

'Instant Karma' and express answers to prayers are gratifying phenomena, but we notice in whomsoever or whatever controls such things a tendency towards literal-mindedness. Henry F. Kretzer's *Lightning Record*, 1895, includes the story of an open-air meeting at Walnut Ridge, Arkansas, in August 1894, at which a fire-and-brimstone preacher was imploring heaven for a sign, right there and then, that all would remember. He was silenced in mid rant by a lightning bolt which exploded a nearby tree, showering the congregation with branches and knocking many senseless.

(Left) A bolt from the blue hit Vladimir Tesitel, climbing in the Alps, pierced his scalp and burnt holes in his feet. (Below) Elijah destroys the messengers of Ahaziah by fire (I Kings 1).

# Coincidences

In the phenomenalist view, single events cannot be isolated from the continuum that embraces all reality and ensures that anything that happens, on any level, anywhere, influences and is influenced by everything else. Thus we criticize nineteenth-century science, which pretended in vain to study objects and events as detached entities. Modern physicists are beginning to reiterate the ancient knowledge that the very act of observation affects the thing observed, and that perception is a powerful act of creativity, in which subjective and objective reality combine to form the event. One class of event illustrates the issue well: coincidences, where two or more chains of cause and effect unite together with the observer, who adds to them a new dimension – meaning.

In *The Unknown*, 1902, Camille Flammarion tells of the experience of his friend, the poet Emile Deschamps. In his childhood, at a school in Orleans, Deschamps shared a table with a certain M. de Fortgibu, who had returned from England with a taste for plum-puddings, then unknown in France. He insisted that Deschamps try one. Ten years later Deschamps passed a restaurant, and saw a plum-pudding being prepared inside. His early taste, long forgotten, urged him to enter and ask for a slice; but the pudding was reserved for another, and Deschamps was obliged to beg the favour from this stranger. It turned out to be M. de Fortgibu, and both were astonished at meeting again for the second time over the same dish. Many years passed again and Deschamps was invited to a dinner party which featured an English plum-pudding; and Des-

champs delighted his hosts with the tale of his extraordinary encounter with Fortgibu. They all joked about the possibility of the old man turning up. During the meal he really did. Fortgibu had also been invited out to dinner, but by the occupant of another apartment in the building, and had lost his way. 'Three times in my life have I eaten plum-pudding, and three times have I seen M. de Fortgibu!' said Deschamps: 'My hair stood up on my head. A fourth time I should feel capable of anything... or nothing!'

Studies of coincidences vary considerably. Jung's *Synchronicity*, 1955, proposes an unknown process which cuts across space-time to order events in the same manner as the archetypes order the pre-conscious contents of the psyche, so that events in both physical and psychological reality take on parallel meanings. Flammarion's interest was para-psychological and arose out of his interest in phantoms as portents of a death. He pointed out that if such visions are merely hallucinations, there is the problem of their synchronization with unknown events far away. Had Flammarion not turned away from his brief excursions into coincidences, he would have anticipated the work of Paul Kämmerer, the ill-fated biologist, who published his work on the 'Law of Series' in 1919. For twenty years he kept a detailed notebook on coincidences, meticulously analysed into categories, and was confirmed in his belief that Seriality is 'ubiquitous and continuous in life, nature and cosmos'.

Buried in Kämmerer's work is the old alchemical notion of affinity, of like

attracting like, a subject we mention also in our FALLS OF FROGS AND FISHES section. Kämmerer also noticed a periodicity of events, a theme picked up and amplified into new area of study by Edward R. Dewey in his *Cycles: The Mysterious Forces that Trigger Events*, 1971. A baby fell fourteen stories in Detroit to fall on Joseph Figlock passing below. A year later it happened again (*Weekend*, London, 19 May 1976). They survived, but some coincidences are deadly. Two brothers in Bermuda were killed by the same taxi and driver, carrying the same passenger, while riding the same moped in the same street, but exactly a year apart (*Liverpool Echo*, 21 July 1975).

Fort said that he was not so much interested in things as in the relations between things, and saw all phenomena as a vastly complex continuity whose peaks occasionally project into the field of our notice: 'Not a bottle of catsup can fall from a tenement-house fire-escape in Harlem, without... affecting the price of pajamas in Jersey City; the temperature of somebody's mother-in-law in Greenland; or the demand in China for rhinoceros horns.'

Not only are coincidences a common factor in everyday life, but according to Ira Progoff (*Jung, Synchronicity and Human Destiny*, 1973) they can to some extent be induced, by keeping a journal as Kämmerer did. The phenomenon is well known to crossword-puzzlers, and also to writers. In his introduction to *The Occult*, 1971, Colin Wilson observed: 'On one occasion, when I was searching for a piece of information, a book actually fell off the shelf and fell open at the right page.' Flammarion recalls (in *The Unknown*) that when he was writing a chapter on the force of the wind for his *L'Atmosphère*, a gust of wind carried his papers off 'in a miniature whirlwind beyond hope of recovery'. A few days later he received the proof of that chapter from his publisher, complete with the missing pages. They had been deposited in a street frequented by the publisher's porter, who often carried Flammarion's material, and who gathered them up under the impression that he must have dropped them (cf. *The Unknown*). On this same subject we could quote widely from personal experience, but refrain.

The most commonly recognized form of coincidences (apart from the 'talk-of-the-devil' effect that so fascinated Flammarion) involves words and numbers. Everyone knows instances of people whose name reflects their interests or occupation: such as the obstetrician, Don Triplett, who recently delivered his third set of triplets (*Weekly News*, 15 May 1976). Fort quotes a classic ('a savage pun mixed with murder') from the *New York Herald* of 26 November 1911: that three men were hanged in

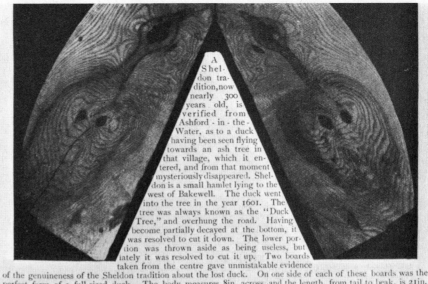

A Sheldon tradition, now nearly 300 years old, is verified from Ashford - in - the - Water, as to a duck having been seen flying towards an ash tree in that village, which it entered, and from that moment mysteriously disappeared. Sheldon is a small hamlet lying to the west of Bakewell. The duck went into the tree in the year 1601. The tree was always known as the "Duck Tree," and overhung the road. Having become partially decayed at the bottom, it was resolved to cut it down. The lower portion was thrown aside as being useless, but lately it was resolved to cut it up. Two boards taken from the centre gave unmistakable evidence of the genuineness of the Sheldon tradition about the lost duck. On one side of each of these boards was the perfect form of a full-sized duck. The body measures 8in. across, and the length, from tail to beak, is 21in. There are holes in both boards at the point where the duck's brains would rest, as if these agencies rotted the timber. This also occurs where the lights and liver settled. The duck appears to have gone head foremost into a hole, which was known to be in the tree, and couldn't get out again.

*(Left) This coincidence of the Union Jack fish and a national flag debate in 1927 reminds us of the comet egg (see p. 59). (Above) An extraordinary coincidence from the* Strand Magazine *(1897).*

## A LOYAL FISH.

## MARKED WITH THE UNION JACK.

The heated discussion in South Africa on whether there shall be an entirely new South African flag, on which the Union Jack would not appear, seems to have spread even to the fish of the surrounding sea.

According to the "Natal Mercury," a fish has been caught off Durban marked with the Union Jack. No fish with similar markings has been caught before. "There seems something uncannily appropriate," remarks our South African contemporary, "about its appearance at this juncture. The marking is readily recognised as a very good effort on the part of Nature to reproduce our national flag."

The fish was caught by an Indian, who was so impressed by its appearance that he took it to the principal fisheries officer. Finally the fish was photographed.

In a letter in the "Fishing Gazette" Mr. W. Thompson, of Durban, declares that the fish is genuine.

Asked by a "Daily News" represen-

**The Union Jack fish.**

tative for his opinion yesterday, the keeper of the fish section at the Natural History Museum said that it was impossible to judge from a photograph.

"I have never seen a fish marked in this way. If genuine, it is very remarkable."

London for the murder of Sir Edmund Berry at Greenberry Hill. Their names were Green, Berry and Hill. There is a punning sense of humour abroad in the world, childish at times, ominous at others. The *Scunthorpe Evening Telegraph*, 26 April 1975, tells of golfer Jim Tollan, who teed off towards the fourteenth hole at the local golf club. His ball hit a 6½-pound mallard in flight and brought it down by the green, called the Mallard after the pub that overlooks it. A striking example of the portentous coincidence occurred with the *Daily Telegraph* crosswords that preceded the Normandy landing on 6 June 1944, and included many of the top-secret codenames for the operations: Omaha, Utah, Mulberry, Neptune and the blan-

ket code for D-day itself, Overlord. Military Intelligence investigations could get no further than the bafflement and protested innocence of the compiler, a schoolmaster. Another schoolmaster was involved in a recent incident, having suggested to the naturalist Sir Peter Scott a scientific name for the Loch Ness Monster, *Nessiteras rhombopteryx*. London papers on 13 December 1975 pointed out with great glee its anagram, 'Monster Hoax by Sir Peter S'.

There is a category of coincidences in which nature appears to follow art, and fact fiction. As phenomenalists, we see little point in arguing out chicken-and-egg-type paradoxes, accepting that in Continuity there is a little of everything in everything else, so that it is difficult to tell where 'hard' and 'soft' realities merge except in an arbitrary and local way. This is a realm of intermediary phenomena that is virtually unexplored. For example: Noel McCabe of Derby was listening to a record, 'Cry of the Wild Goose' by Frankie Laine, when a Canadian Goose crashed through his bedroom window, and two others fell outside (the London *Sun*, 19 November 1974). The villagers of Ruthwell, Dumfriesshire, were watching a TV showing of the film *Around the World in Eighty Days* when there was a sudden power-failure. Outside the village a hot-air balloon had been attempting to land when a gust of wind blew it into the power-lines, 'just as the hero, in the film, was about to set off in his hot-air balloon' (*Weekly News*, 12 April 1975). The Melkis family of Dunstable, Bedfordshire, were also watching a TV film when . . . just as the doomed *Titanic* was about to collide with an iceberg, their house shook under an impact of a large

block of ice that had 'chosen' that moment to fall from the sky and smash through their roof (*Daily Mail*, 8 July 1975). In a *Sunday Times* article Arthur Koestler notes that the *Titanic* incident itself was preceded fourteen years earlier by Morgan Robertson's 1898 novel, *Futility*, in which a giant ship, the *Titan*, collides with an iceberg on her maiden voyage in about the same place in the Atlantic. Koestler also publishes a letter from a man who was at the helm of a ship in 1939, at the exact position of the *Titanic* disaster, when he stopped the ship on a premonition. And just in time, for a giant iceberg loomed up, striking and damaging the vessel, but this time with no loss of life. The ship's name was *Titanian*.

Finally we have noted a form of coincidence that would have amused Fort, that of an expert scientist being on the scene of the unorthodox, as though it were a show put on for him alone. *Science*, 22 April 1949, reports that Dr A. D. Bajkov, an ichthyologist, was bombarded with fish from the sky shortly after breakfast in Biloxi, Mississippi. Dr W. M. Krogman, a pathologist who specialized in fire-deaths, happened to be on holiday nearby on the night Mrs Reeser spontaneously combusted (see SPONTANEOUS HUMAN COMBUSTION). And on 2 April 1973, a meteorologist out strolling in Manchester was nearly brained by a block of ice that fell to shatter at his feet. According to the *Meteorological Magazine*, September 1975, it was one of the best documented falls of ice on record. But now we are touching on another variation, one which has benefited science on many an occasion – the accidental discovery. Just how accidental was it?

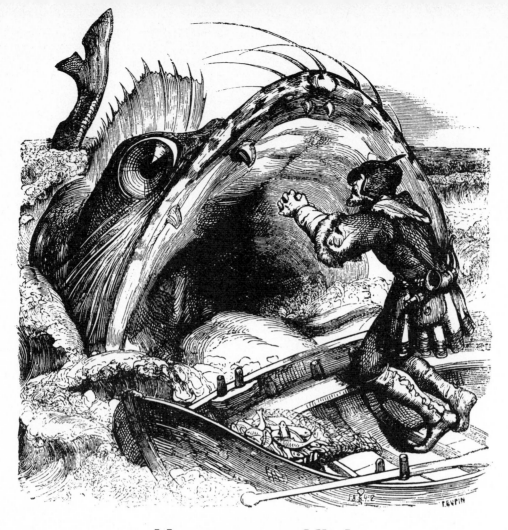

# Honest codfish

On 23 June 1626 Mr Mead of Christ's College, Cambridge, was walking through the city's market when exclamations from a rustic group around a fish stall attracted his attention. On the stall lay a battered book, its sail-cloth binding slimy with fish gut. The fishwife had just pulled it out from the inside of a plump codfish. In a letter to Sir M. Stuteville, Mr Mead wrote excitedly: 'I saw all with mine own eyes – the fish, the maw, the piece of sail-cloth, the book – and observed all I have written; only I did not see the opening of the fish, which not many did, being on the fish-woman's stall in the market, who first cut off its head, to which the maw hanging, and seeming much stuffed with somewhat, it was searched, and all found as aforesaid. He that had had his nose as near as I yester morning would have been persuaded there was no imposture here without witness. The fish came from Lynne.'

In the name of scholarship Mr Mead took possession of the fishy volume. It turned out to be a theological work by John Frith, written while the author was in prison at Oxford. We do not wish to be provocative, and merely for the sake of inclusiveness we record the fact that the

AN HONEST CODFISH.—A sloop, belonging to Rothesay, was recently lying in Lochbroom, the skipper of which, when fishing over the side, lost the keys of his lockers, &c., from his pocket into 10 fathoms of water. Attached to the bunch was a small piece of parchment, on which his name and that of the vessel were written. He, of course, gave up all hopes of ever seeing the keys again, and gazed on their rapid descent into the watery depository with deep regret. Six weeks afterwards the skipper cast anchor off the island of Rassay, about 100 miles from Lochbroom, and again resumed his piscatory employment. Among the results of his labours was a large codfish, which was speedily unhooked and thrown upon the deck; and, to the utter amazement of the skipper, the poor cod, when in the last agonies of death, vomited up his bunch of keys. The parchment, being partly preserved, proved his property beyond a doubt. At the same time, as if conscience-stricken, it disgorged a penknife belonging to a brother skipper, on which his initials were engraved. It is a remarkable circumstance that this fish, in its migratory course, should arrive at the same spot where the sloop was, sacrificing its life, and with its last breath discharging an act of honesty that would have honoured a higher grade or species of animals.—*Greenock Advertiser.*

place of his confinement had been a fish storage cellar where the smell was so overpowering that several of Frith's fellow prisoners had died of it. His book, thus miraculously restored to circulation, was reprinted by the Cambridge authorities under the title *Vox piscis* and illustrated with a woodcut showing the book, the fish stall and the knife which had cut open the fish.

This anecdote perfectly illustrates a principal theme of our book, the way in which certain apparently most unlikely events repeat themselves among all people and in all ages of which we have

record. Some of these stories of lost treasures revealed by a fish we find rather incredible. A tall one is given in William of Malmesbury's *Gesta pontificum*, repeating a slightly different version in the Chronicle of Evesham Abbey. The eighth-century founder of the Abbey, St Egwin, an early Bishop of Winchester, had become involved in some scandal and decided on a voyage to Rome to clear his name. Dramatically, before setting off, he locked fetters to his feet and threw the key into the River Avon. As he sailed to Rome, a fish leapt out of the sea and onto the ship's deck, was opened . . . there was the key. The Chronicle says that the fish was actually caught in the River Tiber. At all events, the Pope took the matter to signify the complete innocence of St Egwin, and he returned to England vindicated.

Among the earliest episodes in Japanese sacred history is the Shinto myth of two brothers, corresponding to Cain and Abel, who divided the country between them, the elder living by the shore and becoming a fisherman, the younger taking to the mountains as a hunter. On a whim they decided to change roles, but neither was any good at the other's trade, and things would simply have reverted to normal had not the younger brother lost the elder one's precious fish hook. Thousands of substitutes were offered, but nothing would do but the original, so the younger brother set out in quest of it to the palace of the fish king. After many adventures, including marriage to the king's daughter, he persuaded the king to summon all the fish of the ocean and to ask whichever one had the fish hook to return it. A mullet which had swallowed the hook obligingly threw it up again, and the brother took it back home.

In medieval versions of this story the object most commonly swallowed and returned by a fish was a ring. St Mungo, bishop and patron saint of Glasgow, who lived in the sixth century, was once applied to by a lady who had dropped her husband's ring into the River Clyde and was suspected of having given it to a lover. St Mungo, after prayer and meditation, asked for the first fish caught that morning in the Clyde to be brought to him. In its mouth was the ring. Another saintly bishop, Gerbold of Bayeux, threw his ring into the sea and retired into a hermitage after the people had driven him out of his palace. Later a man caught a fish. The Bishop's ring was in its belly. The hint was taken; Gerbold was sent for and reinstalled in his palace at Bayeux, which he continued for many years to sanctify, first with his living presence and thereafter with his holy bones.

All these stories, we know, bear a mystical interpretation. In Celtic mythology the salmon is the bearer of wisdom, and the oracular fishes, consulted by the Druids at Irish holy wells, were within recent years still spoken of by the country people. Accounts of being swallowed by a fish, or descending into a cavern or dark hermetic vessel, are allegories of the psychological process in which the soul in its quest for maturity sinks into the perilous depths of the mental underworld to emerge tempered and purified. Christ's descent into Hell and Jonah's adventure in the whale's belly are among the many illustrations of symbolic death as a means to initiation. In *Psychology and Alchemy*, Jung describes an episode from a patient's dream containing all the essential elements in our fish and ring story:

'Then the dreamer is wandering about in a dark cave, where a battle is going on between good and evil. But there is also a prince who knows everything. He gives the dreamer a ring set with a diamond. . . .'

In Jung's interpretation the cave is the unconscious mind, scene of deep mental conflict. The prince is the philosopher's stone, instrument of reconciliation, and in accepting the ring the dreamer is pledging himself to the sacred quest.

Jung's purpose was to show the enduring, archetypal nature of certain themes and images, expressed in universal mythology, poetry and magical symbolism, and also recurring spontaneously in people's dreams, and to construct from them a model of human psychological reality. Ours is to take the matter a stage further by spotting these same archetypes as they emerge from the world of dreams into the world of actual experience. We do not know whether Herodotus was correct in stating that Polycrates, tyrant of Samos, sacrificed his emerald and gold seal on the advice of a holy man by throwing it into the sea and later received it back from the belly of a fish; nor do we know just what truth there is behind the legend that the name of Pickering in Yorkshire comes from a ring lost by an old British king and a pike that restored it. But we keep hearing modern instances of the same thing, reported as fact, though without the detailed references which would make them interesting to record here. Echoes of them are often to be found in odd newspaper reports, and we were lucky enough to come across in an old *Times* an item to typify them all, the absurd story of the Honest Codfish from which this section takes its absurd title. This item we reprint, for the reader to evaluate as he will.

VOX PISCIS:
OR,
THE
BOOKFISH
CONTAYNING
Three Treatiſes which were found in the belly of a Cod-fiſh in Cambridge Market, on Midſummer Eue laſt,
*Anno Demini* 1626.

LONDON,
Printed for IAMES BOLER and
ROBERT MILBOVRNE.
M.DC.XXVII.

*(Left) A transaction with an honest whale (1863). (This page, top left and above). Title page and woodcut reproduced from the 1626 reprint of the lost book found within a codfish in Cambridge market. Illustrated are the market stall, knife, fish and book. (Centre left) A 6th-century legend tells that Nest, wife of King Maelgwn Gwynedd of North Wales, lost the traditional ring worn by the Queens in a pool. At a meal with the bishop, St Asaph, the ring was found in the King's fish, caught in the River Elwy that morning. (Left) Pictish inscribed stone from early Christian Scotland, bearing symbols of the worm bait, fish and mirror ring, reminiscent of the archetypal theme reviewed in this section.*

# Invisible barriers

This section is about unexpected intrusions by strange forces into whatever we mean by normal reality. We are particularly interested in a phenomenon which is surprisingly common yet little studied: the phenomenon of invisible barriers which unaccountably inhibit people, animals and even machines. Modern UFO incidents often feature car engines that stall in the presence of a UFO or when a UFO directs a beam of light at the car. Several writers, notably Roger Sandell (in the *Metempiric UFO Bulletin*, Summer 1976) and Clark and Coleman (in *The Unidentified*), have suggested that this effect continues from the older tradition of fairy and ghost lore. We take it further, back to the Old Testament, to the story in Numbers 22: 21–33 about Balaam and his ass. Balaam's instructions from God forbade

him to take a certain way, which he immediately did. His ass shied away from the path but Balaam beat it back again. A second time it stopped, and backed against a wall, crushing Balaam's leg. More beatings. Finally it lay down in the road, and no blows could persuade it to continue. The Biblical explanation, put into the mouth of the ass, was that its inhibition was caused by a vision of the Angel of the Lord standing in its path.

Fort noted a series of 'attacks on automobiles' in April–May 1927, in which cars were forced off roads into ditches, rivers and lakes. In one incident the driver described how he tried to keep the car to the right as it was being forced mysteriously to the left. We could add many similar modern cases. In Sunbury, Ontario, Mrs Celina Legris was found guilty of driving negligently, causing a

death when her car hit another. The local *Recorder and Times*, 24 January 1969, says that she pleaded that 'some unseen force seemed to pick my car up and violently throw it into the wrong lane just before the head-on collision'. Whether this was true or not, what court would believe her?

Mysterious accidents and stallings of engines have been blamed on equally mysterious 'rays'. One of the earliest cases involved about forty cars stalling simultaneously and unable to restart for about an hour on a road in Saxony (*New York Times*, 25 October 1930). The subject of 'secret rays' which could stop machines was enthusiastically discussed in the popular press of 1923–24, and Grindell-Matthews, the eccentric British genius, even claimed to have invented one (*Daily Mail*, 5 April 1924). Later on, the idea of 'death rays' and machine-stopping rays was revived in the classic rumours of the Second World War.

The effect as of 'invisible rays' occurs frequently in the fairy, ghost and magical traditions. We hear of the inhibiting magical spell which can be lifted only by the person who placed it. In Katherine Wiltshire's collection of tales from the living memory of her English county (*Ghosts and Legends of the Wiltshire Countryside*, 1973), a ninety-year-old shepherd tells of a carter who worked on the same farm as himself at Newton Tony. One day the man was driving a wagon-load of wood and encountered a woman, known locally as a witch, who asked if he would carry her small bundle on his cart. He refused and tried to drive on, but the horses were unable to pull the wagon beyond that point, and he had no choice but to unhitch them and lead them home. The farmer returned with him the next morning, and again the wagon would not budge; it remained stuck until they consented to carry the woman's small bundles of wood. In *Operation Trojan Horse*, 1970, John Keel says that in the 1820s General Andrew Jackson visited the Bell farm in Tennessee, intending to investigate the poltergeist activities there. Suddenly the wheels of his coach 'froze', and no amount of pushing and pulling could budge them. The exasperated members of his party were startled by a metallic voice ringing out in the air: 'All right, General, let the wagon move.' And it did!

In *Weekend*, London, 21–27 October 1970, is a story by several witnesses of a phantom army which had been seen in November 1960 on a road near Otterburn, Northumberland, the site of a fourteenth-century battle. One of the witnesses, Mrs Dorothy Strong, was in a taxi. She said: 'Suddenly the engine died, the fare-meter went haywire and the taxi felt as if it was being forced against an invisible wall. The soldiers seemed to close in on us then fade into thin air.' Several people said it had happened there before.

Frequently we read in accounts of fairy sightings that horses with or without carriages are unable to pass beyond a point in the road adjacent to where fairy music is heard or where fairies are seen at their revels. It is said that St Thomas Aquinas, who learned the art of making magical models from Albertus Magnus (see IMAGES THAT COME TO LIFE) was so disturbed in his studies by the clatter of horses outside his house that he made a brass horse and buried it in the street. Thereafter no horse could be made to travel that way, even under the whip.

Other accounts of invisible barriers come from people who have stepped on a patch of soil on which fairies have placed a spell. Dermot Macmanus devotes a chapter of *The Middle Kingdom*, 1973, to stories of the 'Stray Sod', as this enchanted ground is called. In 1935 his aunt in Mayo hired a girl from a neighbouring village and sent her on an errand which meant passing Lis Ard, a beechwood-capped hill ringed by a famous fairy-fort. As she was homesick and had time to spare, she climbed up the hill into the enclosed wood to gaze at her village from its summit. Then she walked back down the slope towards a gap in the bank. 'She had just got to the opening when she felt a queer kind of jerk, a muscular jerk inside her rather than from outside, and before she realized what had happened she found herself walking quickly in exactly the opposite direction towards the centre of the wood again.' The same thing happened when she tried the gap a second time. She then made for the point at which she had entered, 'but now she received her greatest shock, for she felt as if an invisible wall was there which she could not pass'. She was trapped for hours behind this magic wall, which felt so solid that she could follow it round with her hands. Meanwhile her absence had been a matter of concern; evening passed into night, and four search parties set out. The girl later said that one party had passed within twenty yards of her, but they could neither see her nor hear her frantic yells for help, although she could see and hear them well enough. Some time later she became aware that the barrier had gone and was able to set off home, frightened and exhausted.

Recently there seems to have been an invisible barrier in a car park at Durham in northern England. According to the *Newcastle Journal*, 8 December 1975, Mrs Dilys Cant failed repeatedly to back her car into a vacant space. She said that it felt as if she were always coming up against a kerb, though no obstacle was visible. Her daughter was also prevented from entering the space by 'an invisible force-field'. Two other motorists tried to drive and then to push their cars into the space, but were unable to do so. Typically, by the time officials of the council investigated, the 'haunted' bay had reverted to normality.

According to the London *Daily Mail*, 1 May 1907, an elderly woman in Paris complained to a magistrate that 'something' compelled her to walk on her hands every time she went through the door of her apartment. The magistrate detained her, thinking she was mad, and sent an officer to investigate. He returned with the woman's son, who told the court: 'I do not pretend to explain it. I only know that when my mother, my uncle and myself enter the flat, we are immediately impelled to walk on our hands.' The uncle was sent for, and he too confirmed the story. Finally the magistrate summoned the concierge of the building, who said: 'All you have heard is true. I thought my tenants had gone mad, but as soon as I entered the rooms occupied by them, I found myself on all fours, endeavouring to throw my feet in the air.'

The magistrate ordered the rooms to be disinfected!

(Left) George Pickingill (d. 1909), the last witch of Canewdon, Essex, was said to be able to stop farm machinery with a glance, and was feared throughout the Rochford Hundred. (Above) A lubin bewitches a Norman ploughman. Lubins, like the English boggarts and fairies, could stop animals and carts. (Below) A scene from the film The Day the Earth Stood Still, 1952, in which an alien stops all the machines on earth simultaneously.

# Levitation and spontaneous flight

An unfashionable reminder in the days of supersonic aircraft is that human beings have the inherent ability to fly, autonomously, without artificial aids. We draw our data from several different categories, for the subject is bedevilled by exclusionism. Christians cherish their own levitating saints with no regard for flying mystics of other persuasions. Collectors of folklore delight in stories of people who have ridden off with fairies, but show no enthusiasm for levitations by modern spirit mediums. Orthodox science has no interest in any of them. We are curious about this phenomenon of human flight. There is no doubt at all that it does on occasion take place. In most modern instances it is involuntary; yet sometimes it is premeditated. There is evidently some natural force, unknown to our present science, by which people can achieve levitation; and the further we move away in time and culture from the rationalistic world-view of modern Europe, the more evidence we find that this force has been recognized, studied and made use of. Perhaps it will one day be so again.

Records of levitation in a religious context are legion. In Olivier Leroy's *La Lévitation* are the legends of some 230 Catholic saints to whom this feat – or accident – is attributed. They include St Ignatius Loyola who was inclined to be suspended a foot or so above the ground while meditating, St Adolphus Liguori who was raised into the air in front of the whole congregation in the Church of St John at Foggia in 1777, and the famous Arabian Carmelite, Sister Mary. In the garden of her Bethlehem nunnery she would sometimes be levitated into the treetops. As she rose she would hold onto a branch, like the Indian yogi with his staff in our illustration. In all such cases the person lifted into the air is in a state of trance or religious ecstasy, physical levitation being a secondary effect of mental detachment or 'astral travel'. The phenomenon is not, of course, exclusive to Catholic saints. Moslem levitators include the twelfth-century Iranian dervish, Haydar, noted for his sudden flights to treetops and roofs of houses.

Sometimes this tendency to involuntary flight is an embarrassment to the person afflicted with it. Simple, saintly Joseph of Copertino (1603–63) was shuffled by his superiors from one Franciscan house to another to avoid the publicity he attracted with his spectaclar soarings. He would suddenly cry out and fly up in the air, so disrupting church services that he was barred from public worship and made to celebrate his aerial Masses in private. Once, according to a witness, 'he rose into space, and, from the middle of the church, flew like a bird on to the high altar, where he embraced the tabernacle'. On another occasion he flew into an olive tree, 'and he remained kneeling for half an hour on a branch, which was seen to sway as if a bird had perched on it'.

The Church, having condemned magical flight in pagan and 'savage' religions as diabolistic, has never encouraged such exhibitions among its own saints. It has therefore cut itself off from a branch of knowledge which less inhibited religions seem to have mastered, the art of controlled levitation. If the thing happens spontaneously, under certain conditions, it can presumably be reproduced at will. Where saints have shown the way, spiritualists have followed. In July 1871 the celebrated medium D.D. Home attended an evening of spirit-raising in a London flat in the company of Lord Adair, a cousin of his and of Lord Lindsay's, who described what happened: 'During the

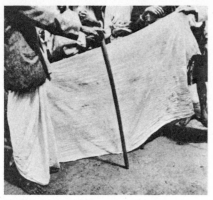

*(Left and above) Two of a series of photographs (1936) showing a Hindu feat of levitation. Before and after the event the stick is unwrapped to show it is not a support.*

*(Above) A drawing by Cades of one of St Joseph of Copertino's ecstatic flights. (Below) Glanvill, author of* Saducismus Triumphatus, *1681, knew of levitation during psychic disturbances, but associated it with witchcraft.*

sitting Mr Home went into a trance, and in that state was carried out of the window in the room next to where we were, and was brought in at our window.' Hume's performances of levitation and other magical acts thrilled the fashionable drawing-rooms of Victorian London, but his powers were by no means unique or exceptional. Many instances are given in Mircea Eliade's *Shamanism* of witchdoctors, shamans and eastern mystics who practise set rituals to induce a state in which the body may rise up into the air. Sometimes a future shaman is marked out by his spontaneous levitation. Thus, in Sumatra, 'he who is destined to be a prophet-priest suddenly disappears, carried off by spirits; he returns to the village three or four days later; if not, a search is made for him and he is usually found in the top of a tree, conversing with spirits. He seems to have lost his mind, and sacrifices must be offered to restore him to sanity'.

When such things happen in traditionalist communities, regulated by shamans or state magicians, the person who has attracted the levitating force is put through a course of initiation in which he learns to control that force and put it to use. In Europe, where spontaneous levitation is either unrecognized or classified in terms of diabolism and the supernatural, its occurrence is unwelcome and often painful to the person affected by it. In the records of the Society for Psychical Research are innumerable instances of people being raised into the air, thrown across the room, and so on, by unseen forces. A letter from a clergyman of Barnstaple, Devon, written in 1683, is printed in John Aubrey's *Miscellanies*. It describes from first-hand experience a series of mysterious and very violent assaults on a young man, Francis Fry, who was a servant at a farm in the parish of Spreyton. Flying missiles and blows were rained on him, and the whole house became so disturbed that a young girl living there had to be sent away for safety. On Easter Eve, 1682, Fry disappeared, was searched for and was found half-naked in a bog, whistling and singing and quite out of his senses. His shoes were scattered one each side of the farm house and his wig was found at the top of a tree: 'Coming to himself an hour after, he solemnly protested that the daemon carried him so high that he saw his master's house underneath him no bigger than a hay-cock, that he was in perfect sense, and prayed God not to suffer the Devil to destroy him; that he was suddenly set down in the quagmire.'

Had Francis Fry experienced this involuntary levitation in tribal society, it would have distinguished him as a chosen seer and spirit medium; at the height of the witchcraft persecutions he might have been burnt. By Aubrey's time, however, the recent hysteria was almost spent, and Aubrey was able to record the curious phenomena he delighted in (like any true scholar) without the necessity for moralistic comment.

Readers unfamiliar with the post-war UFO literature, which is now the main repository for such items, may be surprised at the number of recent cases where a person has undergone a sudden, inexplicable change of location, sometimes combined with an encounter with dream-like creatures who appear to be the agents in his transportation. The case of Travis Walton, described in our section TAKEN AWAY AND BROUGHT BACK, is one such example; another, the subject of an article in the *Flying Saucer Review* of November 1973, and fully reported in Clark and Coleman's *The Unexplained*, began with the disappearance of a Brazilian soldier, José António da Silva, from his tent beside a lake, where he had spent the evening fishing, near the town of Bebedouro. On 9 May 1969, after an unaccountable absence of four and a half days, da Silva found himself suddenly deposited in a lonely spot near Vitória, over two hundred miles from his point of departure. His story was that he had been abducted by humanoid creatures from a flying saucer (see TELEPORTATION).

Going through our files, we find many such instances where swift carriage through the air seems the only possible way of accounting for the short time and great distances involved. With this in mind we are drawn to reconsider the preposterous claims made by the old witches, that they could levitate and fly – a claim which no modern historian of witchcraft has taken seriously, but which was certainly so taken, on the evidence of sincere witnesses, including the accused witches themselves, at many of their trials.

The usual explanation now applied to the witches' claim to flight is that they experienced the sensation of flight through drugs, trances and the power of suggestion, while actually remaining earthbound. Mystics often describe their ascents into the world of prophetic imagination as a flight to heaven. Yet modern tribal shamans, writes Eliade, consider physical flight to be an occasional consequence or extension of flights of ecstasy; they value its occurrences as reminders of the greater powers of their predecessors, who could invoke at will the necessary conditions for levitation of the body. Unless we reject all the documented accounts from every religious tradition of levitating saints and ascetics, we can scarcely deny that some witches may have possessed the same gifts, powers or afflictions. And while the Christian levitators were encouraged to suppress in themselves all tendencies towards aerial exhibitionism, the witches were not so inhibited.

# Strange disappearances

We have many records of people disappearing, suddenly, mysteriously and finally, but from the storyteller's point of view there is something wrong with all of them. They are too short, without proper endings. We can state, for instance, on the authority of the London *Daily Chronicle* of 30 July 1889, that on the thirteenth of that month Mr Macmillan of the famous publishing firm climbed to the top of Mount Olympus. He was seen waving from the summit but, despite careful searches and rewards offered, no trace of him was ever afterwards found. Again, in 1809 Mr Bathurst went to enter his carriage outside a German inn; then, says Sabine Baring-Gould in *Historical Oddities*, 'he stepped round to the heads of the horses – and was never seen again'. In December 1900 the boat from Lewis in the Outer Hebrides went to relieve the three keepers of the lonely Flannan Islands lighthouse. They were not there. Two RAF pilots, Day and Stewart, crash-landed in the Iraqi desert in 1924. Their footprints were clearly visible in the sand some distance from the aircraft, and then suddenly there were no more prints and no further news ever again of the two airmen.

When, as in these cases, no rational explanation is apparent, superstitions arise. There is talk of the devil, particularly when the person disappearing is notorious for an evil life-style. The disappearance of Owen Parfitt in 1769 might be, and indeed commonly was, explained as an instance of the devil's habit of taking his own. Parfitt was a retired nautical villain, a pirate they said locally, who was spending his old age in tactful obscurity in a cottage in Shepton Mallet, Somerset. A stroke had immobilized him, but a kind female relative had wrapped him in a rug and placed him in a chair outside the cottage that he might enjoy the air of a fine summer day. She went off on a short errand, and when she returned, the chair with cushion and rug were still there but the old man had gone; and he had gone for good. In a field just over the way, within sight and hearing of the cottage, haymakers were at work. They were certain that no one had passed the cottage and they had heard and seen nothing unusual.

The devil taking his own does not, of course, serve to explain cases of good or holy men mysteriously disappearing; so we hear of angels and people taken directly to heaven. However, most vanishing people, being neither angelic nor diabolic, can not reasonably be supposed to have been selected for special treatment by gods or devils, so the common explanation used to be in terms of an amoral force, the fairies. We have

referred in previous sections to the universal belief in abductions by fairies or supernatural beings, but in many cases of disappearing people, where this explanation is offered, the agency of such beings is only supposed. Dr Moore, for example, whose adventure is related in our section TAKEN AWAY AND BROUGHT BACK, was drawn away from his friends by a force, invisible to them, which he saw as a troop of men. That this force was fairies was merely the conventional belief of all concerned, and we feel sure that had the incident taken place today instead of in 1678 the flying saucer folk would have been blamed for it. Yet in the modern cases, regularly reported in the *Flying Saucer Review*, of people who have suddenly vanished and later returned to tell the tale, there are many accounts of an impersonal abductive force, not necessarily identified with such conventional agencies as fairies, gods or UFOs. A good example is found in a recent case, reported in the *Flying Saucer Review* of November 1975. Near the Argentine city of Bahía Blanca (a notorious centre of the TELEPORTATION effect) a young waiter, Carlos Díaz, was walking home in the early morning of 4 January 1975 when he was suddenly paralyzed by a beam of light from above. The atmosphere around him started humming and vibrating, and he felt himself drawn up about ten feet into the air before losing consciousness. Some

four hours later he found himself lying on the grass by the side of a road. With him was his bag containing his working clothes and a newspaper he had bought earlier that morning in his home town. Yet he was nowhere near home but some five hundred miles away, outside Buenos Aires, where he was taken to hospital.

To account for the time spent between his disappearance and return, Díaz told a story of a type commonly found in both the fairy and the UFO mythology, though with some peculiar details of its own. Following his ascent into the sky and loss of consciousness, he had been inside a translucent globe in the company of three strange creatures, somewhat like men but green in colour, who had painlessly extracted tufts of hair from his head. At the hospital where he was examined, it appeared that he had indeed lost some hair, removed by some mysterious process without damage to the roots.

No one saw Díaz disappear, and it is only because he came back that his story was told. We wonder how often the same sort of thing happens in cases of mysterious disappearances where there is no return and therefore no story. There are several records of people *almost* disappearing in similar circumstances to those in which Díaz actually did. In the extraordinary case of the French children of Clavaux, reported in *The Times* of 13 January 1843, two little girls were drawn up into the air as if in a vortex. Their parents were on hand, unaffected by the vortex, and dragged them back to earth. Brad Steiger in *Strangers from the Sky*, 1966, gives a detailed account (though without reference to original sources) of the disappearance of Oliver Thomas, an eleven-year-old Welsh boy, from outside his home near Rhayader. It was Christmas Eve, 1909. There was a party going on. Oliver Thomas stepped outside the house, he was heard to cry out for help, and the sound seemed to come from the sky. The whole district was searched. His parents and their guests traced his footprints in the snow to a point seventy-five yards from the house, where they ceased, and nothing more was ever heard of the boy.

Another report in *The Times*, 11 December 1873, tells of an elderly couple, Mr and Mrs Cumpston, who were asleep in a Bristol hotel when they heard noises. Mr Cumpston stepped out of bed onto the floor, which seemed to open, and he was in the act of falling into a black void when his wife seized hold of him and pulled him back. They fled panic-stricken out of the room through the window, and were discovered at the railway station in their night clothes, looking for a policeman.

*(Left and top) Among countless unsolved disappearances in mysterious circumstances are that of the pioneer American aviator Amelia Earhart and that of Colonel Percy Fawcett, who vanished in the Mato Grosso in 1925. (Above) Some disappearances of children were blamed on fairies (see text). (Right) Elijah ascends to heaven without dying, a rare honour.*

A phenomenon which was once, by all accounts, very active, but seems scarcely to have been reported in recent years, is that of the changeling – the abduction by fairies of a human baby and the substitution of a sickly alien child. In one of the extracts from Waldron's *History of the Isle of Man*, reproduced in J.O. Halliwell's *Illustrations of the Fairy Mythology*, 1845, is the story told by a Manx woman whose babies were given to making strange disappearances shortly after their births. On the first two occasions, the disappearances were attended by various noises and disturbances in her house, which brought the neighbours running, and the babies were each found some distance from the bed – dropped by the fairies, as they explained it. Soon after her third baby was born, the woman saw it being levitated out of the room by an invisible force. She cried out and her husband came in and pointed to the baby by her side; but it was a sallow, wrinkled child, not like her own, and it lay naked with the original baby's clothes tied in a bundle beside it. It lived on for a few

years, never speaking, walking or de-fecating, and eating nothing but a few herbs. Wirt Sikes has another good anecdote, here illustrated, in *British Goblins* about Jennet Francis of Ebwy Fawr valley in Wales. One night she awoke to feel her infant son being pulled from her arms. She screamed, prayed and pulled him back, successfully. An interesting detail, in view of the prophetic or shamanistic powers which in many tribes are attributed to people who have been teleported, is that the son grew up to become a famous preacher.

In earlier times, when the existence of an abducting or teleporting force was recognized in the terminology of the fairy faith, local witches or magicians were at hand with the appropriate spells to remedy the 'sudden disappearance' effect. In the case of changelings, the folklore record is full of various procedures by which parents can regain their abducted baby, and other traditions hint at forgotten methods of recapturing older people whom the fairies had taken. Robert Kirk, minister of Aberfoyle in Scotland, described in

*The Secret Commonwealth of Elves, Fauns, and Fairies*, 1691, his own abduction by fairies, and it is said that on the anniversary of his death (or final abduction) he appeared again with the fairy host, and could have been liberated if the right spell had been enacted.

A spontaneous echo of this old belief that an abducted person reappears and may return on the anniversary of his disappearance comes from a report in the *Scottish Daily Express*, 27 December 1971. Six years before, in the early hours of New Year's Day 1966, nineteen-year-old Alex Cleghorn had been walking along Govan Road, Glasgow, in company with his two elder brothers, engaged in the Scottish custom of first-footing (New Year visiting). Suddenly Alex was not with them, nor had they seen him since. On New Year's morning 1972 the two brothers were planning to first-foot along the very same route as six years previously, passing the spot of Alex's disappearance, 'in the vain hope that somehow he may return'. Whether the hope was indeed vain we have not heard.

# Taken away and brought back

People are always vanishing. Some do it fair and square, once and for all, either of their own volition or somebody else's; others turn up again. Not surprisingly, those who return from mysterious absence feel the need to explain, but some of these explanations, far from enlightening, only make us wonder more about the people who did not return.

Some common explanations old and new: 'abducted by fairies': 'murdered by colleagues'; 'went out for a pack of cigarettes and wandered off'; 'taken up by people from a flying saucer'. The phenomenon is the same throughout: a person inexplicably vanishing and unaccountably returning. The explanation, as we keep pointing out, varies with fashion.

Long devotion to the curious history of the law persuades us that no one should be hanged for murder, even in hanging times, without a corpse. There have been too many judicial miscarriages and near-miscarriages. The legal writer Sir Edward Coke, in his *Institutes*, vol. III, refers to a dreadful case in Warwickshire, where a little girl of eight or nine went mysteriously missing. She was an orphan, looked after by her uncle, and at the age of sixteen she was due to inherit the family estate. The uncle was required to produce her, could not do so, and in panic dressed up another little girl and presented her as his niece. He was exposed, charged with the niece's murder, convicted and hanged. Years later the girl, having reached the age of sixteen, turned up and claimed her estate. She had run away, she said, and had been living with some kind people in the next county.

In the records of nineteenth-century folklorists are found several cases where a person's sudden disappearance threatened fatal consequences to his companion. T. C. Croker (*Fairy Legends*, vol. III) repeats a first-hand account he heard in the Vale of Neath, South Wales, of the disappearance of a certain Mr Rhys. One evening Rhys was returning with another man, Llewellyn, to the farm where they worked. They were driving some horses. On the way Rhys fancied he heard music and told Llewellyn to go on ahead with the horses as he wanted to stay behind for a while and have a dance. Llewellyn reached home and went to bed, thinking Rhys had probably gone to the inn, but next morning his friend had not returned, and when searches failed to discover him, Llewellyn was suspected of his murder. Fortunately a local farmer with a knowledge of mysteries persuaded all parties, including Llewellyn and the narrator, to revisit the scene of the disappearance. There Llewellyn heard

the music. His foot was on the edge of a fairy ring. 'Put your foot on mine, David,' said Llewellyn to Croker's informant. The man did so, and the others likewise. Then all heard the music and saw a crowd of little figures dancing in the ring with Rhys among them. Llewellyn dragged him out of the ring and together they forced him to come away with them. It seemed to him he had only been dancing for five minutes or so, and the experience left him so melancholy that he soon died.

A record of an abduction by fairies, reprinted in J. O. Halliwell's *Illustrations of the Fairy Mythology*, 1845, from a pamphlet of 1678 in the British Museum, signed J. Cotham, is the most interesting we know of, on account of its remarkable details and because it is attested to by the man who was taken away and by the witnesses to his disappearance and return. Three weeks before the pamphlet was written, a Dr Moore with two companions was travelling in Wicklow, Ireland, and staying the night at an inn at Drom-

greagh near Baltinglass. He began to speak of fairies, saying that as a child in that country he had several times been taken off by them, on which occasions his mother would call in a local wise woman whose spells were effective in having him brought back. As he spoke it seemed to him, as he said later, that a troop of men entered the room, took hold of him and dragged him off. All that his companions saw was that he was being drawn out of the room by an unseen force. They tried to hold on to him, but he vanished and they raised the alarm. The innkeeper, who was apparently used to such happenings, sent for an old woman who said that Dr Moore was in a wood about a mile away with the fairies, and that if by her magic she could prevent him from eating or drinking during his absence, he would be restored unharmed; otherwise he would return in a consumptive state and would soon pine away. Early the next morning Dr Moore reentered the inn, hungry and thirsty from a night spent in rapid travel between places of fairy

(Left and far left) Travis Walton of Arizona with an artist's version, from his own and other witnesses' accounts, of his abduction by a luminous flying object. (Below) Dragged from the fairy ring. Experiences such as Walton's (see text) repeat those recorded in folklore of abductions by fairies. The fairy ring in some accounts is a shimmering sphere. In both modern and ancient accounts, the person taken away is often brought back curiously changed in personality.

feasts and revelry. Every time his abductors had offered him food, he said, it had been unaccountably struck out of his hand – presumably through the woman's magic – and at daybreak he had found himself alone within sight of the inn.

Local traditions everywhere are full of such incidents, and the theme continues in the many similar reports of our own time. Sometimes, as in Dr Moore's case, there is direct evidence from participants and witnesses. The *Daily Express*, 15 November 1975, printed an interview with a young American forester, Travis Walton. Ten days earlier he had been in a truck, driving back to work with five mates from the woods near Snowflake, Arizona. Hovering just above the trees they saw a bright light (there are similar things in our MYSTERIOUS LIGHTS section). Travis Walton did not think of angels or fairies, he thought of UFOs. When he and his brother were boys they had been followed by one, and they had determined never again to be frightened of such

things. The driver of the truck, Mike Rogers, pulled up, and Walton jumped out and ran towards the light. The others saw a bright flash and Walton falling to the ground, and they drove off in panic. When they returned there was no sign of the man, and for five days a thorough, massive search of the countryside was conducted in vain. Inquisition by the electric lie-detector at the Sheriff's office failed to discredit the men's story, and there were no murder charges. On the fifth day Walton reappeared in Heber, a few miles from Snowflake. He gave a detailed account of the flying saucer in which he had found himself after being knocked out by the light. He described its occupants, some human, some 'weird . . . like well-developed foetuses', and he described their curious treatment of him before they let him go not far from where he had first been taken.

We can think of many such stories in recent years. There are some in every book on UFOs, mostly the same stories repeated, for in copying and plagiarizing each other the UFO authors are the

equals of the folklorists. Nor is this so surprising, for they are dealing with essentially the same material. Rhys in the earlier Welsh account had been brought up in a world of fairies; Walton was a child of the SF and UFO age. Both went through the experience of abduction by the unknown, and both explained, as Fort put it, 'in terms of the familiar'.

The threat of murder charges, which is an ugly feature of many of these abduction cases, became a terrible reality in 1660 during one of the strangest disappearances on record. On 16 August of that year, William Harrison, a man of seventy, for many years the trusted agent of Lady Campden of Chipping Campden, Gloucestershire, set out to collect rents. When night fell and he had not returned, a servant, John Perry, was sent out to look for him. He was nowhere to be found, but a search party later came across his hat, comb and scarf, lying in the road, cut and bloody. Perry was suspected of having murdered him and was held in custody, where he confessed, involving also his mother and brother in the murder. These two strongly denied having done any such thing, but Perry persisted with his confession and accusation, and next year, despite the absence of a corpse, all three were sentenced by an inexperienced judge and publicly hanged on Broadway Hill.

Two years later, the 'murdered' man, William Harrison, returned to Chipping Campden with his fantastic explanation. On the night of his disappearance he had been attacked by two armed horsemen, who ran him through the side and thigh with swords and took him, thus wounded, on a long journey through England to Deal, where he was put on a ship and taken off to sea. The ship was captured by Turkish pirates who sold Harrison as a slave to an elderly Turk living in Smyrna. This old man on his death-bed gave Harrison his freedom and a silver bowl, by selling which, and after many adventures, he made his way back to England and Chipping Campden. The judge, Sir Robert Hyde, who had hanged the Perrys on the sole evidence of one false confession, died full of honours and has his monument in Salisbury Cathedral.

No commentator has ever taken Mr Harrison's account seriously. Why should an unremarkable old man be thus elaborately kidnapped in the heart of England, and not even robbed but, by his own account, given money by his captors? Popular opinion, expressed in a contemporary broadsheet which is reprinted, together with other documents and opinions on the case, in Sir George Clark's *The Campden Wonder*, 1959, was that Harrison had been magically transported to a rock off the Turkish coast by a witch – none other than Perry's mother who had been hanged.

# Teleportation

Teleportation is the name coined by Charles Fort to describe the phenomenon of people or objects transferred without physical agency from one place to another. Under our present system of belief this, of course, is not supposed to happen, but in previous sections we have quoted cases where we must surely suppose that it actually has; and we are impressed by the voluminous evidence from centuries of human experience which indicates that living creatures and things are occasionally transported vast distances in the proverbial twinkling of an eye.

An early report, long buried among Spanish legal records and resurrected by the pioneer UFO writer M. K. Jessup, is of the trial by the Inquisition of a soldier who, on 25 October 1593, appeared suddenly in a confused state in the main square of Mexico City, wearing the uniform of a regiment stationed nine thousand miles away in the Philippines. He could only say that moments before his appearance in Mexico he had been on sentry duty at the Governor's palace in Manila, the Philippine capital. The Governor, he said, had just been assassinated. How he came to be in Mexico he had no idea. Months later a ship from the Philippines confirmed the news of the assassination and other details of the soldier's story.

The sad fate of the man from Goa, referred to earlier (see p. 7), supports our view that teleportation, and indeed everything, however irrational, which long, repeated experience shows is liable to happen, should be acknowledged as part of phenomenal reality, so that people who find themselves involved in these happenings are not burnt, sacked from their jobs or otherwise persecuted for adventures which are beyond their control.

A simple experience of the teleportation effect is claimed by the late respected mystic, Wellesley Tudor Pole, in his book, *The Silent Road*, 1962:

'On a wet and stormy night in December 1952, I found myself at a country station some mile and a half from my Sussex home. The train from London had arrived late, the bus had gone and no taxis were available. The rain was heavy and incessant. The time was 5.55 p.m. and I was expecting an important trunk call from overseas at 6 p.m. at home. The situation seemed desperate. To make matters worse, the station call box was out of order and some trouble on the line made access to the railway telephone impossible. In despair I sat down in the waiting-room and having nothing better to do, I compared my watch with the station clock. Allowing for the fact that this is always kept two minutes in advance, I was able to confirm the fact that the exact time was 5.57 p.m. Three minutes to zero hour! What happened next I cannot say. When I came to myself I was standing in my hall at home, a good twenty minutes walk away, and the clock was striking six. My telephone call duly came through a few minutes later. Having finished my call, I awoke to the realization that something very strange had happened. Then much to my surprise, I found that my shoes were dry and free from mud, and that my clothes showed no sign of damp or damage.'

The implication here is that Major Tudor Pole was miraculously transported home in response to his strong desire to be so, but without any conscious magic on his part. Yet if it could so happen spontaneously, why not at the direction of the will? We think of witches and spiritualists and particularly of the incident – rather an absurd one and naturally much ridiculed at the

*(Left) 'Transit of Venus': a satirical view of Mrs Guppy's teleportation (see text). (Top) Mary of Agreda (see text). (Above) A Welsh news story of 1887. (Below) Witchcraft teleportation (1681).*

time – of the hefty, seventeen-stone (240-pound) medium Mrs Guppy, who on 3 June 1871 'was instantly pre-cipitated from her home at Highbury (London) to a house in Lamb's Conduit Street, some three miles away, where she came down bump right in the middle of a séance' – dressed in her underclothes. We hurry on from this seductive pheno-menon to examine the most remarkable feat of TELEPORTATION, or bilocation, ever recorded of a Christian mystic.

The Venerable Mary of Jesus of Agreda was never known to leave her Spanish convent, yet between the years of 1620, when she was a girl of eighteen, and 1631 she was officially estimated to have made over five hundred trips to America, where she converted to Chris-tianity the Jumano Indians of New Mexico. This estimate was not given lightly. Indeed, the Catholic authorities, made wary by the delusive claims of religious hysterics, did all they could to dissuade Sister Mary from insisting on the reality of her trans-Atlantic flights, until the testimony of missionaries to the Mexican Indians forced them to authen-ticate her experiences. In 1622 Father Alonzo de Benavides of the Isolita Mission in New Mexico wrote to Pope Urban VIII and to Philip IV of Spain asking to be told who had forestalled him in his mission to convert the Jumano Indians. They themselves declared their knowledge of Christianity to have come from a 'lady in blue', a European nun who had left with them crosses, rosaries and a chalice which they used for celebrating Mass. This chalice was afterwards found to have come from Mary's convent at Agreda.

It was not until 1630, when Father Benavides returned to Spain, that he heard of Sister Mary and her fantastic belief that she had converted the Jumano Indians. He obtained leave to examine her and did so closely, receiving from her exact accounts of her visits to the Indians with details of their appearance and customs. She kept a diary of her experiences, but burnt it on the advice of her confessor. In it she described many details of her travels, including a vision of the planet earth as a sphere (a heretical view at the time), revolving on its poles. In his *Life of the Venerable Mary of Agreda*, James A. Carrico concludes:

'That Agreda really visited America many times is attested to by the logs of the Spanish conquistadors, the French explorers, the identical accounts by different tribes of Indians a thousand miles apart. Every authentic history of the Southwest of the United States records this mystic phenomenon un-paralleled in the entire history of the world.'

A memorandum of Mary's includes a detail that will delight all phenomen-alists. As the folk traditions of all lands warn the traveller into fairyland against taking fairy gifts, eating fairy food, or lusting after fairy women, so Mary was warned by God, 'that neither by thought, word nor deed must I presume to long for or touch anything, unless it were God's express will that I should do so'.

Within recent years some remarkable cases of involuntary teleportation have been reported, mostly within the UFO context, many of which are summarized in John Keel's *Our Haunted Planet*, 1971. For example, Dr Geraldo Vidal and his wife were driving in their car near Bahía Blanca, Argentina in May 1968. The next thing they knew was that they were in Mexico, many thousands of miles away, although only forty-eight hours had passed. They had no idea where they were nor how they came to be there. The only clue was that their car was scorched on the outside. Another case, described in detail in Clark and Coleman's *The Unidentified*, is that of Jose António da Silva, aged twenty-four, who turned up on 9 May 1969 near Vitória, Brazil, shocked and dishevelled, having been near Bebedouro, some 500 miles away, four and a half days earlier. His story, that he had been captured by creatures about four feet tall, taken by them to another planet and then returned to earth, sounds fantastic, but the case, like several others where similar claims have been made, was thoroughly investigated, and no one doubted that da Silva's account was sincerely given. The significant feature of all these UFO-linked teleportation cases is that the victim reappears in a state of shock, trance or semi-amnesia, exactly as is reported of fairy abductees of an earlier generation.

Many instances of teleportation have occurred spontaneously, as uncon-trolled, random effects; others were evidently directed, though uncon-sciously, by the wills of highly sensitive people, of whom Sister Mary and Major Tudor Pole are two dissimilar examples. The man who was teleported from Goa to Portugal in 1655 was evidently judged by the Inquisition to have procured the effect by magic, and he was therefore burnt for the prohibited use of occult powers. No one then doubted the exis-tence of such powers, and the further back in history we go, through times of witches and tribal shamans to the power-ful state magicians of archaic civiliz-ations, the more exact is the knowledge claimed of controlled techniques of teleportation and magical flight. Even when unrecognized, the phenomenon continues as an occasional chance hap-pening, and instead of flying mystics and the aerial transport of great stone slabs by the builders of Stonehenge we hear of a teleported motor car and a bewildered couple in Mexico who should have been in Argentina.

# Miraculous provisions

In his article on 'Miracles' in *Man, Myth and Magic*, A.R.G. Owen writes that Christ's miraculous feeding of the multitudes tends to be interpreted today as a parable of 'spiritual feeding' rather than as a factual record of five thousand or so people who dined adequately off five loaves and two fishes divided between the lot of them. If it is indeed the modern tendency to explain sacred irrationalities this way, we deplore it. Though the details do seem rather exaggerated, the feat as reported is by no means unique. The feeding of very many on very little is called theologically a 'miracle of abundance' and merits a whole chapter in Pope Benedict XIV's definitive guide to mystical phenomena, *De servorum Dei beatificatione et canonizatione*. Father Herbert Thurston re-examines a number of these in *The Physical Phenomena of Mysticism* and concludes that the phenomenon of multiplication cannot be lightly dismissed as belonging solely to the domain of legend.

The most recent worker of miracles of abundance we know of is the Indian holy man Sai Baba. In *Sai Baba : Man of Miracles*, Howard Murphet gives an account of a party after a religious ceremony at the house of Mr and Mrs Ramachandran, near Poona. A hundred guests had been catered for, but about a thousand turned up. Sai Baba was present and saved the day by miraculously multiplying the food tenfold during its serving so that all were fully satisfied. At other times, Murphet writes, the saint could instantly produce sweets still hot from cooking. Prolific feats of edible magic were attributed to St Angiolo Paoli (d. 1720), who delighted in multiplying small quantities of food to distribute to the poor of Rome and rarely refused any genuine request. In his *Life* (1756) by Cacciari, the saint is described as being frequently seconded to picnics arranged by the sponsors of some of the Carmelite missions. On one hot June day the Father took a group to a garden party where he provided lettuces and radishes for a salad, a tart, and a basket of strawberries for dessert, all of which during the current drought were very scarce. Cacciari gives several other similar incidents.

One of the most authoritative cases of multiplication procured the beatification of St Andrew Fournet (d. 1834), founders of Les Filles de la Croix, a house for educating the poor at La Puye, in Poitou. One year, about 1824, the sisters at La Puye were in dispair because they had very little corn in their granary and no money to buy any more. After admonishing their lack of faith in a sermon about Christ's multiplication miracle, St Andrew bid them gather what corn they could find into two heaps, around which he walked in prayer. The sister in charge of the granary would draw daily enough to feed some 200 sisters, and for the next two and a half months the heaps did not diminish at all. According to the *Summarium* for his beatification, St Andrew performed this miracle on several occasions, and kept the house in cornflour from July to December. Auffray's *Life of Blessed John Bosco* also quotes from beatification documents evidence of this saint's miracle of abundance. One day in 1860 Don Bosco was informed there was nothing for breakfast in the Salesian house in Turin in which he was staying. The eyes of three hundred hungry boys were on him as he asked for all the scraps of bread of any size to be found to be brought to him. Everybody there could see there were only fifteen or twenty small pieces of bread in the basket he held as he walked among them – yet he managed to give each person there a piece.

Sometimes we hear of the miracle taking place in the dough while the bread is being made. For example, in the hard winter of 1845, the Bon Pasteur convent at Bourges was faced with supplying the daily needs of 116 people from a depleted granary. Blessed Mother Pelletier inspired the nuns to pray for the intercession of St Germaine Cousin, who died in 1601, confident that the small supply would be replenished. The cooking sisters were urged to use about a third of the customary amount of flour; and behold! Within minutes the dough had swollen to overflow the kneading trough with enough for twice the usual number of loaves. This was repeated many times between November 1845 and February 1846, during which time the nuns did not have to buy any more flour. The documentation of these wonders was thorough enough to be cited for the canonization of St Germaine in 1854, and the beatification of Mother Pelletier. It is interesting to note that traditional folklore stories of Christ's and St Peter's wanderings on earth include variants of this phenomenon. G. W. Dasent's *Popular Tales from the Norse*, 1903, says that they came to a baker's house and begged some bread from the wife. She took a small piece of dough because she thought they were merely ordinary beggars. The piece expanded to cover the whole griddle, and not wanting to give away so much she broke off another small piece. This too expanded, and she decided not to give it away at all. Christ angrily turned her into a woodpecker.

Miracles of abundance go back to well before Christian times and are referred to in legends of magic cauldrons and fairy cups and vessels all over the world; they could never be drained of drink and everyone served from them would have whatever he wanted to eat or drink. At the risk of being thought literal-minded, we give our opinion that there may be grains of truth in these tales, but we also believe that these miraculous provisions must have come from somewhere. Being aware of the TELEPORTATION effect (see also MATERIALIZATION AND FLIGHT OF OBJECTS), and suspecting it to have been used by the old magicians and also, if

*(Left) The materialization of the Holy Grail, in Malory's* Morte d'Arthur*, brought each knight generous helpings of his favourite food and drink. Similar beliefs were held about the magical cups and cauldrons of fairies and witches. (Above) Among well-documented angelic transportations of the Host to the communicant's mouth is that of St Catherine of Siena (d. 1380).*

*(Above) Mosaic of loaves and fishes on the altar of the Church of the Multiplication, where Jesus worked the miracle. (Below) A modern Grail miracle (1975).*

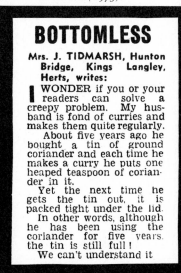

**BOTTOMLESS**

Mrs. J. TIDMARSH, Hunton Bridge, Kings Langley, Herts, writes:

I WONDER if you or your readers can solve a creepy problem. My husband is fond of curries and makes them quite regularly.

About five years ago he bought a tin of ground coriander and each time he makes a curry he puts one heaped teaspoon of coriander in it.

Yet the next time he gets the tin out, it is packed tight under the lid.

In other words, although he has been using the coriander for five years, the tin is still full!

We can't understand it

unconsciously, by more recent saints, we look around for corresponding stories of missing provisions. We could fill this book with accounts of food and other objects and living things which vanish from one place and appear in another. The world is busy with a constant toing and froing and in these sections we have only begun to hint at its extent and variety. Let us keep to the subject of the flour for the bread.

In FALLS OF CREATURES AND ORGANIC MATTER we mention cases of seeds, all of one kind, falling from the sky onto a specific area of land. These falls were seen and recorded. Imagine a fallow field that lies waiting for seed, like the empty ponds that yearn for fish (see SHOWERS OF FROGS AND FISHES), and an unobserved fall of seed which later sprouts. In 1919 there were two recorded instances of the mysterious appearance of a full field of wheat: the *Cardiff Evening News*, 1 July, said that in a field in Lincolnshire which had been fallow since its last crop of barley ten years before, there appeared a crop of wheat said to be finer than that in surrounding fields; and the London *Sunday Express*, 24 August, tells that after a drought had killed off a field of wheat near Ormskirk, Lancashire, the previous year, 'one of the best crops of vigorous young wheat' one farmer had ever seen had appeared without his re-seeding the field. We have looked for records of vanishing seeds, but this subject hardly merits the attention of the newspapers these days, if records are kept at all. In 1974 some farms in Worcestershire and Shropshire faced a bill of £2000. Their sugarbeet seeds had vanished in the fields and they blamed a plague of mice. Despite elaborate precautions, like flattening the furrows and laying poison, the seeds continued to vanish. The *Sunday Mercury*, 26 May 1974, said that the experts had tried all they could and remained baffled. Whether the mice were responsible there or not we don't know, but we have another modern tale of a phantom crop of wheat appearing unexpectedly. A farmer near Milan noticed the fine crop in a 2½ acre field. According to the *Daily Mirror*, 29 April 1968, this had happened several times in preceding years, and as soon as the crop ripened it vanished overnight despite careful watches on the field. We wonder if the grain ever materialized in some destitute convent's granary. Perhaps it was also miraculously threshed; we have many reports of strange falls of straw.

Legends of the ever-full cups of the fairies are continuous with stories of teleported wine in the lives of the saints. It is said that St Dominic, who died in 1221, blessed a cup of wine from which 26 people drank. It was then carried to a convent, where 104 nuns each swallowed a mouthful. It was returned to the saint still full.

# Materialization and flight of objects

In December 1894 a house on Lord Portman's estate at Durweston, Dorset, was the scene of inexplicable events. The residents told of objects rising into the air and being propelled toward their dwelling. The gamekeeper, Newman, investigated, and inside the house saw beads and a toy whistle come up and hit a window without breaking it. He decided to wait and see what developed, and later told this story to the Society for Psychical Research, which printed it in *Proceedings*, 1897–91:

'I sat down and was looking at the door opening into the garden; it was wide open leaving a space of 15 inches between it and the inner walls when I saw, coming from behind the door, a quantity of little shells. They came round the door from a height of about five feet, one at a time at intervals varying from half a minute to a minute. They came very slowly and when they hit me I could hardly feel them. With the shells two thimbles came so slowly that in the ordinary way they would have dropped long before they reached me. Both thimbles struck my hat. Some missed my head and went just past and fell down slanting-wise (*not* as if they were dropped). Those that struck me fell straight down.'

This suspension of the laws of motion and gravitation is by no means unique, especially in accounts of the activities of the so-called 'noisy spirits' (*Poltergeister*) who disturb domestic life by throwing furniture and utensils around. By

using this word we do not intend to commit ourselves to belief in the agency of a *Geist* or spirit. Though there may sometimes appear to be intelligence or purpose behind 'poltergeist' outbreaks, we are inclined to see them as evidence of some unrecognized universal force rather than of wilful persecution by ghosts and demons. This unidentified force offers the most exciting challenge to science, because it not only bypasses or appears to suspend what we think of as established laws of how matter should behave, but it also suggests a multiplicity of other universes beyond the causal one in which these 'known laws' are familiar to us. There are two peculiarities in Newman's story which particularly interest us: the materialization of objects (presumably from somewhere else), and their strange, slow flights through the air.

On the matter of strange flights of projectiles, apparently without projectors, we have many good reports of objects that fell or flew, either faster or slower than would normally be expected, often swerving to evade grasping hands. Professor Sir William Barrett addressed the Society for Psychical Research on this subject in 1911; and the Jesuit scholar Father Herbert Thurston, from a lifetime's study of the phenomenon, was moved to confirm this with many cases in his *Ghosts and Poltergeists*, 1953. For instance, he cites a case from Germany in 1718, in which 'On one occasion a large stone seemed to be

falling perpendicularly and with great velocity right on the minister's head. One of the maids who was looking on shrieked in terror, but the stone turned aside in full career, though at the cost of a pane of glass through which it passed into the court outside.'

As an instance of materialization, Thurston quotes a German pamphlet about a doctor whose house was virtually demolished in 1713 by a constant bombardment of missiles that became solid and visible seconds before they hit anything. During this harassment the doctor took to swiping about him with his sword, and once, upon re-sheathing it, found the scabbard stuffed full of dirt. A lengthy disturbance in 1928–29, involving the eight-year-old adopted son of an Indian family at Poona, was reported in *Psychic Research*, May 1930, by Miss H. Kohn, a teacher, who, with her sister, lodged with the family. One day both sisters counted some eggs into several baskets and shut them in a cupboard. Almost immediately an egg shot past the girls from the direction of the cupboard to smash on the floor. Looking in the cupboard, they found one egg missing. As they cleaned up the mess, another egg smashed nearby, and again an egg was missing from the baskets. Three more eggs suffered the same fate, and then one basket containing forty-two eggs vanished out of the cupboard and was never seen again. Several times the girls saw coins fall: 'At first we could not always see the coins in mid-air, but merely saw them fall, being startled by the contact of the coin with the floor. Soon, however, we were able to observe more closely, and actually saw the money appear in the air.' Compare this with our accounts of coin-falls in FALLS OF ARTIFACTS, in which there was no apparent poltergeist-type agency.

The term 'apport' is applied by the Spiritualists to the objects materialized at seances. To give a couple of unusual examples: Guy Lyon Playfair in *The Flying Cow* says that the famous Brazilian medium, Carlos Mirabelli, was asked to locate the missing remains of a woman who had died insane. A seance was held at which, according to the sworn testimony of Enrico de Goes, director of São Paulo Municipal Library, there was a foul smell of decomposition as numerous bones of human arms, legs and thorax fell on the heads of those present along with a gruesome rain of hair and other remains. More pleasantly, we note many instances of the materialization of flowers and living plants, some out of season at the time. The phenomenon is a stock item in the spiritualists' repertoire; and outside the seance-circle is the record of a blue marsh-land flower, said to have materialized from heaven and given to Alexandra David-Neel in mid-winter in Tibet (*My Journey to Lhasa*). Similarly,

it is recorded that appearances and falls of flowers were among the first of the miracles attributed to the modern saint Sai Baba.

Universally regarded as a spirit, the 'poltergeist' and its disturbances are commonly dealt with by exorcism. Sometimes this treatment is effective, yet the phenomenon is not always respectful of religious people and their rituals. Quite the reverse. The twelfth-century English saint, Godric, was pelted by all the moveables in his hermitage, including his Mass articles. In his *Itinerarium Kambriae*, Giraldus Cambrensis recorded a case in Pembrokeshire in 1184 in which a 'foul spirit' threw excrement at the exorcizing priests and ripped their vestments. Martin Luther was tormented by '*poleter geister*'; so was John Wesley; and both Barrett and Thurston mention many other incidents in which holy articles vanished, flew away or were otherwise disturbed by 'poltergeist' activity.

Charles Fort was inclined to replace the notion of poltergeists, angels, etc. with the less anthropomorphic concept of TELEPORTATION as a universal force responsible for many of the reported aberrations in normal reality. As an example we have the unequivocal passage by the Tudor annalist, Stowe, quoted by Harold T. Wilkins in *Strange Mysteries of Time and Space*, 1958, concerning a teleported clump of trees: 'On Sunday, 3 January 1582, in the valley of the Cerf Blanc, Dorset, a piece of earth suddenly quitted its place of former time, and was transferred forty yards to another paddock, in which there were alders and willows. It stopped the high road leading to Cerne. Yet the same hedges which surrounded it still enclose it today, and the trees that were there are still standing. The place this bit of land occupied is now a great hole.'

Such mysterious transplantations are reported of all manner of objects, creatures (see our various FALLS sections) and even human beings (see TELEPORTATION). About AD 1200, Gervase of Tilbury wrote in his *Otia imperialia* of a merchant from Bristol who lost his favourite knife over the side of his ship while on a far ocean. When he returned to port, his wife told him that one day, while she was sitting in her parlour, his knife fell in through the skylight and stuck in the table below. Both had kept a record of the disappearance and reappearance of the knife, and the times were found to be 'simultaneous'. Wilkins tells a modern version: the story of a man working on electric power-lines in a field at Brockworth, Gloucestershire, in February 1956. At lunchtime the man found to his annoyance that he had forgotten to pack a knife in his lunchbox. Suddenly he noticed a knife at his feet. It was a brand new table-knife which was not his and which he claimed had not been there seconds before. He kept it; and, Wilkins was told, on the man's death it vanished forever.

*(Left) An illustration from Harry Price's* Poltergeist over England *of the typical curving flights of unlikely objects, moving with a fine disregard for conventions. (Above) During Professor Zoellner's tests, at Leipzig University in 1877–78, on the American medium Henry Slade, these solid wooden rings, threaded on a sealed string, vanished to reappear on the central pillar of a table, apparently travelling through solid material. (Below) A rare photograph of a poltergeist in action (in France in 1955).*

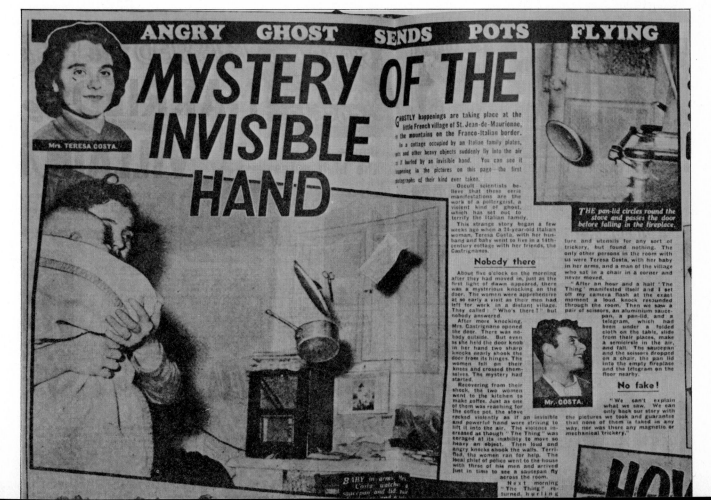

# Children brought up by animals

Several mythologies embody the theme of human children cared for by animals. Miletus of Crete, son of Apollo, is an example. It was once respectably believed that Romulus and Remus, founders of Rome, were suckled as infants by a wolf; but by the nineteenth century, during which there seems to have been a sort of competition among scholarly and scientific people to see how much of popular lore and old history could be discredited, such reports were regarded as fables, amusing for children but too absurd for the attention of serious people. Yet at the same time as they were being rationally proved impossible, more and more cases of humans fostered by animals kept being reported. Several were supported by good evidence and reliable witnesses. Finally in 1920 the carefully documented history of the wolf children of Midnapore (see below) convinced all but the wilfully sceptical that children may indeed be nurtured by wild animals.

We have many cases of children raised by wolves or bears, and less frequently by leopards, antelopes, goats, pigs, cattle and sheep. In all cases the children have acquired more or less permanently the natures, habits, abilities and even some of the physical features of their animal guardians. There is scarcely an example of a child taken from wild animals becoming fully reconciled to human ways, and the few who have managed to speak even a few words have invariably used them to express their preference for their old animal home above their present human one. It might therefore seem kinder not to force them away from their animal families – something which is often done for religious reasons in connection with theories of the human soul – but it is a strange fact that instances of feral children of more than about ten years old found among animals are rarely reported. Perhaps they fail the initiation test for adult life.

It is generally supposed that such children have been stolen or found abandoned by a mother animal in milk and adopted by her, but their remarkable physical abilities, their speed or strength in the case of antelope or bear children, and such features as the luminous, wolf-like eyes of, for example, the Midnapore children, have suggested another and (even to us) rather fantastic theory, that some are truly the children of animal parents, but monstrosities, corresponding to the known monstrous births of animal-like offspring to human mothers. Despite the evidence – or perhaps out of ignorance of it – many anthropologists are still unwilling to accept the phenomenon of the rearing of humans by animals, which does indeed have many unexplained aspects, and prefer to believe that all animal children are idiots who have been found wandering near the animals supposed to have fostered them. Autistic children often have characteristics in common with those taken from animal homes.

In his *Systema naturae*, 1758, the great systematizer, Linnaeus, identified the wild man, *Homo sapiens ferus*, as a sub-species of humanity (see WILD

*(Above) The she-wolf with Romulus and Remus. A detail from Rubens's painting. (Below) The crest of Stanley, Earl of Derby, features an ancestor brought up by an eagle. (Top, right) A boy adopted by a bear in 17th-century Poland; an Indian wolf-boy held in a Mission. (Right) Tissa, the Monkey Boy of Ceylon (1973).*

PEOPLE). He characterized him as 'four-footed, dumb and hairy', and cited as examples nine historical cases, among them the following:

Two little boys were seen by some hunters among a group of bears in the Lithuanian forests. They caught one of about nine years old, strong, healthy and handsome, and took him to Warsaw where he became the pet of the royal family and the nobility. He could not be taught to speak or to give up his bearish nature, but he did learn to raise his eyes and arms to heaven at the name of Jesus. Several times he escaped to the woods, and was once seen exchanging affectionate hugs with a wild bear notorious for having killed two people. There seems to have been a rash of bear children in Lithuania at the time. This first case was in 1661, and there are two others recorded in Dr Connor's *History of Poland*. One, taken in 1694, was seen by Connor himself, who found him unable to talk or walk upright, though he later acquired both arts imperfectly; another such captive had been inspected by a Dutch diplomat in Warsaw some years earlier.

It is strange that such a proverbially bad-tempered creature as the bear should be so tolerant of human cubs; yet it is credited with more adoptions than any other animal apart from the wolf. The most recent case was reported in *The American Weekly*, 5 September 1937. George Maranz, the writer of the article, 'Raised by a She-bear that Stole Her When a Baby', described his visit to a girl in a Turkish lunatic asylum who had just spent eight years with a bear family. One of a party of hunters near Mount Olympus had shot a she-bear and had been then violently attacked by a powerful little 'wood spirit'. Finally overcome, the spirit turned out to be a human child, though utterly bear-like in her voice, habits and physique. When Mr Maranz saw her, she was much the same as at her capture, though somewhat more docile, and starvation had made her accept cooked food. In 1767 hunters from Fraumark in lower Hungary were pursuing a large bear when they noticed human footprints in the snow in a part of the mountains where they thought no humans had ever before penetrated. These were followed to a bear's den, and there was discovered a real Goldilocks, a girl of about eighteen, tall, healthy and brown-skinned. Her behaviour was 'very crude', and when taken to an asylum she refused to eat anything but raw meat, roots and the bark of trees. Another bear-girl of about three years old was found in India in 1897, and a case of a bear-boy occurred early in the seventeenth century in Denmark.

Feuerbach in his book on Kaspar Hauser, 1833, gives a sad account of a pig-girl:

'Dr Horn . . . tells that he saw in the infirmary at Salzburg, but a few years ago, a girl of twenty-two years of age, and by no means ugly, who had been brought up in a hog-sty among the hogs, and who had sat there for many years with her legs crossed. One of her legs was quite crooked, she grunted like a hog, and her gestures were brutishly unseemly in a human dress.'

The first historical (i.e. of contemporary record) case of a wolf-boy occurred in Hesse in 1341. The boy, taken from the wolves by hunters, ran on all fours and leapt prodigiously, and died from being forced to take a civilized diet. Three years later in the same district a wolf-boy was captured and successfully educated, living on to the age of eighty. He said he had been adopted by wolves when three years old; they had fed him, sheltered him and taught him their ways, and he was very sorry to have been parted from them.

The majority of wolf-children recorded since the early nineteenth century have come from India, the jungles of Bengal in most cases. The best documented is the history of the Mid-

napore children, written by their discoverer and subsequent guardian, the Rev. J. Singh, and included in a book by (we are not kidding) Singh and Zingg, *Wolf-Children and Feral Man*, in which many of the cases here mentioned are quoted in detail. The Rev. Singh, a missionary of the Midnapore Orphanage, was in the habit of making regular evangelical trips to the aboriginal tribes of his district. On one such expedition in 1920, he was told of two little ghosts with blazing eyes that haunted a mound containing a wolf den some distance from a village, terrifying the villagers. Bravely he took a party to investigate. From a vantage point in a tree they observed the ghosts leaving the wolf den in company with the wolves. Mr Singh decided they were human and ordered the den to be dug out. Excavations began on 17 October. At the first strokes of the spade two wolves bolted out into the jungle. Then the mother wolf appeared and fiercely attacked the diggers. Before the Rev. Singh could intervene, one of them killed her with an arrow. Inside the den they found a ball of cubs, two wolves and two little girls, clinging together. One girl was about one and a half years old, the other about eight. The Rev. Singh took it as a nice compliment to the human species that the she-wolf should have been so pleased with the first little girl as to adopt a second. The wolf cubs were sold off by the Indians and the little girls dragged to the Orphanage. The younger died within a year, never speaking or walking upright; but the elder girl, lovingly cared for by Mrs Singh, survived her capture for nine years, during which she lost some of her animal nature and gradually learnt to stand, to eat civilized food and even to speak a few words.

The latest feral child to come to our attention is the 'sturdy' seven-year-old ape-boy found in the Central African Republic of Burundi in 1973; a colour photograph appeared in the London *Observer* magazine section, 28 March 1976. Two other cases came to light in

1973. In the London *Sunday Times*, 26 August 1973, a monkey-boy found in the jungles of northern Ceylon (see illustration) is compared with Rocco, a wolf-boy from the Abruzzi mountains of Italy, who 'is speechless, grunts in a half-wolf, half-goat way, and bites and claws at anyone who shows him affection'.

More interesting are two recent gazelle-boys. The *Sunday Times*, as above, describes one case: 'A Syrian "gazelle-child", discovered by a local prince on a hunting party, was said to be capable of running at 50 mph with the gazelles. He also had superb eyesight and very acute hearing.'

Another was reported in the London *Daily Mirror*, 1 February 1971. He was seen in the Spanish Sahara, not far from Río de Oro. He was said to move in leaps and bounds, though 'not as fast or as graceful as his companions'. Jean-Claude Armen, the distinguished (and kindly) anthropologist, reported to the Life Institute, Geneva: 'I have watched him approach gazelles and lick their foreheads in a sign of recognition'. A delightful book by Armen, *Gazelle Boy*, has recently been published. Apparently, despite attempts by American scientists to capture him, the boy is still at large.

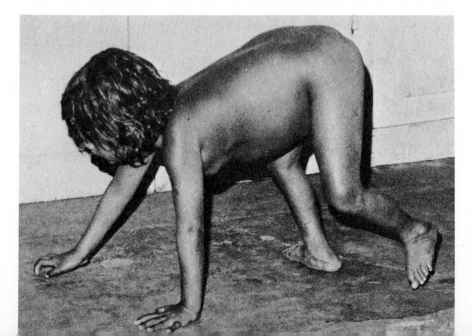

# Wild people

In September 1731 a formidable little figure strode into a French village to become one of the nine specimens classified by Linnaeus as *Homo sapiens ferus*. A book of that name by Räuber in 1888 describes her first dramatic appearance: 'A girl of nine or ten years, suffering from thirst, entered the village of Songy at dusk. The village is four or five leagues from Châlons in Champagne. Her feet were naked, her body was covered with rags and skins of animals. Instead of a hat she wore a piece of bottle-gourd on her head. She carried a club in her hand, and when someone in the village set a dog at her she gave it such a heavy blow on the head that the animal fell over dead at her feet.'

When finally captured and examined, she was found to have extra large thumbs which was attributed to her Tarzan style of swinging from tree to tree. Several hot baths revealed that her skin was white. Some even identified her as an Eskimo. She was speechless, but she ran and swam wonderfully and caught and ate small animals, also raw fish and – appropriately for a French wild girl – frogs. A remarkable feature in the case was that until recently she had had a wild companion, a young Negress, who continued to be seen in the neighbourhood but was never captured. She had quarrelled with this girl over an ornament they had found and had broken her head with her club. In later life, when she had learnt to talk, she could give no account of her previous existence apart from some vague remembrance of a large water animal and of having twice crossed the sea. For one brief period of her life she had been taken in by a woman who had given her some clothes; before that she had been naked.

Captivity damaged the wild girl in health and spirit. The food she was given made her teeth fall out, she was often ill and became worse through the bleedings ordered by the doctors to weaken her savage nature. She was no idiot. She was taught to speak and behave like a civilized female of the time, and she finally gratified her benefactors by becoming a nun in a Paris convent.

The mystery of how two wild girls, one a Negress, the other apparently an Eskimo, could suddenly appear in eighteenth-century France has never been solved. Yet this is no isolated case. Similar examples of *Homo sapiens ferus* have been recorded in every century and in every part of the world. Another French wild child was caught in the woods of Caunes, Department of Aveyron, on a date given in the language of metrication as 19 Thermidor of the year VIII, which we believe to be 7 August 1800. As in all such cases his appearance, behaviour and diet were entirely animal-like, but under the care of Dr Itard, whose book, *The Wild Boy of Aveyron*, was published in 1832, he eventually learnt to speak a little and lived on to the age of about forty. In the *American Weekly* of 27 October 1935 is an account of a wild boy found naked in the Salvador jungle. He was about five years old, lived off raw fruit and fish, and spent his nights in the trees to avoid predatory animals. A strange report from Suffolk is quoted from Grose's *Antiquities* in Lady Camilla Gurdon's *Suffolk Folklore*:

'A curious story relating to Orford is told by Ralph of Coggeshall (abbot of the monastery there in the early part of the thirteenth century). Some fishermen on this coast (AD 1161) caught in their nets one stormy day a monster resembling a man in size and form, bald-headed, but with a long beard. It was taken to the Governor of Orford Castle, and kept there for some time, being fed on raw flesh and fish, which it "pressed with its hand" before eating. The soldiers in the Castle used to torture the unhappy monster in divers fashions "to make him speak"; and on one occasion, when it was taken to the sea to disport itself therein, it broke through a triple barrier of nets and escaped. Strange to say, not long afterwards it returned of its own accord to its captivity; but at last, "being wearied of living alone, it stole away to sea and was never more heard of". A tradition of this monster, known as "the wild man of Orford", still exists in the village.'

There seems no reason to doubt the genuineness of this report. The incident would still have been a living memory at the time Abbot Ralph was writing, and the behaviour of the wild man was in character with others of his kind, as also was the uncomprehending way in which he was treated. When it comes to explanations, however, we are no wiser than the Orford people of the time. Perhaps their visitor was a sealion-man or a were-seal or an old sea god or a teleported Finn or a lunatic fisherman. We are not happy with these or any other explanations for the repetitive wild man phenomenon, and we sympathize with Linnaeus, who, avoiding all explanations, dealt with the problem by classifying, as a separate order, THE WILD PEOPLE.

The existence of wild people in the forests and waste places was commonly recognized throughout the Middle Ages. Known as 'woodwoses', they figure in Gothic carving and heraldic ornament. A supporter on the arms of the Earl of Atholl of the Murray family is a woodwose in chains, commemorating

The wild man in chains, supporting the arms of the Earl of Atholl, represents an actual wild man captured on the family estates by a 17th-century ancestor.

the capture of a wild man among the rocks of Craigiebarns by a seventeenth-century Murray who was rewarded with the hand of the Atholl heiress and the succession to the title. The wild or green man of the woods is frequently displayed on inn signs. At Sproughton in Suffolk the Wild Man Inn, built in the sixteenth century, was named after a wild man who terrified the builders in a nearby waste. From the same county comes the well-known but inexplicable report by an old chronicler, William of Newburgh, of two children, a boy and a girl, greenish in colour and eating only beans, who suddenly appeared in a field near Woolpit, having apparently emerged from some underground workings there. Their story was that they came from a place called St Martin; they had been watching their father's sheep when they had heard a loud noise, and the next thing they knew was that they were mysteriously in the fields of Woolpit.

Charles Fort was a great collector of wild man reports. In Lo! he quotes from the New York Times of 19 January 1888 an account of five wild men and one wild girl who appeared in Connecticut on about the first day of that year; and he claimed to have records of no less than ten wild men in England during the winter of 1904–05. One of them, of unknown origin, appeared naked in the streets of Cheadle, Cheshire, and was decently placed in a sack by a policeman and dragged off to the police station. Another carried a book with drawings and writings in an unknown language, and speaking the same unknown language himself. His case is reported in the East Anglian Daily Times of 12 January 1905. There was a report in the Chatham News, 10 January 1914, that in bitterly cold weather a man was found running naked about Chatham High Street. He was arrested, but like a true Homo ferus could give no account of himself. He appeared suddenly, he was unknown, he was declared insane.

Fort regarded these wild men appearances in much the same way as he regarded showers of fishes and frogs. Wild men, like falling fishes, must come from somewhere, and both these phenomena, so Fort suggested, were due to a mysterious force in nature which he was the first person in modern times to identify and name: the force of TELEPORTATION. His idea was that there may be a relationship, as of one end of a tube to another, between the places where people inexplicably vanish and the places where 'wild men', in states of shock, trance or amnesia, suddenly turn up. Thus, in every case of a strange appearance, one should look for another of a strange disappearance. In one of his outrageous fantasies, Fort looked forward to the day when the workings of teleportation would be understood and made use of to transmit not merely occasional frogs or wild men but people and goods from one part of the earth – or universe – to another.

One modern piece of evidence has since emerged to support Fort's view of the origin of wild men. In our TELE-PORTATION section reference is made to a young Brazilian, José António da Silva. It is recorded that after being set down near Vitória, miles from the spot from which he had mysteriously vanished some four days earlier, his first impulse was to retire into the woods and to live off the wildlife.

# Werewolves

Werewolves are people who turn into wolves and then back into men again. We are not doctors, but we believe this sort of thing is physiologically impossible. If we were lawyers, however, we should have no option but to believe in werewolves because of the vast amount of legal precedent for convicting and executing the creatures. Evidence against people accused of transforming themselves into savage animals and committing crimes while in that shape has often been given by unanimous witnesses of good repute, firmly convinced from personal experience of the accused's ability to assume animal form. On the one hand werewolves are impossible; on the other they actually occur. Here again is a phenomenon which can not be reconciled with any rational system of explanation.

The most direct evidence of werewolves is from people who have actually seen the transformation taking place. One of these was said to be Pierre Mamor, a fifteenth-century Rector of the University of Poitiers in France, whose writing on the subject is quoted in the Rev. Montague Summers's book, *The Werewolf*. The learned Mamor contributes a disgusting story of a peasant's wife in Lorraine who saw her husband at table vomit up a child's arm and hand which he had devoured while in the form of a wolf. This event is explained by Mamor as a 'demoniacal illusion', because his theory is that werewolves are actual wolves possessed by the spirits of men, whose bodies meanwhile are safely hidden away, all this being the work of evil demons. This theory does not account for such cases as the one recorded in Olaus Magnus's *Historia de gentibus septentrionalibus*, 1555, as having happened some years earlier. A nobleman's wife was heard by her slave to deny the possibility of men becoming wolves. The slave disagreed and proved her wrong by there and then making the transformation. He was at once set upon by dogs but managed to shake them off and flee away in wolf's shape after they had torn out one of his

eyes. The next day the slave appeared, human but one-eyed. A more recent account is quoted in C. Dane's *The Occult in the Orient*. In 1960 Mr Harold M. Young, a former official in the Burmese administration and at the time proprietor of the zoo at Chiengmai, Thailand, was hunting in the Lahu mountains near the Burmese-Thai frontier when he encountered one of the locally dreaded 'taws', a jungle werewolf. Entering a village he was told there was a taw nearby. A shriek was heard, and Mr Young ran over to a hut where in the bright moonlight he saw the taw chewing the neck of a dying woman. He raised his gun and shot the beast in the flank, but it escaped into the jungle, leaving a trail of blood. In the morning Young and others followed the trail which led out into the jungle and then back to the village to a hut, in which they discovered a man with a bullet wound in his side.

This modern account repeats in detail the classical werewolf story which recurs in all times and places with remarkable consistency. We do not know what happened to Mr Young's taw, and we pass on the story at second hand, but we have direct evidence of the careers and

fates of many European werewolves from the most satisfactory sources, the contemporary reports of their trials. In December 1521 two French peasants, Burgot and Verdun, were accused at Poligny of a long series of cannibalistic murders committed by them while in the shape of wolves. Both confessed. Burgot said that he had long been in the service of the devil and had extended his activities to shape-shifting with the encouragement of Verdun, who was a practising werewolf and a member of a witches' coven. Verdun was the more agile of the two and could change his shape with his clothes on, while Burgot had to strip naked and be rubbed with werewolf ointment which they obtained from their diabolist superiors. This special ointment for effecting transformations is often referred to in these cases. Montague Summers suggests it was composed of such bewitching drugs as belladonna, aconite, hemlock or henbane. Whatever it was, its influence on Burgot and Verdun was bestial. They attacked and devoured many locals until Verdun was wounded by an armed traveller, who followed the bloody wolf-spoor to a hovel where Verdun was having his wound bandaged by his wife. Both men were executed together with another local werewolf, and it is said that portraits of all three were to be seen in the Jacobin church at Poligny.

Throughout the sixteenth century werewolves were rampant in Europe. So many of those caught and burnt in France during that period were also practising witches, and claimed to have learnt the art of transformation from others of their coven, that we suspect some traditional magic ritual was involved, inherited from ancient times and still active in remote districts of Europe almost to the present. Many of the classical authors on the subject of werewolves refer to this traditional knowledge. In eleventh-century Ireland it was the practice of the inhabitants of Ossory always to have two of their people in the shape of wolves, each pair serving seven years. Giraldus Camb-

(*Top left*) *Werewolves in battle from Olaus Magnus's* Historia de gentibus, *1555.*
(*Bottom left*) *The grisly symptoms of lycanthropy, whose sufferers behave like ravening beasts.* (*Above*) *Goya's painting of the ritual transformation of men into beasts.* (*Right*) *The werewolf lives on in science fiction and horror comics. This specimen is from the film* The Werewolf of London.

rensis, who gives this information in his *Topographica hibernica*, tells of an Irish priest who spoke with one of these Ossory werewolves in 1182. He was on a journey between Ulster and Meath, passing the night in the woods, when he was approached by a large wolf who explained his circumstances and asked the priest to come and bless his dying wife. The priest was unwilling to extend religious privileges to a she-wolf, but the wolf reassured him by pulling back his wife's wolfskin and revealing an old woman beneath it.

Fort on werewolves: 'I think that the idea of werewolves is most silly, degraded, and superstitious: therefore I incline toward it respectfully.' From the *Cornhill Magazine*, October 1918, Fort quotes the experience in northern Nigeria of a Captain Shott, DSO. Hyenas had been raiding a native village. Hunters who followed their tracks were surprised to find that at a certain point the animal prints gave way to human ones. One night Captain Shott's party wounded a particularly large beast, shooting off its jaw. The trail of blood was followed to another village where next day a man died of a terrible wound. His jaw had been torn off.

Reports of werewolves from all times and continents are innumerable, and so

are were-tigers, foxes, hares, bears, cats and weasels, enough to fill an alternative menagerie. The phenomenon as experienced is as well established as anything could be. What everyone wants to know, of course, is whether the transformation from man to animal takes place in actual fact, in defiance of the doctors, or whether it is an illusion affecting the senses of both the person transformed and the people who see him (some light is shed on the matter of physical transformation in BODILY ELONGATION). It may make little difference to a man having his throat torn out by something which looks and behaves like a wolf whether the creature is actually a wolf or merely seems like one, but this question has been disputed by the learned from very early times. Paracelsus thought the change was actual and physical, taking the magical view that the power of human will and imagination could be concentrated to affect external reality through the medium of the spiritual substance of the universe. Other authorities disagreed, explaining the phenomenon as an effect of drugs, magic or 'glamour'. They in turn were contradicted by Sponde in 1583, who reasoned that 'if a herb and the power of evil can have such control over the higher part of man, his reason

and his immortal soul, why can not man's body be subject to similar disturbances?' An old explanation, put forward as early as the second century AD by the Roman medical writer Marcellus Sidetes, is in terms of the unpleasant affliction known as lycanthropy, whose victims become convinced that they are savage wolves and behave accordingly; though whether it is, as Marcellus thought, a 'species of melancholy', to be treated with cold baths and a diet of curds and whey, or whether it is a form of diabolic possession, as Summers and many others have believed, is a question which may never finally be resolved. In any case the lycanthropy theory accounts for only one half of the werewolf phenomenon, the delusion of the werewolf himself, and says nothing about the delusions of the witnesses who see him in his wolf's form. The same objection of incompleteness can be brought against other popular explanations in terms of self-hypnosis and the ritual wearing of animal skins. The Viking 'berserkers' wore bear skins while transforming themselves into savage killers by invoking the spirits of beasts, and members of the secret leopard-men societies, still active in east Africa, practise the same sort of rites. A certain Mr K., whose story is quoted, though without reference to its original source, in *Fate and Fortune* magazine, no. 6, was present early this century at a ritual in Orissa, India, where a local youth was transformed before his very eyes into a were-tiger. It is impossible to understand the effectiveness of these ritual transformations through any of the part-explanations already mentioned, such as lycanthropy, hypnosis or illusions created by the wearing of make-up and animal skins. Not that we reject any of these; we accept them all, in combination with other causes, as contributing towards the production of a magical effect which, whatever the degree of physical reality one may choose to attribute to the transformation, has a terrible reality indeed to the man who seems to change into a savage beast and to all who come within the sphere of his activities.

While browsing through the werewolf literature we came across the following item in Frank Hamel's *Human Animals*, and we include it here as of particular interest to Forteans. In July, 1603 there was a heavy hailstorm which wrecked the fruit trees in the French district of Douvres and Jeurre. With the hail appeared mysteriously three large wolves. As is characteristic of werewolves they had no tails, and they passed through a flock of goats and cattle without harming them; on which account it was locally said that they were magicians who had come to inspect the damage caused by the storm they had raised.

# Family retainers, weird and ominous

Viscount Gormanston is a very charming and handsome man, but even his best friends do not deny that he does look a little like a fox. Foxes run in his family. There is one running on the Gormanston crest, and another, erect, supports the coat of arms. It is also a matter of repeated record that when the Viscount Gormanston of the day is on his death bed, foxes gather round the castle to honour the passing of one whom they evidently regard as their human representative.

In the *New Ireland Review* for April 1908 is an account of events at Gormanston Castle on the night of 8 October the previous year, when Jenico, the fourteenth Viscount, was dying in Dublin. At 8 p.m. the gardener and coachman saw about a dozen foxes lurking about the castle and its chapel. They were barking and 'crying'. Two days later, at three in the morning, Jenico's son, Richard Preston, was in the chapel watching over his father's body. Outside he heard stealthy footsteps, whimperings and scratchings. He opened a side door and saw a large fox sitting just outside. There was another one behind it, and others could be heard in the bushes. Preston then went to the end door of the chapel, opened it, and there were two more foxes, one so close he could have kicked it. For two hours the foxes continued to haunt the chapel and then suddenly departed.

Earlier records of the Gormanston foxes are summarized in *True Irish Ghost Stories*:

'When Jenico, the twelfth Viscount, was dying in 1860, foxes were seen about the house and moving towards the house for some days previously. Just before his death three foxes were playing about and making a noise close to the house.... The Hon. Mrs Farrell states as regards the same that the foxes came in pairs into the demesne, and sat under the Viscount's bedroom window, and barked and howled all night. Next morning they were found crouching about in the grass in front and around the house. They walked through the poultry and never touched them. After the funeral they disappeared.

'At the death of Edward, the thirteenth Viscount, in 1876, the foxes were also there. He had been rather better one day, but the foxes appeared, barking under the window, and he died that night contrary to expectation.'

There is something about these Gormanston foxes which makes them seem more like werefoxes than natural ones. The incident in which they passed harmlessly through the poultry is like the story of the strange wolves at the end of our WEREWOLVES section. In many of the cases in our collection of family death omens, the office is performed by something other than a natural living creature. There is a merging here between animals and wraiths. At the death of a Scanlon of Ballyknockane, County Limerick, strange lights appear to illuminate their residence and have always so appeared ever since the time of a seventeenth-century Scanlon who was King of Ossory. They were last seen in 1913. Many other pedigree Irishmen are warned of their deaths by the moanings or apparitions of that dread female spectre, the Banshee. In England we hear of knocks. According to Dr Plot's seventeenth-century *Natural History of Oxfordshire*, a death in the family of Wood at Brize Norton was always preceded by 'knockings on doors, tables, or shelves'; the Cumberfords of Cumberford Hall were similarly affected by rappings, while the Burdets foretold the end of one of their number by a drumming sound issuing for several weeks from their chimneys. From other sources we are informed that the Roman Catholic Middletons of Yorkshire see a ghostly Benedictine nun before dying, and that the Breretons are similarly advised by a mysterious tree trunk floating in the lake before their mansion.

Returning to living creatures, real or spectral, as family death omens: a white owl performs this service to the Westropp family in Ireland, its last recorded appearance being in 1909; the Arundels of Wardour were also warned by owls, two remarkably large ones which perched ominously on the battlements

of their castle; and the Cliftons of Nottinghamshire had as their death omen a rare sturgeon swimming up the Trent past Clifton Hall. In the ancestral park of the Ferrers family of Chartley near Lichfield dwelt – and maybe still dwells – an ancient herd of white cattle. To the Ferrers the birth of a black calf into this herd was fatal. The *Staffordshire Chronicle* of July 1835 gives details:

'The decease of the seventh Earl Ferrers and of his Countess, and of his son, Viscount Tamworth, and of his daughter, Mrs William Jolliffe, as well as the deaths of the son and heir of the eighth Earl and of his daughter, Lady Francis Shirley, were each preceded by the ominous birth of the fatal-hued calf. In the spring of 1835 a black calf appeared at Chartley, and before long the beautiful countess, second wife of the eighth Earl, lay on her death-bed.'

The see of Salisbury is not an hereditary post, but its incumbent inherits a family death omen. When a Bishop of Salisbury is dying, white birds are seen on Salisbury Plain. They are unusual. Kathleen Wiltshire describes them: 'They are large birds like albatrosses, with dazzling white wings which do not move as they fly.' The first recorded incident was in 1414. The Bishop of Salisbury died abroad, attending the Council of Constance. A great flock of strange white birds descended on the roof of the hall where he lay in state and stayed all night making harsh noises. It was called 'a great sign of the birds'.

Miss Moberly, the Bishop's daughter, saw the white birds fly up out of the Palace gardens as her father lay dying in 1885. Again, on 15 August 1911, Miss Edith Olivier, returning from a village choir outing near Salisbury, saw two curious white birds, flying but not moving their wings. She knew nothing of the bird-bishop connection at that time, but on reaching home she was told that Bishop Wordsworth had suddenly died. Her report of the white birds was then recognized as the conventional omen.

Quite the best and longest-documented history of a family haunted at times of death by a particular creature relates to the white bird of the Oxenhams. The origin of this family's connection with their white bird is lost in antique mists. An old country ballad in Devonshire tells of Sir James Oxenham preparing for the wedding of his daughter, Margaret. In the background is a jilted lover. Sir James gives a banquet. A white bird appears and Sir James shudders at the omen which, even in those legendary times, was long known in the family. Next day Margaret and her bridegroom stand at the altar. The jilted lover steps forward, stabs her and then himself. As she dies the white bird flies through the church.

The first historical record of the white bird was just before the death of Grace Oxenham in 1618. Twenty-three years later her son, James, published a tract, shown on this page, about the circumstances of certain recent deaths in his family. His son, John, aged twenty-two, had suddenly died two days after a bird with a white breast had appeared in his room and hovered over the bed. Five days later, on 7 September 1635, James Oxenham's wife, Thomasine, fell ill, saw the white bird and died; the same thing happened soon afterwards to her little sister, Rebecca, aged eight, and on 15 September Thomasine's infant daughter also died, the ominous bird having previously been seen in her bedroom. James Howell in *Familiar Letters*, 1646, claims that he saw in a London stonemason's a marble slab about to be sent into Devonshire, with an inscription that 'John Oxenham, Mary his sister, James his son, and Elizabeth his mother, had each the appearance of such a bird fluttering about their beds as they were dying.'

Up to 1873 the white bird was still faithful and active. On 15 December of that year Mr G. N. Oxenham died in Kensington. According to a statement by his nephew, the Rev. Henry, reproduced in F. G. Lee's *Glimpses of the Supernatural*, flutterings were heard in the dying man's chamber, and a week before his death there was an odd incident when his daughter and a friend, who knew nothing of the family tradition, heard a commotion, opened the window and saw a strange bird, like a pigeon but larger and white, perched on a bush just outside. Some workmen were trying to drive it away by throwing their hats at it. In Dr Mogridge's *Descriptive Sketch of Sidmouth* is an account of the death of old Mr Oxenham of Sidmouth in the second decade of the nineteenth century. Just before he died, the couple who waited on him, a gardener and his wife, saw a white bird fly in at the door, pass over Mr Oxenham's bed and disappear into one of the drawers of his writing-desk.

(*Far left*) Lord Gormanston and family fox crest (*see text*). (*Below left*) Appearances of the white bird of the Oxenham family, 1641 (*see text*). (*Above*) On the coat of arms of the Duke of Argyll is the fatal galley that attends the death of the senior Campbell. Details p. 64.

We had intended to compare this sort of thing with various anthropological phenomena such as totemism and tribal affinities with animals, hoping thus to provide some reasonable background for our collection of family death omens. But there are certain aspects of this family-animal connection which defy comparisons and hint at the existence of some guiding – or occasionally interfering – principle behind life on earth, some principle which, whatever its other qualities, is certainly not lacking in a sense of humour. There is an old Border family called Herries. Their crest is a hedgehog because, say the heralds, it is a pun on their name, *hérisson* meaning hedgehog in French. Somehow this joke has penetrated to the hedgehogs themselves, for whenever a Herries is dying the little creatures turn up in droves to haunt his dwelling.

The Fowlers are an ancient family, and ever since the time of the Crusades their crest has been an owl. The following story was told to Mr William Fowler of Cumberland by his father; we quote from Kathleen Wiltshire's *Ghosts and Legends of the Wiltshire Countryside*. It is a story which tends to confirm our notion that there is a sense of humour abroad, that the guiding or interfering principle referred to above enjoys the sort of joke that the superior among us might find rather infantile.

'The Reverend W. W. Fowler, a canon of Lincoln, retired to a rectory in Wiltshire to write a book on ornithology. On the day he died, all the owls in the neighbourhood seemed to have gathered around his house, perching on the roof, gareposts, pinnacles, or any convenient place. There they remained till he was dead, when they all disappeared. On the day of the funeral, however, when the coffin was being carried under the lychgate to the church, a large white barn owl swooped down, almost touching the coffin before disappearing into the large yew trees in the churchyard.'

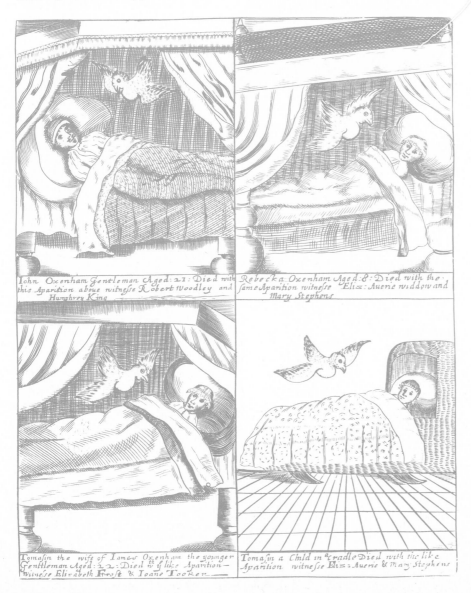

Iohn Oxenham Gentleman Aged: 21: Died with this Aparition aboue witnesse Robert Woodley and Humphrey King

Rebecka Oxenham Aged: 8: Died with the same Aparition witnesse Eliz: Auerie widdow and Mary Stephens

Tomasin the wife of Iames Oxenham the younger Gentleman Aged: 22: Died wth if like Aparition witnesse Elizabeth Frost & Ioane Tooker

Tomasin a Child in cradle Died with the like Aparition witnesse Eliz: Auerie & Mary Stephens

# Little people

If we were to write a history of Europe from a phenomenal angle, drawing our material from contemporary records of the things people experience in different ages, part of the general pattern of events would be that from the earliest time there was intimate contact between our race and another, more diminutive and less material; that the link between the two peoples gradually weakened; and that the smaller race retreated from areas of human habitation into the wilder regions, finally retiring into the upper atmosphere from which they now and then descend on brief visits, transporting themselves in luminous discs or globe-shaped vessels.

The 'fairy' phenomenon, which was still quietly active even through the darkest days of rationalist scepticism, made a remarkable come-back in the middle of the twentieth century. The little people who, by unanimous report, played an intrusive part in daily life up to the Middle Ages, had long been dwindling from their accustomed haunts when suddenly they reappeared, airborne and technologized (being traditionally fond of aping their human contemporaries) and up to all their same old tricks. We refer of course to the 'UFO people'.

Customs until recently surviving show how close and balanced was formerly the relationship between our people and the other race. We read of saucers of milk placed outside the door at night, fairy ground preserved uncultivated, and fairy paths kept clear of houses and obstructions; and from the other side rewards and good luck to men who respected fairy ways. The decline in this state of affairs is generally agreed to have been due in the first instance to the activities of Christian exorcists, the zealous friars and 'limetours' who penetrated into every part of the country blessing houses, barns, woods and streams. 'This maketh that there bin no fairies,' explains Chaucer.

'For thir as wont to walken was an elf,
Thir walketh now the limetour himself.'

Dr Ingram, a famous preacher who died in 1879 at the age of 103, is said to have driven the last of the trows, the local fairies, out of the Shetland Islands, forcing them to migrate to the Faroes. John Nicholson, author of *Some Folk-Tales and Legends of Shetland*, was told this by an islander who had it direct from an old trow-woman, too feeble or obstinate to make the journey with the rest of her race. Yet if we are to believe Mr W. E. Thorner of Luton, Bedfordshire, whose letter is printed in Marwick's *The Folklore of Orkney and Shetland*, the trows of the northern isles are not quite extinct. Mr Thorner, who spent some time in the Orkneys during the Second World War, came across a party of them one stormy winter's day on the high cliffs of Hoy. There were about a dozen of them, 'wild men' with sallow complexions and long dark hair, small in stature with unkindly looks on their faces. They were dancing.

These creatures would have fitted in well with the theory put forward by David MacRitchie in 1890 that the fairy Fin Folk of northern Scotland, and fairies in general, were memories of actual Finns or Eskimos or some other small aboriginal race. If so, it would explain the unkindly looks directed at Mr Thorner. John Buchan wrote a terrifying story on this theme about a man kidnapped in Scotland by a troglodyte tribe of left-over Picts. Such a survival into the present day would seem an unlikely explanation for modern 'little men' reports, particularly since they have taken to space travel. Yet, come to think of it, the fairies' craftmanship was always known to be more delicate than human work and their knowledge of natural science profounder. As evidence of this is the exquisite glass vessel, the Luck of Edenhall, taken from the fairies by a butler to the Musgrave family of Cumberland and preserved by them (now in the Victoria and Albert Museum, London). There is also in the Royal Irish Academy, Dublin, an ancient medical treatise which was presented by the fairies to a Connemara man whom they took away to their land of Hy Brasil and later restored to his people, having initiated him into all the secrets of medicine. With the skills generally attributed to them, there seems no reason why fairy technology should not be equal to constructing the aerial globes in which the little people are now so commonly reported to travel.

We take this fairy-UFO connection seriously. The 'little man' phenomenon is too well documented in times both ancient and modern to be unfounded; and we can not sympathize with the folklorists of an older generation who delighted in hearing quaint expressions of the fairy faith from unlettered rustics while ignoring or disdaining any repetitions of the same 'superstition' in a modern context. The academic world today has inherited their prejudice, and it has therefore been left to the post-war school of writers on flying saucers and allied enigmas to record phenomena which, had they been experienced a

(Left) A most curious exhibit in the Museum of Antiquities, Edinburgh, is the cache of 'fairy coffins', delicately made and containing dressed, wooden effigies, discovered in a cleft below Arthur's Seat in 1836. Some had rotted almost away, from which it was thought that a series of burials had been made over many years. (Above) One of the fairy photographs taken by two young Yorkshire girls which excited Conan Doyle, who investigated the case in 1920, to announce 'the coming of the fairies' (see text). (Below) Traditional view of mound-dwelling little folk.

(Below) Objects of fairy origin are preserved in many family and museum collections. They include several chalices shamefully acquired in the manner here illustrated.

couple of hundred years ago, would now be proudly displayed in the scholarly folklorist's cabinet of curiosities. For modern accounts of fairies and the like we must turn to such books as Charles Bowen's *The Humanoids*, 1969, or *Flying Saucer Occupants*, 1967, by C. and J. Lorenzen, or a recent book, *The Unidentified*, 1975, by Clark and Coleman, where a common phenomenal source for both the fairy and the UFO legend is emphasized.

In the second of these books we can select from some fifty reported encounters with 'little men' in the 1950s and 1960s, and as many more with other types of fairyland creatures, each one associated with a spherical or disc-shaped airship, and all described in detail by named witnesses. To quote just one example, at noon on 20 August 1965 an engineer, Alberto Ugarte, his wife and another man were visiting Inca ruins near Cuzco, Peru, when they saw a shiny disc, only about five feet in diameter, come down from the sky and land on an ancient stone terrace. Some little creatures, described as of strange shape and dazzling brightness, stepped out of the craft, but seeing people they climbed back in and departed.

Evidence of the actual existence of a fairy race is deficient in only one respect. Considering the number of contacts reported there are very few material souvenirs. Certain objects, like the cup and the medical treatise mentioned above, are alleged to have been received direct from the little people, and there are many instances of scorched or flattened grass or depressions in the ground discovered at the spots where their craft have been seen to land. Finds have been reported, but rarely substantiated, of tiny bones unearthed at fairy burial grounds. Adjacent to Lewis in the Outer Hebrides is the Little Isle of Pigmies, which local tradition claims as the former residence and graveyard of the little people. The Rev. Dean Monro dug there in the sixteenth century and found

miniature skulls and bones. In 1630 Captain John Dymes dug. He also found bones and skulls, but decided they were too small to be human, which seems to us to be rather begging the question. Early this century the Hebridean historian Mackenzie dug at the same spot and found bones, but his bones were of sea fowl and small mammals and he explained earlier finds in terms of these, presuming that the pigmy legend was based on the inability of the locals to distinguish between skeletons of familiar birds and of humanoids.

Photographs purporting to show fairies and such are generally few and poor, but one case is exceptional. In the Christmas number of *Strand Magazine*, 1920, Sir Arthur Conan Doyle, who spent his royalties from the Sherlock Holmes stories on psychical research, announced an event so sensational as to 'mark an epoch in human thought'. Printed with the article were photographs of two young girls with elves and fairies. Their names, not disclosed at the time, were Elsie Wright of 31 Lynwood Terrace, Cottingley, near Bingley, Yorkshire, and her cousin, Frances Griffiths. Behind 31 Lynwood Terrace was a fairy glen. The girls liked to play there, making friends with its tiny inhabitants, and when Elsie was sixteen and her cousin ten, in the summer of 1917, she borrowed her father's camera to photograph them. They obtained some fine portraits. Photographic experts could find no fault with them, and the circumstances in which they were taken seemed to exclude the possibility of fraud. Frauds however they must be, said other experts, because, since fairies do not exist, no honest camera could take pictures of them. At that time, of course, Ted Serios (see PROJECTED THOUGHT FORMS) was unknown. A tough reporter from the *Westminster Gazette* was sent to Yorkshire to track the girls down and expose them. He found them and their family radiating honesty, and retired baffled. A friend of Sir Arthur's, Mr Edward Gardner, also went to Yorkshire with a camera and marked photographic plates. The girls took this equipment to the glen and came back with more fairy photographs. The most stringent examination of both photographs and photographers has ever since failed to support any other conclusion but that both were genuine. Proclaiming 'The Coming of the Fairies' in a book of that name, Conan Doyle wrote:

'It is hard for the mind to grasp what the ultimate results may be if we have actually proved the existence on the surface of this planet of a population which may be as numerous as the human race, which pursues its own strange life in its own strange way, and which is only separated from ourselves by some difference of vibration.'

# Lake monsters and sea-serpents

The mode of existence illustrated in these sections relates to what we call phenomenal reality. In this category we place all those sights, visions, experiences and happenings which recur repeatedly over long periods of time yet continually elude scientific analysis. Elusiveness is the significant feature of such things, the feature which links such apparently disparate phenomena as the unidentified objects which people see in the sky and the serpentine monsters which people see in lakes and oceans.

These water monsters are curious indeed. By all accounts – and there are good accounts from people of undoubted good faith and mental health – large unknown creatures exist in lakes all over the world as well as in the sea. Yet modern science, which claims to have studied and classified almost every form of life, however rare or microscopic, has found no physical evidence at all of such creatures, no body, bone, tissue or any other relic. There are photographs which, together with the reports of many excellent witnesses, prove that aquatic monsters are *seen*, but there is nothing to prove they physically *exist*. In the same way we have indisputable records of ghostly apparitions seen and even photographed, but nothing for the laboratory. We find this comparison significant, and though nothing imaginable is impossible, we feel that the chances of seeing the Loch Ness Monster drawn through the streets of Inverness are about the same as of seeing any other phantom thus paraded.

No doubt lake and sea monsters exist, phenomenally. They are reported both inland and offshore from Scotland, Ireland, Scandinavia, Canada, Africa, New Zealand, everywhere indeed where there is accommodation for them – and even where there is not. One of the objections raised by biologists to the Loch Ness Monster is that the Loch is too small to support a colony of such creatures. Yet there are many lakes much smaller than Ness where the evidence of monsters is equally good. Captain Leslie spent years investigating the legendary and still commonly reported monsters of Connemara in the west of Ireland, denizens of lakes no more than half a mile long. On 16 October 1965 he set off an explosion in Lough Fadda and was rewarded with the sight of a monstrous shape threshing about in the water about fifty yards offshore. In the same lake in 1954 the librarian at Clifden, County Galway,

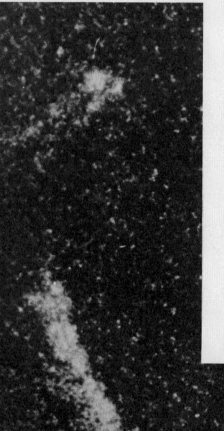

Miss Georgina Carberry, together with three friends, had been terrified by the sight of a great black serpentine monster which swam with open mouth to within twenty yards of them. F. W. Holiday in his book on phenomenal creatures, *The Dragon and the Disc*, 1973, describes his investigations at small Irish lakes, scarcely more than ponds, such as Lough Nahooin near Clifden whose dimensions are only some hundred by eighty yards yet which has a record of monster sightings. Holiday, one of the most perceptive of 'monster' writers, draws attention to the paradox behind the whole affair:

'Although everything suggested that Peistes [the old Irish name for phantom lake creatures] were indigenous to these lakes there was nothing to indicate what they ate. Nahooin contained a stable population of small brown trout. However to suppose that a creature the size of a crocodile lurked in the pool and fed on these fish was obviously nonsense. The fish would have been cleared out in a few days.'

The 'SURREY PUMA' has the same ability to live in the country though apparently not off it. Holiday points to another curious feature of the Loch Ness Monster investigation which the UFO spotters have also noticed. The phenomenon seems purposefully to evade the photographer, or photographs do not develop or mysteriously vanish, or the camera was left in the car. The only good cine-camera sequence of the Ness creature, taken in the 1930s by a Dr McRae, has never been shown publicly or to experts. Then there is the curious ill luck which dogs the Loch Ness Investigation Bureau. In all the years since 1965, when its observation post was set up to keep continuous watch over the Loch for six

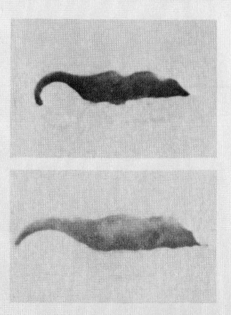

months in the year, nothing very remarkable has been recorded. Yet at the same spot in 1964 there were two good sightings by multiple witnesses. In 1965 the Monster showed itself on the one day the Bureau's camera was out of order, and on another occasion in 1970 it appeared minutes after the observer had packed up for the evening. In 1971 Tim Dinsdale, an enthusiastic monster hunter, was manning an observation post with no less than five telephoto cameras when a serpentine neck broke surface only 200 yards away. He was paralysed with shock and missed the photograph. This inhibiting effect of phenomenal creatures was noticed long ago. In 1857 Lord Malmesbury was told by his stalker of a monster he had seen in Loch Arkaig, but when he proposed to go and shoot it the stalker said, 'Perhaps your Lordship's gun would misfire.'

Modern literature on the Loch Ness Monster and its kin mostly concerns itself with the futile question of whether or not such things exist physically. The majority of writers, from Gould in 1934 to the latest, Costello, argue for its hard reality, while others, notably the great monster debunker, Dr Maurice Burton, try to explain in terms of error, hoax or psychology. Throughout this book we suggest that such polarization of opinions is unnecessary. Between the hard and the psychological there is an intermediate reality, the reality of phantoms. In earlier times, before the doctrine of materialism was given precedence over people's experience, this world of intermediate reality was recognized as a product of the reaction between thought and form and thus susceptible to magic.

There are many references in old histories to the same water monsters that are seen today, and they are always represented as being different from ordinary creatures, elemental rather than faunal. An early history of St Columba describes how in about AD 565 the saint summoned up and then banished the Loch Ness Monster. Similar magical feats of controlling or exorcizing such apparitions are recalled in many local legends, and the archetypal nature of the act can be seen in the universality of the myth of the solar hero defeating the serpent or dragon-like monster. We respect the opinion ascribed to a friend of W. B. Yeats (probably George Russell, the Irish seer known as 'AE') that 'these terrible creatures so common in lakes were set there by subtle enchanters to watch over the gates of wisdom'. This was a mood and theme perfectly captured in the brooding Gothic romances of Arthur Machen and H. P. Lovecraft at the beginning of this century; their stories seem to have anticipated many of the strange phenomena in this book.

*(Above) One of a series of drawings to illustrate various sightings of the Loch Ness Monster, from the* Illustrated London News. *(Below) A Scottish sea-serpent report from* The Times, *March 1856.*

THE SEA SERPENT IN THE HIGHLANDS.—The village of Leurbost, parish of Lochs, Lewis, is at present the scene of an unusual occurrence. This is no less than the appearance in one of the inland fresh water lakes of an animal which from its great size and dimensions has not a little puzzled our island naturalists. Some suppose him to be a description of the hitherto mythological water-kelpie; while others refer it to the minute descriptions of the "sea serpent," which are revived from time to time in newspaper columns. It has been repeatedly seen within the last fortnight by crowds of people, many of whom have come from the remotest parts of the parish to witness the uncommon spectacle. The animal is described by some as being in appearance and size like a "huge peat stack," while others affirm that a "six-oared boat" could pass between the huge fins, which are occasionally visible. All, however, agree, in describing its form as that of the eel; and we have heard one, whose evidence we can rely upon, state that in length he supposed it to be about 40 feet. It is probable that it is no more than a conger eel after all, animals of this description having been caught in Highland lakes which have attained a huge size. He is currently reported to have swallowed a blanket inadvertently left on the bank of the lake by a girl herding cattle. A sportsman ensconced himself with a rifle in the vicinity of the loch during a whole day, hoping to get a shot, but did no execution.—*Inverness Courier.*

*(Far left) The photograph, taken in the depths of Loch Ness in 1975, which prompted some biologists to dignify the Monster with a Latin name, but left others unconvinced. (Left) Morgawr, the double-humped Cornish sea-monster, photographed near Falmouth in February 1976. (Below) Pictorial records of two sea-serpent sightings, the lower one showing the monster seen from HMS Daedalus on 6 August 1848. Sir Richard Owen, who was not there to see it, said it was a seal!*

*(Below) Sea monsters are reported in many shapes other than the serpent. This creature, like a humanoid squid, is called by Japanese fishermen the* Umi-bozu. *Print by Kuniyoshi.*

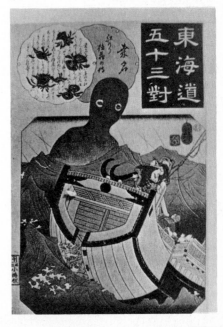

# The Great American Monster

All over the world, wherever there are wastes and mountains, there are monsters, creatures unknown to science but quite familiar to the native inhabitants. They are described by people who have seen them as huge, hairy beings, half men, half apes, of supernatural intelligence and extremely elusive. Their giant footprints have been seen and photographed from the Himalayas to the mountains of North America, but not one of these creatures has ever been caught.

Everyone has heard about the Abominable Snowman or Yeti of the Himalayas, the man-like creature that lives high up in the snowy peaks. The local people know it well, and it has even been seen by Europeans. A classic sighting was by the famous British mountaineer, Don Whillans, in the summer of 1970 at a height of 13,000 feet in the mountains of Nepal. One night, after he had spent the day photographing the tracks of some large, unknown animal in the snow, he saw in the bright moonlight the creature which might have made the tracks moving along a ridge opposite his tent. It was like an ape and moved on all fours.

A good account of the Yeti was given to Lord Hunt by the Abbot of Thyangboche Monastery who had watched one playing in the snow outside his residence. It was about five feet tall, with grey hair. The other monks became very excited and drove it off by blowing conch shells and bugles.

Despite innumerable reports by Sherpas and others, the evidence most acceptable to science for the existence of the Yeti is the footprints. On 8 November 1951 Eric Shipton, on one of his Everest expeditions with Michael Ward and a Sherpa, Sen Tensing, came across some remarkable tracks in the snow at an altitude of 18,000 feet. They were of a creature that walked like a man and, if it were of human proportions, would have stood about eight feet tall. The tracks continued for about a mile and disappeared on some ice. Many other Himalayan explorers, including the *Daily Mail* expedition of 1954, have recorded similar footprints; the most dramatic were those discovered in Sikkim in 1915 and reported by a forestry officer, Mr J. Gent. The prints were between 18 and 24 feet long; according to Gent's native informants, who identified them as belonging to one of a local race of giant wild men, the toes pointed in the opposite direction to that in which the creature was moving.

Similar to the Yeti are the hairy wild men of Soviet Central Asia, one of which was clearly seen in 1957 by a scientist from Leningrad University, A. G. Pronin. It was in the Pamir mountains, and Pronin, who saw it again a few days later, described it as reddish-grey, hairy, long armed and of shambling gait. The local Kirghizh herdsmen had long known of the creature's existence, but neither they nor any of the Soviet expeditions dispatched to the region have ever managed to catch one.

There have been sightings of unidentified hairy giants in mountainous districts all across Asia, but the firmest evidence of these creatures' existence comes from the western parts of North America. The first European settlers in California, Oregon and Washington were told by the local tribes about the strange wild man of the mountains which the Indians of British Columbia called the Sasquatch. Ever since the explorer David Thompson came across tracks attributed to this creature, each print 14 inches long, near Jasper, Alberta, many thousands of inexplicable footprints have been discovered and the hairy beings have often been seen, even photographed; and continuing the Indian tradition that the Sasquatch is inclined to abduct human beings, several modern Americans have claimed this experience, the most recent in 1976. The earliest was in 1924: Albert Ostman, a lumberman, was camping opposite Vancouver Island when he was lifted up, sleeping bag and all, and carried some twenty-five miles to the lair of a Sasquatch family, consisting of Father, some eight feet tall, Mother, a foot shorter, and two children. They treated him well, and after six days he escaped. Fearing mockery he kept the experience to himself until 1955.

There was an account in the *Seattle Times*, 16 July 1918, of 'mountain devils' attacking a prospector's shack at Mount St Helens in the State of Washington. The devils were said to be members of a local race, intermediate between men and animals, with magical powers and the gift of invisibility at will. In October 1940 the Chapman family of Ruby Creek, British Columbia, was approached by an eight-foot-tall, hairy male creature, which caused them to flee their house and left behind it 16-inch footprints and an overturned barrel of salted fish. Many other such incidents and sightings are recorded in the books of Ivan T. Sanderson, John Green and other writers on the 'Bigfoot' phenomenon, and all the evidence to date for the existence of these unknown giants in north-west America is soberly analysed in *Bigfoot*, a book by the famous anthropologist Professor John Napier. The most convincing proof he recognizes is the half-mile trail of 1,089 footprints, $17\frac{1}{2}$ inches in length and 7 inches wide, found in 1969 near Bossburgh, Washington. The right foot of the creature that made them was crippled, but at one point it had stepped easily over a 43-inch high fence.

A report in the *New York Times*, 30 June 1976, gives the experience of a logger, Jack Cochran, on 12 May 1974 in the Hood River National Forest, Oregon. At a distance of fifty yards he saw a 'big, hairy thing' standing silently. Following his first, remarkable notion that it might be one of his fellow workers, he realized that the creature could only be the legendary Bigfoot. It finally walked away 'gracefully, like an athlete' into the trees. Next day two other loggers of the same party were walking in the woods and disturbed the same or a similar creature. It ran away on

two legs while they pursued it throwing rocks. Members of the Bigfoot Investigation Center at The Dalles, Oregon, later visited the site and found huge footprints with those of the loggers running alongside.

The most striking record ever made, or claimed, of the Great American Monster is the film shot by Roger Patterson while on a Sasquatch hunt at Bluff Creek, Northern California, on 20 October 1967. It shows at a distance of about 100 feet a hairy man-like creature walking upright in full view of the camera. Experts who have examined the film can find no flaws or evidence of fakery, and it seems worthy of a place along with the classic UFO and Loch Ness Monster photographs as one of the rare photographs of a phantom.

We speak of phantoms bearing in mind the saying of the great anatomist Sir Arthur Keith that the only class of beings which are constantly seen but never present themselves at the dissecting table belongs to the world of spirits. In America the Bigfoot hunters are quite as active as the UFO and Loch Ness Monster people in the pursuit of evidence for the physical existence of their phenomenon; and they have had just the same degree of success or non-success: tracks, sightings, noises, strange feelings, mystical legends – and above all, elusiveness. As we write, July 1976, there is news in the American papers of a 'secret expedition', organized by North American Wildlife Research, setting out to the wilds of British Columbia, where a 'computer study' indicates that the Sasquatch is most likely to be located. Their destination is the spot where a fisherman recently heard and found tracks of the monster, and they intend to tranquillize one with a drugged dart, fit it up with a radio transmitter and then track its subsequent movements. We wish them luck but think they might as profitably, and far more comfortably, come to England and hunt THE SURREY PUMA.

Supporting our belief in the phenomenal reality that links so many of our sections is the following early Bigfoot record which Warren Smith quotes in *Strange Monsters and Madmen* from a diary shown to his friend, Brad Steiger, by the grandson of the man who wrote it, Mr Wyatt of Tennessee. Grandfather Wyatt, a woodsman in Humboldt County, wrote in his diary for 1888 that the local Indians were in contact with strange, hairy beings they called 'crazy bears', which were brought down to earth from time to time by spacemen in the modern classic mould, complete with shining UFOs and silvery, close-fitting outfits. The explanation, as Wyatt understood it, was that the space people were experimenting with stocking the earth with the animals they most liked to eat.

*(Far left) John Green, the American 'Bigfoot' investigator, displays his collection of monster footprint casts. (Top) Still from Roger Patterson's film of an unknown hairy creature in California, 1967. (Left) Jack Cochran's view of the Oregon monster he saw in 1974. (Above) An ice-pick gives the scale of one of the 'Yeti' footprints photographed by Eric Shipton in the Himalayas, 1951.*

# Black dogs

A phantom is something which can be seen but not captured, a definition which covers many of our phenomena. Folklore studies show that there is scarcely a corner of the British Isles without its traditional phantom. There is a tide of fashion in such things. The old coach with its headless horses and driver, once regularly reported, seems to have been driven off the road early in the motor age, but in its place we have plenty of reports of phantom motor cars. Nothing has really changed. Our stock of native phantoms remains undiminished. Through the shifts of fashion there is continuity.

In the case of THE SURREY PUMA we see continuity: a large, dark, mysterious beast roaming the English countryside. There is nothing new in this. The creature is mentioned in every volume of local folklore, and it is so much a part of people's experience that in each part of the country it has its own familiar name: Black Shuck in Norfolk, the Pooka in Ireland, the Gurt Dog in Somerset, and so on, picturesquely. Whatever it is called, the phenomenon is everywhere the same, a fearful creature haunting certain spots and old tracks, the sight of which can make a man faint with horror. ''Twas awful. It had four legs, and it was black, and had great fiery eyes as big as saucers.' This description is of a black dog seen in 1907 by a Somerset man near Budleigh Hill. It sounds like one of our modern pumas, but this was no ordinary beast, for 'it ran on until it came to where the water crosses under the road, and they things, of course, can never abide running water, so it just couldn't get across, and it went up in the air like a flash of fire.'

Similar to this was the experience of a Devon farmer. We quote from the fine collection of black dog myths, legends and modern sightings in Patricia Dale-Green's book, *Dog*. This farmer was on Dartmoor (no date or other details are given) when he heard the footsteps of an animal coming up behind him. It was a large black dog. He made to stroke it but his hand touched nothing. The creature ran off while 'a stream of sulphurous vapour issued from its throat'. The farmer chased it to a crossroads, where it seemed to explode in a blinding flash, throwing him to the ground.

This is not the sort of story one tells one's drinking companions of the evening before, but there are too many sincere accounts by people who have seen the black dog without benefit of DTs for the thing to be merely an effect of liquor. There are strange features of this black dog apparition which link it with several of our other types of phenomena. Its habit of vanishing in an explosive flash,

for instance; in this detail it resembles the fire-balls, will-o'-the-wisps and corpse candles in our MYSTERIOUS LIGHTS section. Like them, it is connected with churchyards, crossroads, watercourses and stretches of old roads. It is also commonly taken as an omen of death. In the Somerset volume of *County Folklore* is a reference to the black dog, haunting a road from St Audries to Perry Farm, which was said in 1960 to have appeared recently to two people just before their deaths. The luminosity of many black dogs and the evil appearance often attributed to them have caused them to be identified as the devil or his agents: 'In some places it is said that, when spots where Black Shuck has been seen are examined, they are found to be scorched and smelling strongly of brimstone,' writes P. Dale-Green. The same effect is mentioned by a correspondent in *Notes and Queries*, 18 May 1850, on the subject of East Anglian black dogs. One witness, 'on bringing his neighbours to see the place where he saw it, found a large spot as if gunpowder had been exploded there.' In another incident at Hatfield Peverell, Essex, a waggoner went to hit a large black dog that was blocking his path in a country lane, with the result that he caught fire and was burnt to ashes along with his horse and waggon. Another case is recorded of a farmer near Aylesbury, Buckinghamshire, who struck out at the two eyes of a black dog glowing in the dark. The dog and its bright orbs vanished instantly; the farmer was left speechless and paralyzed, never to recover.

We would like to be rational and identify the black dog with one of those familiar though still unexplained atmospheric phenomena such as ball lightning. The difficulty is that all the black dog witnesses are unanimous that it is definitely in the form of an animal.

There can be no misunderstanding here. Nor is the creature always said to be a dangerous force. The Pooka of Ireland (strange the similarity between Pooka and puma) is often represented in a favourable light as a companion or guide to country people on dark, lonely roads. Another reference to a friendly protective aspect of the black dog is in the book of Somerset folklore. In the 1930s women in the isolated valleys of the Quantock hills allowed their infants to roam the hillsides in the secure knowledge that the Gurt Dog up there would keep them from harm. It is a general rule that the more simply and unhysterically people accept their local phantom the more amicable it becomes.

In the Suffolk volume of the Folk-Lore Society's county series the local black dog is described in the words of an old writer:

'Old Shock is a mischievous goblin in the shape of a great dog, or of a calf, haunting highways and footpaths in the dark. Those who are so foolhardy as to encounter him, are sure to be at least thrown down and severely bruised, and it is well if they do not get their ancles sprained or broken; of which instances are recorded and believed.'

The most terrible outbreak of black dog in Suffolk, involving worse than broken ankles, took place on 4 August 1577 on a Sunday. An account of what happened was published in a pamphlet by some of the witnesses. Between 9 and 10 a.m., while the people of Bungay, Suffolk, were in church, there was suddenly a most unusual thunderstorm of extreme violence. The sky darkened, the church quaked, and the parish clerk who was cleaning out the gutters on the roof was struck to the ground by lightning, though not seriously hurt. In the church a fearful prodigy appeared – a black dog.

(Left) A black dog, eyes glowing, invades the study of Cardinal Croecentius. (Above) A modern black dog story from Country Life.

and terrible Wunder wrought very late in the parish Church of Bongay, a Town of no great distance from the citie of Norwich, namely the fourth of this August, in ý yeere of our Lord 1577. in a great tempest of violent raine, lightning, and thunder, the like wherof hath béen seldome séene.

With the appearance of an horrible shaped thing, sensibly perceiued of the people then and there assembled.

Drawen into a plain method according to the written coppy. by Abraham Fleming.

(Left, above and bottom) The Suffolk black dog (see text). The marks on Blythburgh church's north door are still visible and the Bungay market weathervane records the event.

Illuminated by lightning flashes it was clearly seen by the whole congregation, and the contemporary record is insistent that it was in the form of a dog. It ran down the church aisle and through the congregation. It passed between two people on their knees praying, and both were instantly struck dead. Another man whom it touched was shrivelled up like a drawn purse but stayed alive. The machinery of the church clock was left twisted and broken, and there were found marks like the scratches of claws on the stones and the metal-bound door of the church. On the same day, at Blythburgh about seven miles from Bungay, a black dog also ran down the church, smiting the congregation and killing two men and a lad as well as 'blasting' others.

Like many other black dogs this Suffolk fiend was obviously something elemental, but something which defies rational explanation as being an effect of natural forces in the atmosphere while at the same time having the form of a recognizable animal. Such a creature of paradox must belong to the realm of magic and witchcraft. Not that this should put it beyond further inquiry. Magicians are no less bound than anyone else by the laws of nature; they merely understand them better. No witch can invoke what is not there in nature to be invoked in the first place. If phantom shapes can be conjured up by magic there must be a phantom potential in nature for the magic to act upon; and if there is this potential it may on occasions manifest itself spontaneously. The dreadful black dog of Bungay was evid-

ently a spontaneous manifestation, but there are many cases of black dogs reputed to be witches' familiars or sorcerers disguised as were-animals. K. Wiltshire, who in her book of Wiltshire legends cites over forty instances of black dogs in that county alone, says she has heard that Norfolk witches can still produce these saucer-eyed creatures by the power of concentrated thought.

Our latest example of black dogs in witchcraft is an item in the *Sunday Express*, 23 November 1975, referring to the trial for attempted manslaughter of five tinkers, a father and his four sons, for trying to burn an alleged witch near Varasdin, Croatia. They claimed that the old woman had attacked them in the form of a large black dog with blazing eyes, knocking one of the brothers from his bicycle. Neighbours disturbed them as they were lighting the bonfire beneath the stake to which they had tied her.

A survey of all our black dog material suggests that these apparitions belong to a side of nature which was better recognized in the past than it is today. There is a pattern in the peculiar association of black dogs with water, bridges, underground streams, buried treasure, old churchyards and certain lengths of road, which is shared by some of our other phenomena and hints at one mysterious principle behind them all. We go further into the matter in the next section. Meanwhile, if anyone should see a large black dog with bright eyes and a sinister appearance, our best advice from the experience of others is to stand well clear and not to touch it.

# The Surrey puma

Animals that are supposed to be extinct but are not extinct; that should not exist but do exist – occasionally at least; that live in one part of the world but turn up in another. We refer to animals 'occasionally' existing because that seems the only way to account for certain peculiar features in the distribution of the world's fauna which are rarely mentioned in textbooks of biology and natural history. We have searched in vain through our *List of British Mammals* for reference to the intermittently indigenous Surrey puma, finally turning to the only authoritative work on this creature, the Day Book of the Godalming Police. Here are listed, just for the two years September 1962 to August 1964, no less than 362 sightings of mystery animals commonly identified as pumas. These records are not for public inspection, but published press reports alone supply a dossier (printed with sources and details in *Info* journal of May 1974 and *The News*, January 1976) of over eighty 'pumas' and mystery animals from 1962 to the present. This is, however, a mere fraction of the total phenomenon. As well as those known to the police, many of which are not publicized, and the cases recorded in the Surrey Puma file kept by the Zoological Society of London, there are many sightings which pass unrecorded for the good reason that people hesitate to make themselves look foolish by admitting to having seen what reason and the experts tell them is impossible, a large unknown beast in the domestic scenery of southern England.

To illustrate the phenomenon for the benefit of strangers to the subject, here are some typical data. We could give many examples for every year since the early 1960s, and for every southern county from Norfolk to Cornwall, but here we shall keep for the moment to the classic puma country of Surrey and neighbouring counties, and to one year when the phenomenon was in its infancy, 1964.

On 4 September 1964 a blackberry picker at Munstead, Surrey, saw a creature about five feet in length excluding its long tail, dark golden brown, with a cat-like face and a black stripe down its back. Later on Munstead Common large animal tracks were found clearly marked in the sandy soil and followed for about half a mile to a point where the creature had jumped over a high fence into some bushes; 23 and 24 September brought more news from Surrey of a roe deer found dead with a broken neck and deep scratches on its body as if from the claws of a powerful beast; also a heifer, still alive but deeply wounded, with flesh torn off and claw marks. The following day a motorist near Dunsfold identified a strange beast that ran across the road in front of his car as a puma. In October, news from neighbouring Sussex. A woman who had been walking her dogs in the woods described to the *Midhurst and Petworth Observer* her encounter with a puma about six feet long with golden-brown fur. Her dogs chased it into undergrowth from which came 'spitting, screeching sounds'. Paw marks were later found nearby. The same month a gamekeeper fired at a 'black, slit-eyed creature' at Farley Mount near Winchester, Hampshire; a similar animal – by now the conventional 'puma' identification had stuck – was seen by another gamekeeper in the same district, and several more such reports were received from Crondall near the Hampshire-Surrey border. The London *Evening News* mentioned this puma outbreak in two articles on 24 and 28 October. The next sighting was by two policemen. Their puma was in the churchyard of Stoke Poges, Buckinghamshire, near the monument to Thomas Gray who wrote his *Elegy* there, and their experience was described in the London *Observer*, 20 November. On that day a puma was seen at Nettlebed, Oxfordshire; two days earlier one had been reported from Littleworth Common, Buckinghamshire, and on 15 December there was another at Ewhurst, Surrey.

By January 1965 the Surrey police had received so many reports of puma sightings that they issued a warning to the public to beware of Hurtwood Common where the animal was thought to be wintering.

And so it goes on. On 5 July 1966 *The Times* carried a report from Worplesdon, Surrey, that on the preceding day several policemen and other witnesses had watched at a range of some 100 yards as a ginger-brown, Labrador-sized 'puma', with cat face and long, white-tipped tail, stalked and killed a rabbit. The sighting lasted for about twenty minutes. A photograph was published in the London *People*, 14 August. Armchair experts, uninhibited by personal observation, decided that what had been seen was a dog, fox or feral cat; to which Police Inspector Eric Bourne, an original witness, replied: 'I am not up the pole. I know a badger or a fox from a puma, and this was definitely a puma.'

People have been hanged on shakier evidence than this; and here we note a feature which runs through many of our phenomena, the persistent, decidedly arrogant belief of urban authorities that country people can not be trusted to distinguish between familiar local animals and those of, say, South America.

The Surrey puma continues unexplained to the present. There was an impressive series of sightings in 1975 between 6 and 9 March, beginning with a 'large, cat-like animal' running across fields at Brooks Green near Horsham, Sussex, which made two horses rear up, throwing their girl riders. A police search of the area discovered hair on a fence, also paw marks which the RSPCA reckoned must have been made by a 90–120 pound animal, not a dog. In the days that followed a puma-like beast was seen several times, once beside the motorway at Pease Pottage. As we write (April 1976) the *Bath Chronicle* reports another puma in west Wiltshire.

There is a mystery here which has attracted and successively defeated rationalizing scientists, big game hunters (yes, they too have been sighted in Surrey), farmers' and police searches and the investigations of occult and UFO students. In the Munstead case, mentioned above, the local police sent casts of the paw marks to the London Zoo where they were positively identified as those of a puma. However, Dr Maurice Burton, veteran debunker of the Loch Ness Monster and other such lore, identified them as marks of a bloodhound; although the creature as seen was in appearance and behaviour quite unlike any dog. If we were to believe the evidence of other people's eyes we would say that beyond doubt the commuter country around Surrey was infested with alien wild beasts, pumas or something very like them.

Yet it simply can not be so. There are clues, but they are all inconclusive: track marks, hair, a few lacerated cattle and some ambiguous snapshots. No bodies and above all no sign of the massive,

sustained slaughter of local cattle and wild life which a colony of real pumas would necessarily cause. Authorities say that a puma eats about 300 pounds of meat a week, equivalent to about five roe deer. To sustain this diet in Surrey is an ecological impossibility. Even one puma at large would take an intolerable toll of local livestock. The problem is just the same as the one UFO spotters face. The evidence is phenomenal, not physical. We can not disbelieve in UFOs and English pumas, because of the frequency and certainty of their sightings; but neither can we believe in them in the same way as we believe in aeroplanes and foxes because it seems to be part of their nature that they can never be caught and scientifically studied. In another section we look at a related phenomenon, BLACK DOGS, often seen but never killed or captured; we think of 'poltergeist' ani-

mals such as the headless black bear which tormented a seventeenth century Somerset village, of WEREWOLVES and shape-shifting animals or men, of witches' familiars, of the PROJECTED THOUGHT-FORMS conjured up by eastern mystics, and of the endless legends of mystery creatures coming from every continent and ocean.

From all this we have brewed a theory, which like all our theories is temporarily and loosely held. It is that creatures now extinct which once inhabited a certain district continue after their extinction to haunt that district in phantom form, varied with occasional real, physical appearances, until the time comes to re-establish themselves. There are some remarkable cases of apparently extinct species which have returned as it were from the dead. The Bermuda petrel, a conspicuous flying bird, was well known to the island's early settlers who by 1621 had exterminated it. So it was thought; at least for over three hundred years the petrel was not seen on its richly populated native island. In 1951 it suddenly reappeared from nowhere. A colony with seventeen nests was found on Bermuda, where the bird now flourishes. In his book, *On the Trail of Unknown Animals*, Heuvelmans gives several instances of the tendency of extinct species to spring up again from their native soil. Most dramatically he includes some good modern sightings of the Siberian mammoth.

In England we have the mysterious renaissance of the wild boar, supposedly extinct here for between two to three centuries. On 5 August 1972 a large wild boar was caught after a long chase near the motorway north of Hartley Wintney. None was missing from any zoo; but had this been a one-off incident we should have thought little of it. On 10 August, however, another wild boar was seen in the same district and unsuccessfully hunted by police and dogs. Six days later another was seen running with horses in a field, dark grey with a pointed head and long tasselled tail. On 7 September a $2\frac{1}{2}$ hundredweight wild sow was shot by a farmer near Bramshill, Hampshire, an action that caused zoo authorities to refrain from announcing the location of *another* wild boar they knew about. These wild boar incidents took place in the area of the Hampshire, Surrey, Berkshire and Sussex borders – 'Surrey Puma' country. The latest report of a boar is from Scotland, where, according to the *Daily Telegraph*, 16 March 1976, one was killed in a collision with a car on the estate of the Earl of Cawdor near Nairn.

There were wild boars and large-toothed 'tigers' in Pleistocene Britain, and probably more recently; and when Worplesdon is no more and the commuter train no longer runs to London Bridge, perhaps there will be again.

*(Left) The Zoological Society of London compared a footprint cast of one of their pumas with one of the 'Munstead Monster', with obvious differences (puma on the right). (Right) Two ex-police photographers staked out a field at Worplesdon, Surrey, in which a large sandy-coloured cat-like creature was seen several times, and took this photograph – The People, 14 August 1966. They saw it only 35 yards away and are certain it was not a feral tomcat. (Below) This map shows how 'Surrey Puma' sightings of 1962–72, on the Hampshire/Berkshire/Surrey/Sussex border, relate to wooded country.*

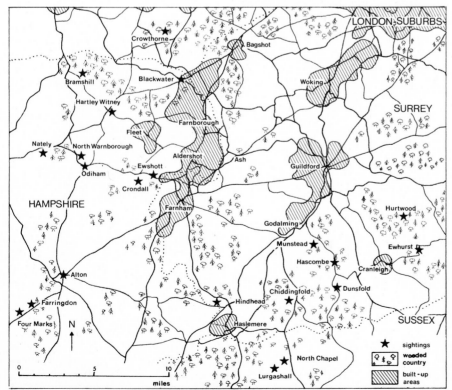

## Acknowledgments

We would like to acknowledge, with grateful thanks, the following, whose unstinting help contributed directly to our researches and data collection.

*In the United Kingdom :* Lionel Beer; Janet and Colin Bord; Ivan Bunn, editor of *Lantern*; James Chambers; Harold S.W. Chibbett; Mrs J.M. Cowland, of the Meteorological Office Library, Bracknell; Paul Devereux, editor of *The Ley Hunter* (*TLH*); Robert Forrest; Carl Grove; Bro. Alan LeMay, of the Catholic Central Library, London; Steve Moore; Peter Rogerson and Roger Sandell, of the *Metempiric UFO Bulletin* (*MUFOB*); Anthony Smith; Nigel Watson, of the Scunthorpe UFO Research Society (SUFORS); Chris Williams; Peter Zinovieff.

*In the USA and elsewhere :* Stan Barets of *Imagine*, Paris; Jerome Clark; Loren Coleman; Ronald Dobbins; David Dunthorn; Lucius Farrish; Livingston Gearhart; William N. Grimstad; Chris J. Holtzhausen; Stella Lansing; Anders Liljegren; Robert J. Schadewald; Dr Berthold E. Schwarz; Warren Smith; Paul J. Willis, president of the International Fortean Organization (INFO); MX, of the Canadian Res-bureaux.

Our appreciation also extends to the editorial team at Thames and Hudson, and to many others too numerous to list whose aid was no less valuable.

## A note on UFO and Fortean sources

Charles Fort wrote four books: *The Book of the Damned* (1919); *New Lands* (1923); *Lo!* (1931); and *Wild Talents* (1932). These were collected into one volume by the Fortean Society and published as *The Books of Charles Fort* (1941); recently reprinted as *The Complete Books of Charles Fort* (1974).

Readers interested in current discussion, reports and study of strange phenomena are encouraged to write to the following journals for further details. Many of these are put out on small budgets as a service to serious students, circulating and preserving data, encouraging research. A word of praise must be given to their many unsung contributors, without whose vigilance for the 'odd story' we all would have very little to go on.

*Fortean Times* (formerly *The News*), Robert J.M. Rickard, ed.; Box 152, London N10 1EP, England.

*INFO Journal,* Richard Hall, ed.; Box 367, Arlington, Va. 22210, USA.

*Pursuit,* John A. Keel, ed.; SITU, RD1, Columbia, N.J. 07832, USA.

*MUFOB,* John Rimmer, ed.; 11 Beverley Rd, New Malden, Surrey KT3 4AW, England.

*Lantern,* Ivan Bunn, ed.; BSIG, 3 Dunwich Way, Oulton Broad, Lowestoft, Suffolk, England.

*The Ley Hunter,* Paul Devereux, ed.; Box 152, London N10 1EP, England.

*Flying Saucer Review,* Charles Bowen, ed.; *FSR* Publications Ltd, West Malling, Maidstone, Kent, England.

*Bigfoot News,* Peter Byrne, ed.; Box 632, The Dalles, Ore. 97058, USA.

## Special note on strange phenomena

Research into a wide range of strange phenomena is continuing. It is largely dependent on the first-hand testimony of people who have experienced for themselves some of the effects of Phenomenal Reality in their lives. If you have experienced any of the phenomena discussed in this book, or any similar non-ordinary events, the authors invite you to send an account to Robert Rickard at the *Fortean Times* address above. All correspondence will be treated in confidence.

## Sources of illustrations

Although every effort has been made to trace the owners of copyright illustration material, this has not always been possible.

*Page*

1 Raining Cats Dogs & Pitchforks!!!, etching by G. Cruikshank, 1820. Victoria and Albert Museum, London. Photo E. Tweedy.

2 Psychic photograph. Copyright 1975 in U.S.A. and under UCC by Messrs Joseph, Fred, Richard Veilleux.

3 See p. 12 top.

4 See p. 33 top l.

5 See p. 117 top r.

11 Sea serpent, engraving from P. H. Gosse, *The Romance of Natural History*, 1860.

12 Headpiece to chapter *De lapsu piscium ranarum murium vermium & lapidum* (On the Fall of Fishes, Frogs, Mice, Worms and Stones), woodcut from O. Magnus, *Historia de gentibus*, 1555.
Account from *Philosophical Transactions of the Royal Society of London*, 1698. Photo British Library Board.

13 Account of toadfall, USA, 20th-c. From *Nature*, 19 September 1918.
Fishfall in Transylvania, and John Lewis and fishfall, both from *Popular Science Monthly*, July–December 1932. Photo British Library Board.

14 *Pluie de sauterelles* (Rain of Locusts), engraving from C. Flammarion, *L'Atmosphère*, 1888.

Israelites gathering manna, woodcut from Bishop Odo of Cambrai, *Expositio Canonis Misse*, 1496. Photo Radio Times Hulton Picture Library.

15 Rain of blood in Lisbon, from C. Lycosthenes, *Prodigiorum ac ostentorum chronicon*, 1557.
*Worcester Daily Times*, 30 May 1881. Photo E. Tweedy.

16 Birds raining stones on the Yemenite army, manuscript illustration from *Siyar al-Nabi, c.* 1594. Topkapi Saray Museum, Istanbul.

17 Mr and Mrs Wildsmith, and the ice that damaged their car, from *Harrow Observer*, 29 March 1974. Photos Middlesex County Press.

18 Rain of crosses, woodcut from C. Lycosthenes, *Prodigiorum ac ostentorum chronicon*, 1557.

19 Metal ball, from *Midnight*, 7 August 1972.
Cylindrical meteorite, from *Popular Mechanics*, 1910. Photo E. Tweedy.

20 Bleeding statue at Mirebeau, from *Daily Herald*, 23 March 1920. Photo E. Tweedy.

21 Weeping statue at Syracuse. Photo Religious News Service.
Bleeding statue at Eddystone, Pa., from *National Enquirer*, 20 January 1976.

22 Engraving from D. Stolcius, *Viridarium chymicum*, 1624.

23 Witches rainmaking, from U. Molitor, *De laniis et phitonicis mulieribus, c.* 1624.

Photo Radio Times Hulton Picture Library.
Oil at Swanton Novers rectory, from *Daily Mail*, 3 September 1919. Photo E. Tweedy.

24 Mohammed's vision of Gabriel, manuscript illustration from Ahmed Mustafa, *The Apostle's Biography, c.* 1368. Topkapi Saray Museum, Istanbul.

25 Miracle of St Francis of Paola, painting by F. Luzi (1665–1720). Church of San Francesco di Paola, Rome.
Kirlian photograph of finger aura. Photo D. A. Keintz.

26 Fireball at Salagnac, engraving from W. de Fonvielle, *Thunder and Lightning*, 1868.
Fireball at Basle, 1907. Photo M. Bessy.

27 Marsh light, engraving from R. Burns, *Address to the Deil*, 19th-c. edn. Photo Mansell Collection.

28 St Anne of Jesus, painting, School of Rubens, Couvent des Carmélites, Brussels.

29 Bradley Shell. Photo Dr B. E. Schwarz.
Josephine Giraldelli, 19th-century engraving. Photo Mary Evans Picture Library.
Anandamayi Ma. Photo R. Lannoy.

30 Firewalker Chief Terrii Pao. Photo Keystone Press.

31 The Attempted Martyrdom of Saints Cosmas and Damian, painting by Fra Angelico (1387–1455). National Gallery of Ireland, Dublin.